NATURE
AT
YOUR DOOR

Connecting with the Wild and Green in the Urban and Suburban Landscape

SARA A. GAGNÉ

Photographs by William Garcia

STACKPOLE BOOKS

Essex, Connecticut
Blue Ridge Summit, Pennsylvania

STACKPOLE BOOKS

An imprint of Globe Pequot, the trade division of
The Rowman & Littlefield Publishing Group, Inc.
4501 Forbes Blvd., Ste. 200
Lanham, MD 20706
www.rowman.com

British Library Cataloguing in Publication Information available

Library of Congress Cataloging-in-Publication Data Available

ISBN 978-0-8117-7226-6 (paperback)
ISBN 978-0-8117-7227-3 (electronic)

∞™ The paper used in this publication meets the minimum requirements of American National Standard for Information Sciences—Permanence of Paper for Printed Library Materials, ANSI/ NISO Z39.48-1992.

For Truman

The point is seeing—the grace
beyond recognition, the ways
of the bird rising, unnamed, unknown,
beyond the range of language, beyond its noun.
Eyes open on growing, flying, happening,
and go on opening. Manifold, the world
dawns on unrecognising, realising eyes.
Amazement is the thing.
Not love, but the astonishment of loving.

From "Growing, Flying, Happening" by Alastair Reid

CONTENTS

SIDEBARS

ACKNOWLEDGMENTS

THANK YOU TO ALL THE SCIENTISTS whose excellent research I describe in this book. Their passion and hard work have transformed how we perceive the world around us. Each of them has helped humanity move one step closer to a more harmonious relationship with nature. Most especially, thank you to Luke, Truman, Shari, and Paul for their loving support. This book could not have been written without it.

CHAPTER 1

INTRODUCTION

On summer Saturdays when I was a kid, my father would take me to the Morgan Arboretum near our house to hunt for salamanders. We'd bring nets and jars and head down to an old rock quarry surrounded by maples, hemlock, and beech. The quarry had been hewn into the side of a small hill, leaving a sheer granite wall overlooking a shallow depression that filled with water in the spring. I would wade into the water from the opening facing the wall into a pool teeming with the most mysterious and amazing creatures I had ever seen. Large green frog tadpoles with two pairs of legs scattered as I approached. Much smaller and deep-black American toad tadpoles swarmed in the sunshine, like a flock of starlings in the fall. Eastern newts hung just below the water's surface, legs dangling and flat, keeled tails slowly moving from side to side. But best of all, blue-spotted salamanders, their dark, shiny bodies mottled electric blue, swam in the deep, seen only if they were unfortunate enough to end up in my net.

It was these salamander hunts that started me on the path to becoming the ecologist and professor I am today, and to writing this book. To my young eyes, the strange and beautiful creatures I encountered in the quarry pond were ambassadors of a world so full of intriguing permutations and possibilities that it baffled my imagination. Here were animals that, in a single lifetime, swam and breathed like fish underwater and walked and breathed like me on land. They could even breathe through their skin, and some did so all the time because they lacked lungs. Some, like adult newts, could pick and choose their lifestyle, remaining fully

1

aquatic from egg to adult, or moving from the water to land and back again twice over depending on local conditions. To top it all off, we now know that salamanders fluoresce green in blue light—I won't even speculate on my reaction to a quarry pond filled with fluorescent salamanders—and can regrow severed limbs and regenerate parts of their brains and spinal cords.[1]

It astounded me that the seemingly superpowered creatures I encountered on these trips with my father lived such very different lives from my own, and, more so, that these incredible animals inhabited the same bustling Island of Montreal that I and approximately 1.8 million other people at the time called home. While blue-spotted salamanders were busily travelling to and from breeding ponds, I was riding to and from school, until that point oblivious to their existence. The glimpse I got at the quarry pond of frogs, toads, newts, and salamanders in all their glory awakened my mind to the myriad non-human lives being lived all around me. The world beyond my doorstep instantly became much more complex, beautiful, and interesting, and one which now held countless fascinating secrets waiting to be discovered.

My wish for you as a reader of this book is that you come away from the experience the same way I did after I netted my first salamander. I'd like you to experience your everyday world with new eyes that see the diversity of animals and plants that surround you where you live. Just like my newfound knowledge that a salamander or toad is living out its extraordinary life in a pond near my house, my goal with this book is to help you become aware of the birds nesting in your yard, the variety of trees along your street, the butterflies in your park, the otters in your local creek, and the coyote in your neighborhood (yes, there most likely is one, no matter where you live). In short, after reading this book, I'd like you to go about your day where you live, work, and play astounded and thrilled by the other species you live amongst. I've looked at my urban and suburban living spaces this way ever since my first outing to the quarry pond. In writing this book, I hope to share with you the joy I experience when I notice a turkey vulture peering down at me from a neighbor's roof, the bright epaulette of a red-winged blackbird at rest in my park, or sun-loving painted turtles in my stormwater pond.

A multitude of species live right under our noses in the urban and suburban places we call home. A hotel for cavity-nesting bees in my local park.

Two painted turtles in a stormwater pond.

Red-winged blackbird in an urban park.

A suburban turkey vulture.

The way I have chosen to share my experience of the natural world in urban and suburban places in this book is by focusing on the connections each of us has with the species where we live. Spending an average of twenty-two hours each day indoors or in vehicles, as Americans do, it's easy to overlook the innumerable ways in which we may interact with other species in our day-to-day lives.[2] Our indoor culture has led us to lose touch with nature, like a friend that you haven't spoken to in a long time and you no longer know where they live, what they do for a living, or whether they have a partner or kids. We can no longer name the species around us—case in point, few if any of my students year after year recognize the house finch, one of the most common species on campus that they surely would have seen at home as well since childhood. We also no longer realize how much our health and well-being depend on nature: to what extent trees clean and cool the air, help to reduce violent crime, and improve our immune systems; the capacity of species-rich wild nature to relieve stress and boost happiness; and the potential of nature to clean and manage urban stormwater and limit flooding. By showing you your reciprocal connections with nature where you live—how your activities, and human activities in general, affect nature and how, in turn, nature influences your and your neighbors' health and well-being, my aim is to foster a deeper relationship between you and nature that is full of awe, beauty, appreciation, and respect. Ultimately, I hope a realization of the intertwining of our lives with those of wild species, even in the most developed of places, will motivate you to act to enhance nature in your living spaces and across your city, town, or county.

Taking action to foster nature in urban and suburban landscapes is central to this book. Each of us can contribute to making the cities, towns, and developed counties where we live healthier environments for ourselves, our neighbors, and our children. As you'll see in the sidebars with recommendations in each chapter, there are many practical ways, small and large, that you can make your living spaces more welcoming to wild species. Most of us live in landscapes of lawn and asphalt where streams are buried or sunken from view and woodlands and grasslands are relegated to nature preserves or the edge of a local park. In my view, precisely because wild nature has been largely excluded from them, our

We've lost touch with nature where we live. Many people cannot recognize or name even common suburban and urban species, like this brightly colored house finch.

developed landscapes are blank slates just waiting to harbor a native flowering plant attractive to pollinators, an eastern phoebe on the hunt for an insect meal, or a curious chipping sparrow. To be sure, developed landscapes are first and foremost where people live and therefore must satisfy resident preferences and needs. But there is so much room to include wild nature in our neighborhoods in ways that are safe and enjoyable and improve our health and well-being. I've tried to include as many as I can think of in this book, but there are likely very many more yet to be imagined.

Why do we need to act? Quite simply, because animals and plants are disappearing from the planet at a rapid rate, a devastating loss of beauty and wonder from the world that also threatens our very existence. According to the World Wildlife Fund's Living Planet Index, which combines population estimates for over four thousand vertebrate (mammal, fish, bird, amphibian, and reptile) species around the world, the

Carpenter bee on butterfly weed.

Eastern phoebe.

Chipping sparrow.

average vertebrate population has declined by two-thirds, or 68 percent, between 1970 and 2016.[3] To put this in perspective, Kenneth Rosenberg at the Cornell Lab of Ornithology and his colleagues estimated widespread declines of birds in North America during the same time period, from larks to finches to starlings, totaling 29 percent of the continent's individuals.[4] That's less than half of the Living Planet Index, but it's still three billion—yes, *billion* with a *b*—birds. There is also evidence that invertebrates, those animals without a backbone such as insects, are disappearing. The biomass, or collected weight, of Puerto Rico rainforest arthropods (a group that includes insects and spiders) has shrunk substantially from what it was in the mid-1970s, and in protected areas in Germany, flying insect biomass has diminished by 78 percent since 1989.[5] In the oceans, live coral cover on reefs has declined by nearly half in the past 150 years, and more than half of ocean area is now being subject to industrial fishing. As a result of such dramatic decreases in wildlife populations, an increasing proportion of species are now threatened with extinction. Of the animal and plant groups that have been sufficiently studied, the average proportion of species at risk of extinction is 25 percent (the proportion varies from over 40 percent of amphibian species at risk to 10 percent of insect species).[6] These values indicate that the global rate of species extinction is at least tens of times higher than the average rate over the last ten million years and that millions of animal, plant, and fungi species on Earth are at risk of disappearing forever, some within decades.

Surprisingly, some of the best places to mitigate these worldwide declines are the urban and suburban places we call home. This is in part because urbanization is a major cause of species loss, so that working within developed landscapes, we can diminish its negative impacts. It's also because, contrary to what you may assume, urban and suburban places are exceptionally biodiverse. In chapter 2, "The Urban Ecosystem," I'll describe how places with high human population density also have many animal and plant species, including threatened species. For instance, 170 bird species have been observed at Morgan Arboretum, where I netted salamanders, including the yellow-billed cuckoo, the bobolink, and the Cape May Warbler, that, according to the North American Breeding Bird Survey, have declined by 34 percent, 56 percent, and 70 percent respectively, since the mid-1960s. Focusing on urban and suburban places as priority sites for nature conservation also addresses the fact that protected areas alone will not be sufficient to lessen the loss of species. The Morgan Arboretum is a tiny six hundred acres that represents just 0.5 percent of the heavily developed Island of Montreal, home to myriad species. In the United States, just 13 percent of the land area is conserved for biodiversity, but 38 percent is estimated to need conservation attention to effectively safeguard wildlife.[7] This 38 percent includes protected areas such as national parks, but also the land where roughly forty-three million Americans live. Clearly, slowing the loss of species requires envisioning and enacting different ways to build, travel, and manage land in our settlements so that more space can be made for the wildlife we live amongst. This book is a contribution in that direction.

Urban and suburban places are critical locales of nature conservation for one more, and perhaps the most important, reason: They are where most people live. Worldwide, more humans now occupy urban areas than rural ones, especially in developed regions. In America, 86 percent of us live in urban cores or suburban areas.[8] Therefore, it is in urban and suburban places that the large majority of Americans regularly experience the natural world, in their yards, on their way to work, and in parks and greenways. This proximity sets the stage for sustained and meaningful interactions between people and nature—those I hope to foster in this book and many more. These interactions will, over time, develop and deepen people's knowledge and understanding of wildlife and its ways, and lead to a lasting appreciation and respect for nature in all its forms. Urban and suburban places, then, are where most Americans can build strong connections with nature. And a strong connection with nature is exactly what is needed to motivate people to take action to protect and enhance nature locally and globally. As I describe in chapter 3, "Your Yard," the global conservation of species critically depends on people's relationships with nature in the most developed parts of the planet, the urban and suburban landscapes we call home.

HOW TO USE THIS BOOK

The organizing concept underpinning this book is the urban ecosystem, the interconnected web of living and non-living things in urban and suburban places in which humans play a central role. In the next chapter, "The Urban Ecosystem," I'll show you that the interdependent relationships that comprise an urban ecosystem link all the natural elements where you live—the multitude of other species you live amongst and the physical environment—and all the human elements—our built structures, people's activities, behaviors, preferences, and attitudes, and the workings of our social systems and institutions. The human elements have an outsized influence on urban ecosystem structure and functioning. By this, I mean that how we build our cities and towns and what we do in them have large effects on the characteristics of their urban ecosystems, such as air quality and tree cover, and how they work—for example, how easy it is for you to get to the park nearest where you live and how often flooding inundates your home or interrupts your daily commute. This outsized influence can be harnessed to fundamentally change the way cities and other urban and suburban places are conceptualized, designed, and planned to create healthy habitats for our and other species. At the same time, the many direct and indirect relationships between the human and natural elements in an urban ecosystem mean that how each one of us acts in relation to nature makes a difference.

The urban ecosystem concept is thus an excellent basis for a book about connections between people and nature where we live. The concept is also scalable, in that it works equally well to describe these connections across an entire city as it does for a single yard. I've capitalized on this flexibility in this book to show you how you are connected to nature in the different places you are most likely to experience it. Each chapter focuses on a different location: your yard, your street, your park, your greenway, your neighborhood, and your city (or town). In each, informed by my own and fellow scientists' research, I first show you how what you do, or what the community of which you are a part does, affects the presence and quality of nature in the space in question. I follow this by doing the same thing but in reverse, showing you how the presence and quality of the nature in the space in question directly or indirectly affects you. Each of these chapters shares two main messages with you: one about how you affect nature and one about how it affects you. You can find these main messages as subheadings within chapters and summarized in chapter 9, "Conclusion." Each chapter, as well as chapter 2, "The Urban Ecosystem," also includes several sidebars with recommendations that list practical actions you can take to enhance nature around you, to experience its benefits, or to manage its potential drawbacks. These sidebars and their page numbers are tabulated after the Contents page.

To make the most of the knowledge, insight, and recommendations for action in this book, use it as you would a handbook. By all means, feel free to read the book from start to finish. But each chapter also stands up well on its own, as does each chapter half that describes one direction of the two-way interaction between you and nature that is the overarching theme of this book. Read just one chapter or a chapter half as time and interest allow. Or simply use the book for the sidebars listed in the front matter. I've designed the book to hopefully be as useful as possible and as a reference that you can easily return to as needed. I hope my efforts to share my enthusiasm and expertise about urban nature with you in this way enriches your urban or suburban experience, as writing this book has mine.

CHAPTER 2

THE URBAN ECOSYSTEM

IMAGINE YOU ARE IN A PLANETARIUM. YOU ARE RECLINING IN A CUSH-
ioned chair, expectantly waiting for the surrounding lights to dim and
disappear. Suddenly, as if you hadn't known it would happen all along,
the room goes dark. The ceiling above you comes alive with the luminous,
swirled surface of the Earth. You marvel yet again at how blue the planet
appears; how small the continents look. As you begin your journey and
start to pull away and move into space, Earth becomes a bright globe in
the darkness. Other planets in the solar system come into view—Mars,
Jupiter, Saturn—and then shrink in turn. Soon you are floating in the vast
Kuiper Belt beyond the orbit of Neptune, getting a close-up look at the
icy balls of gas that are the precursors of comets and dwarf planets like
Pluto. The sun is now just one of many stars peppering the ceiling, and
somehow, you feel physically smaller than you did when you sat down. As
your journey continues, the Orion Arm of the Milky Way coalesces out
of the starry sky. It, too, quickly becomes smaller and smaller until you
can see the spiral galaxy in its entirety and realize it is just one of hundreds of billions of other galaxies, multicolored shapes that have replaced
the stars. At this point, the enormity of the universe in which you live
makes you feel tiny indeed.

There certainly aren't hundreds of billions of species on Earth; a
reasonable estimate is at least eight million, but all the same, your place
in the constellation of living things surrounding you is analogous to
Earth's position in the universe.[1] Most likely unbeknownst to you, you
share your home and yard with thousands of other species. Early in the

A constellation of species surrounds you where you live (from top to bottom on this and the next page): box turtle, brown thrasher, bullfrog, blue dasher, green anole, eastern kingbird, rat snake, black swallowtail, yellow passionflower vine hanging from Joe Pye weed, white-tailed deer.

COVID-19 pandemic, Matthew Holden, Russell Yong, and Andrew Rogers, three young scientists at the University of Queensland in Australia and sharing a house in the suburbs of Brisbane, decided to pass their time in lockdown by cataloguing their additional "roomates."[2] They regularly searched the vegetation in their yard, looking under leaves and occasionally shaking plants to see what emerged, monitored their porch light for visiting moths and beetles, and even made forays under the house to look for spiders. A year and a half later, their tally has exceeded one thousand species, including 556 insects, 95 plants, 40 birds, 34 spiders, 8 mammals, 7 reptiles, and 2 amphibians. Of the insects, just under half are moth species (249 species), 35 species are wasps, and 33 are butterflies. What's more, this astounding biodiversity has been sharing a property that is just a tenth of an acre. A tenth of an acre is about one-tenth the size of the average American grocery store or about the same size as a double row of thirteen parking spaces facing each other. Albeit not all the species that Holden, Yong, and Rogers found were living with them all year round, each one of those species partook of resources, such as food and shelter, made available on the property.

Holden credits their ability to identify all the different species he and his housemates found in part to iNaturalist, an app that uses artificial intelligence and the power of community to catalogue wild animals and plants. The app originated in 2008 as the final project of three University of California at Berkeley master's students: Ken-ichi Ueda, Nate Agrin, and Jessica Kline. Today, iNaturalist is a joint initiative of the California Academy of Sciences and National Geographic and boasts over a million community members. iNaturalist is an instance of citizen or community science, science performed by nonprofessionals that is revolutionizing the amount and type of data available to help solve pressing environmental challenges. People around the world use the app and their phone's camera to identify the species they come across, helped along by image-recognition software that suggests possible matches for the organisms depicted in photographs. The member community, which includes some of the foremost naturalists in the world, can then weigh in on what was spotted, thereby improving the accuracy of species identification. In other words,

How to use iNaturalist

iNaturalist is a database of species observations and a community of people interested in the natural world. You can use iNaturalist to log observations of species, to identify other users' observations, and to explore the natural world around you.

Creating an observation

The purpose of an observation is to record the presence of a species. The most useful observations are those that are accompanied by photographs or sound recordings, but it's not necessary to associate media with your record. When you create an observation, iNaturalist will want to know what you observed; the day, time, and location of the observation; and whether the species is captive or cultivated. What you observed can be as simple as "vine" or as detailed as "yellow passionflower." iNaturalist will suggest groups or species that most closely match your observation input and provide more information about each possibility, including its Wikipedia page, a map of its distribution, its seasonality, and a link to similar, nearby observations. You have the option to remove or change the automatically generated date and time of your observation, and the ability to choose whether the location of your observation is associated with precise coordinates of latitude and longitude or a more general area. Importantly, you can add your observations to projects aimed at better understanding the species that occur in a particular place, like the Metro Phoenix EcoFlora project, or even create your own.

Identifying other community members' observations

You can help improve the accuracy of iNaturalist by adding your own identifications to other users' observations. You can find other observations by simply exploring where you live or by searching for specific species or groups. Once at least two-thirds of identifiers agree on the identification of a species and the observation is accompanied by a date, latitude and longitude, and photograph and/or sound recording, and isn't captive or cultivated, the observation gets classified as "Research Grade." Research Grade observations are enabling scientists to map changing patterns of species occurrence much faster and over much larger areas than was possible just a few years ago. For example, iNaturalist data have been used to track the expansion of disease vectors such as ticks and mosquitoes and to map the incursion of pumas into urban areas during the pandemic.[3]

even if you have absolutely no idea what that weird-looking insect on your deck is called, iNaturalist and its members can help you find out (see the sidebar *How to use iNaturalist*).

Exploring the map of my location in iNaturalist on my phone just now brings me back to my cosmic analogy likening the plethora of species all around you to the stars and galaxies in the universe. To the thousand species Matthew Holden and his housemates identified in their home and yard, we can add an average of nine thousand more fungi and bacteria living in the dust collecting on the upper trim of doors in homes across the United States, making where you live something like the Pleiades cluster of stars in the sky.[4] Zooming out to my neighborhood on iNaturalist—a mushroom-obsessed neighbor seems to be identifying all the fungi he spots on his walk, from eastern jack-o'-lantern to hare's foot inkcap—I'm reminded of bright pinpoints of light coalescing into the Orion Arm of the Milky Way. Zooming out even further brings me to the galaxy that is my city and its myriad of species, including, at last count, at least 899 species of moths.[5]

For the past three years, my city has participated in the City Nature Challenge, a community science initiative like iNaturalist but focused exclusively on urban places. The City Nature Challenge began in 2016 as a friendly competition between the Natural History Museum in Los Angeles and the California Academy of Sciences in San Francisco to determine which city could document the greatest number of species of any kind during an intensive eight-day search, or "bioblitz." The yearly event has grown from the two founding cities in the United States to 419 cities spread across every continent except Antarctica in 2021 (going back to my analogy, you can think of cities as multicolored and variously shaped galaxies spread across the globe). In that year, 52,000 people made nearly 1.3 million observations and identified more than 45,300 species in total. The number of species identified in each city varied from 4,466 in Cape Town, South Africa, to just one in Anta District in Peru. In the United States, the event seems to have struck a chord with Texans in particular—many of the largest numbers of species and participants were from the state where sixteen cities joined the challenge, nearly as many as California, New York, and Florida combined. Despite Texans' love of urban biodiversity, the species totals per city are low in comparison to the roughly ten thousand species of animals, plants, fungi, and bacteria estimated to inhabit homes and yards. As more people participate in the program, each helping to find and identify species, these numbers will surely grow. Interestingly, even with the relatively few species identified in each city, the City Nature Challenge inventoried more than two thousand rare, threatened, or endangered species, such as the Blainville's horned lizard in Orange County, California, and the witches' cauldron fungus, also known as the charred-pancake cup, in Russia.

The fact that people are finding rare, threatened, or endangered species in cities may seem counterintuitive. Current wisdom dictates that places where people congregate are devoid of nature, especially rare species that depend upon a narrow set of environmental conditions to thrive. When we think of where we live, we tend to focus on the built environment, the places we use and are familiar with, and we overlook the natural nooks and crannies hiding along stream edges, in the patches of forest interspersed among our houses, and throughout the old fields and abandoned, brushy lots on our commute. These places, as well as our homes, bridges, and buildings, host a multitude of species. In fact, if you calculate the correlation, or association, between the number of species and the number of people in an area, you will find that this correlation is positive. Gary Luck, an adjunct professor at Charles Sturt University in Australia, took it upon himself to compile all such correlations to determine whether the overall association between the number of species in an area, or species richness, and human population density was positive or negative, regardless of variation across individual studies, like where the study was carried out.[6] He found that, contrary to what most people assume, places with high human population density had high species richness. This positive association holds for birds, mammals, plants, geographically restricted species, and threatened species.

If we rightly assume that most species don't flourish on pavement, then it doesn't make sense that places with the highest density of human beings, and therefore built structures, host many species. The key to this

19

paradox lies in the size of the area under consideration. Most of the studies included in Luck's analyses measured human population density and species richness in relatively large areas of about one thousand square miles, equivalent to a square area thirty-three miles across. The easiest way to picture landscapes of this size is to think back to your last take-off in an airplane in clear weather and the view of the mosaic of houses, forests, and fields below you. The reason areas this big can have lots of people and species is simply because they have room; there is room for houses and habitats. In addition, the more room there is, the more habitat types there are, and consequently, the more different species that depend on these habitats. This explanation is not meant to discount the positive association between the locations of people and species, since a concur-rent study carried out by Marco Pautasso, currently at the European Food Safety Authority, found that the positive association persisted in areas as small as 1 kilometer, or two-thirds of a mile, across.[7]

There are several reasons why people and other species are found in large numbers in the same places. Humans and other species may be responding to the same underlying gradients of energy availability, eleva-tion, and/or spatial heterogeneity. The availability of energy from the sun, along with water availability, powers natural systems through the process of photosynthesis that transforms photons into plant matter. The more energy and water that are available, the greater the number and diversity of plants, and ultimately of herbivores and predators, including humans. Humans and other species also reach high densities at low elevations for the similar reason that environmental conditions at low elevations are more amenable to a good life. Finally, places with many different environmental conditions, resources, and habitats provide humans with more resources overall and thus permit larger populations and represent a greater diversity of niches that more species can fill. These explanations are simplistic in that they do not consider human cultural, economic, and settlement patterns, or other reasons for humans to aggregate in certain areas. But they do hint at why dense human habitations also have lots of other species. And where there are many species, there are likely to be more rare species, such as those with restricted geographic ranges assessed by Gary Luck.

The creation of novel habitats, like this new stormwater pond, is one of the reasons why areas with many people also have many species. This pond hosted a large breeding population of Fowler's toads in its second spring.

Other explanations for the positive association between human population density and species richness are that humans import a lot of species—Luck also found a positive association between human density and the number of non-native plant species—and that humans actually create a diversity of novel habitats—think of all the greenways, gardens, hedges, stormwater ponds, forest patches, railway corridors, streetscapes, industrial sites, and office parks packed into a relatively small urban or suburban area—that attract a diversity of species. The good news from this unexpected, positive association between the density of humans and the number of species is that we live among a truly dazzling array of natural wonders that, in the case of some species and some cities, occur nowhere else on Earth. The bad news is that our activities can and do lead to the loss of some of the native species we live amongst, the rare ones being the most vulnerable, as evidenced by the positive correlation between the number of threatened species and human density reported by Luck. In reconciling these two realities, I like to think that the places where we live represent a life-changing opportunity to embrace nature in our day-to-day lives. It's an opportunity that is not easily seized, but that once acted upon, will improve our health and well-being and that of the planet.

⸻

At this point, I hope to have shown you that you share your yard, sub-division, and city with innumerable other species. My point in doing so is to introduce the organizing concept of this book: that you, and all the other species that occur where you live, are part of an urban ecosystem, an interconnected web of living organisms and the physical environment in which humans play a large role. As a part of an urban ecosystem, you regularly interact with other species, and you and other species respond to, and influence, your common physical environment. I've chosen the urban ecosystem concept as the basis for this book because it is funda-mentally concerned with these relationships—all the myriad connections that link people, other species, and the air, water, and minerals upon which we all depend. As a result, it's a great way to situate the reciprocal relationships between people and nature that occur where you live and that I'll be focusing on in each chapter. In the next few pages, to give you a better idea of what an urban ecosystem is, I'll first provide you with the classic definition of an ecosystem that dates from the beginnings of the field of ecology. Then, I'll describe a forest ecosystem and the inter-actions that define it in order to compare these to the interactions that are characteristic of an urban ecosystem, in this case a neighborhood in Vancouver, Canada. I'll show you how urban ecosystems are similar to, but also very different from, natural ecosystems, most importantly with respect to the outsized influence of people. I'll also define exactly what I mean by "urban," since ecologists use the term much more broadly than it is generally understood.

The classic definition of an ecosystem is a community of organisms and their physical environment interacting as an ecological unit. The term "ecosystem" originated with Arthur G. Tansley in 1935 at a time when ecology was a young field of study and adepts were focused on bringing

Urban ecosystems are where human and natural elements in all their forms interact.

order to the search for a better understanding of the living component of the natural world.[8] In contrast to those who maintained that relying on the concept of the community, a group of organisms of different species occurring in an area and interacting among themselves by means of predation and other such relationships, was the most productive way to advance ecological understanding, Tansley argued that organisms were inseparable from the physical environment and, therefore, a useful unit of ecological organization must incorporate both living (the community) and non-living (the physical environment) components. Only by explicitly accounting for the ways in which organisms respond to and shape the physical environment in an ecosystem could we hope to advance our understanding of why plants, animals, and other types of organisms occur and persist where they do.

A forest ecosystem is probably the example with which most of us are most familiar. Picture yourself walking through a pleasant, open stand of trees. It's fall, as it is now as I'm writing this, and leaves are slowly falling from the branches overhead. You regularly hear a dry shuffling as squirrels forage for acorns in the leaf litter. Small birds flit among the nearly nude branches, and a woodpecker's tapping reverberates through the woods. If you're in luck, you might even see a doe and fawn ambling in the sun-dappled distance. All these elements, and the air, water, and minerals surrounding and within them, compose the forest ecosystem. However, none of them would exist without interacting with one or more of the others.

The interactions among the living and non-living components of a forest ecosystem are myriad and complex. A focal point for many of these interactions is the trees. Trees perform photosynthesis, the process by which energy from the sun and carbon dioxide and water from the air are chemically transformed into glucose and oxygen. Glucose is combined with nutrients from the soil and underlying bedrock to form the matter in tree trunks, branches, and leaves. Fallen leaves accumulated on the forest floor are broken down into nutrients by armies of invertebrates and bacteria and an intricate network of filamentous fungi. Insects, birds, and mammals that eat tree leaves, nectar, and nuts are themselves transformed into nutrients when they die. They also eat and are eaten by other animals. And most living things are continually respiring, or burning their stores of carbohydrates, protein, and fat to produce energy, taking in oxygen and emitting carbon dioxide and water in the process.

An important thing to note about these interactions is that they are often reciprocal. For example, trees both absorb and emit carbon dioxide when they photosynthesize and respire, respectively. The nutrients ingested by squirrels in the form of acorns are returned to the soil once the squirrel or its predator dies, to be taken up by the tree once more and turned into more acorns. Put another way, the tree in part creates the conditions for the squirrel to occur and thrive, and the squirrel returns the favor in time. I'll return to this interdependence of elements when I describe the relationships between people and nature that form an urban ecosystem.

When ecologists study ecosystems, they focus on the interactions that define them by quantifying the flow of energy and/or nutrients among the elements. For forest ecosystems, the nutrient most commonly quantified is carbon. Trees and other plants "fix" the inorganic carbon in carbon dioxide in the air by adding it to oxygen and hydrogen to make glucose, a sugar used for energy and as a building block of more complex organic molecules such as carbohydrates and protein. When leaves fall from tree branches to the forest floor, carbon is being transferred from one ecosystem "pool" to another. It is these pools and transfers, or fluxes, that ecosystem ecologists measure. For example, Suzanne Simard at the University of British Columbia and her colleagues recently estimated the amount of carbon in different pools in a sixty-eight-year-old fir-cedar-hemlock forest near the city of Vancouver in order to assess the effects of logging intensity and climate on forest carbon stocks.[9] About 65 percent of the total carbon in the forest was held in aboveground pools, including live (50 percent) and dead (9 percent) trees, woody debris such as logs and twigs on the forest floor (7 percent), understory plants (0.15 percent), and stumps (0.04 percent) (the sum of values exceeds 65 percent because I averaged measurements from multiple sampling sites). The other third or so of carbon was located in tree roots (11 percent), in leaf litter (19 percent), and in mineral soil under the litter (8 percent). In another study nearby, Elyn Humphreys, then at the University of British

Carbon circulates among reservoirs, or pools, in forest ecosystems, such as trees, leaf litter, and dead branches on the forest floor.

Columbia and now at my alma mater, Carleton University in Ottawa, Canada, estimated the exchange of carbon dioxide between a fifty-three-year-old Douglas fir stand and the atmosphere.[10] In one year, the stand absorbed 2 kilograms of carbon per square meter and emitted 1.75 kilograms of carbon per square meter, for a net sequestration or storage of carbon of 0.25 kilograms per square meter. That's equivalent to the weight of an AA battery for every square foot of forest per year.

The last point I'd like to make about the ecosystem concept before turning to how it has been applied to an urban context is that the concept is scalable. By this, I mean it can be used to describe the interactions among organisms and the physical environment in areas of different sizes. One can refer to the ecosystem in a Petri dish, to a pond ecosystem, or to the forest ecosystem of a nature preserve or county. The size of the area under consideration will constrain the elements that are included in any particular instance of an ecosystem and, as a consequence, the types and magnitudes of interactions among elements. However, ecosystems are typically open systems in that they receive inputs and produce outputs that link them with areas outside their boundaries. The ecosystem concept is really a means of understanding how organisms and species depend on one another and their physical environment in a given place at a given time. Think of the ecosystem concept as one of those powerful satellites that are so useful in techy police dramas and spy movies to pinpoint the bad guy's location. With it, you can view entire cities, and in an instant, zoom in to a neighborhood, streetscape, and yard. In an analogous way, the concept and the perspective that it brings will be useful in the following chapters as I examine the connections between people and nature that occur in your yard, along your street, in the places you visit like your local park, and in your neighborhood and city. In each place exists a web of interconnected living and non-living elements of which you are an important part.

In a sense, an urban ecosystem is just like any other ecosystem. It is an ecological unit constituted of the interactions among organisms and the physical environment. When urban ecologists study urban ecosystems, they do so in very similar ways as ecologists trying to understand other types of ecosystems. They focus on the cycling of energy and/or nutrients and define and measure pools of material storage and fluxes, or exchanges of material, among pools. Ronald Kellett and his colleagues at the University of British Columbia did just this for a neighborhood in Vancouver and carbon cycling.[11] Cities are hotspots of carbon emissions to the atmosphere. As a result and given the severity of climate change and its impacts, the sources and magnitudes of carbon emissions in cities are of special interest to scientists and decision-makers, not least because identifying and understanding them may assist in the development and design of avoidance and mitigation measures.

Kellett's case study was a 1.2-by-1.2-mile area in the Sunset neighborhood, an inner suburb of Vancouver, a city of 630,000 people in a metro area home to nearly 2.5 million. The study area is mostly single-family homes with lots of about a fifth of an acre, but also includes commercial, institutional, and mixed-use development, especially along the busier thoroughfares, one of which is a major commuting corridor and truck route. There are three public parks covering a combined 58 acres, or about 7 percent of the study area.

Carbon occurs in many forms in these blocks of house- and tree-lined streets. It's easy to think of carbon as a constituent of tree trunks, branches, and leaves, of the turf grass sandwiching the sidewalks and in backyards, and of garden plants and flowers. It's less intuitive to think of the houses, streets, and sidewalks themselves as pools of carbon. Even less obvious is to think of the inhabitants, the people, as storage units of carbon. Similarly, when we think of the fluxes of carbon among pools, it's easy to remember the two-way transfer of carbon dioxide between plants and the atmosphere and perhaps even to identify heating fuel and gasoline as inputs of carbon to the system. But all the food, paper, and plastic that we consume also contains carbon, as does the waste that leaves the neighborhood every garbage day.

Kellett and his colleagues quantified as many of these pools and fluxes as possible to arrive at an estimate of net storage change in carbon per year in the study area. Based on the availability of data, they were able to estimate the neighborhood carbon stock to be 18 kilograms of carbon per square meter, apportioned in buildings and furniture (72 percent), soil (18 percent), lawns and trees (9 percent), humans (0.03 percent), and fuel tanks (0.03 percent). Of the carbon imported to the system in fuel, food, and materials, 88 percent is emitted into the atmosphere from vehicle tailpipes (44 percent), as heating exhaust from homes and other buildings (37 percent), and by humans (7 percent). The remainder is exported as waste (12 percent). Trees, lawns, and soils contribute 5 percent of all emissions to the atmosphere and generate 8 percent of the total waste (as garden waste). On a yearly basis, only 1 percent of the carbon added to the neighborhood, or 0.09 kilograms of carbon per meter squared, is stored in its vegetation and soils.

A comparison of the carbon accounting in the Sunset neighborhood of Vancouver with that performed by Suzanne Simard and Elyn Humphreys and their colleagues in nearby Douglas fir forests reveals the defining feature of urban ecosystems: the outsized influence of human structures and activities. For a fair comparison, I've excluded dead trees, woody debris, stumps, and leaf litter from the forest ecosystem accounting because these elements were not assessed in Sunset. Otherwise, I'm assuming that the two examples, forest and urban, are reasonable estimates of the major pools and fluxes of carbon in areas with similar climates and types of soil—that is, the major factors other than human activities that affect plant growth and, as a consequence, carbon cycling. Let's start with the total amount of carbon estimated for the two types of ecosystem: Sunset contains 55 percent of the carbon per unit area that a nearby forest does. In Sunset, 72 percent of that carbon occurs in buildings and furniture, whereas 70 percent of the carbon in the forest is part of live trees (from the deepest root to the tip of the highest branch), understory plants, and soil. In the forest, the exchange of carbon dioxide with the atmosphere is carried out by the vegetation and by microorganisms in the soil. In Sunset, trees, lawns, and soil account for only 12 percent of the atmospheric exchange of carbon dioxide, the rest being a result of human activities—heating, transportation, and bodily respiration. As a consequence, the total amount of carbon emitted to the atmosphere in Sunset is three times that emitted by a nearby forest, and the amount absorbed is only 28 percent. These differences result in Sunset's carbon storage per year being a mere third of what it is in the forest.

The International Union for Conservation of Nature lists urban and industrial ecosystems, alongside other, perhaps more familiar, examples such as deciduous temperate forests and semi-desert steppes, in its latest ecosystem typology. Urban ecosystems occur where a relatively large number of people create and maintain habitats for themselves, like houses, backyards, skyscrapers, shopping centers, and parking lots. Adding humans to the organism-physical environment mix of an area brings with it a multitude of new living and non-living elements to the system. The Sunset example brought to light (pun intended) several of the major human-derived elements in an urban ecosystem: buildings, lawns, furniture, fuel, food, and of course, people themselves. Since an ecosystem includes *all* living and non-living elements, we need to also include all the material goods we live with and use, all of the structures we create, and all the animals and plants, from cats to roses to kudzu, that we add to the system, intentionally or otherwise. These human-derived elements interact among themselves and with the existing natural elements of an area to create a diverse and complex set of dynamics where people live. Think back to the idealized forest ecosystem I described earlier. Picture the trees, soil, and animals in your local park as a kind of mini forest ecosystem busily cycling nutrients and energy among its elements and the atmosphere. Now add the jogger who scares away the ground-feeding birds and squirrels every morning; the warmer and more polluted air; the maintenance crew who mows the lawn, regularly removes fallen branches and leaves, and sprays for pests; the paved trail that limits water infiltration; the often-overflowing trash can next to the trail; and the ornamental flowerbeds and fruiting shrubs that attract their own suite of animals, and you'll begin to have an idea of the new and varied interactions that characterize urban ecosystem functioning.

But what is "urban"? It's straightforward to think of city centers, especially large ones, as urban. Same goes for the inner suburbs of large cities, like Vancouver's Sunset neighborhood, or Staten Island, New York, which has about the same housing density. However, most Americans do not live in large city centers or their inner suburbs. As of 2018, the Pew Research Center estimated that 55 percent of Americans lived in suburban counties in small metropolitan areas of fewer than a million people (30 percent of Americans) or in suburban counties in larger metropolitan areas (25 percent of Americans).[12] The remainder lived in urban cores (31 percent) or rural areas (14 percent). When urban ecologists refer to "urban" ecosystems, they are thinking of the urban core counties and the suburban ones. These places contain a relatively large number of people—at least fifty thousand in the classification used by the Pew Research Center—living and working in an environment dominated by human structures and activity, characteristics that conform to my definition above of an urban ecosystem. In this book, I similarly use "urban" to refer to suburbs and city centers alike, the places that 86 percent of Americans call home.

Another aspect of suburban counties, and suburbs in general, is that they occur in what the US Census defines as metropolitan statistical areas (MSAs), agglomerations of one or more cities and their surrounding counties that share economic and social ties, as measured by commuting patterns. For example, the largest MSA in the United States is the New

York-Newark-Jersey City, NY-NJ-PA MSA. These ties can bind otherwise rural-seeming places, such as low-density residential developments far from the urban core, to city centers and thereby qualify such communities as "suburban." In other words, these communities would not exist but for their interactions with the urban core and, as a result, are best understood as an element of the metropolitan area urban ecosystem or as examples of urban ecosystems themselves. Finally, it is important to note that farmed and natural areas within the matrix of a metropolitan area are arguably urban ecosystems as well, or are components of the greater metropolitan ecosystem. This is because they are likely to be subject to the dominating influence of urban-associated human activities that alter species composition and air, water, and soil quality.

So far, I have described the elements of an urban ecosystem and hinted at the various, new interactions that the addition of human-derived elements to a natural system engenders. I've also mentioned that urban ecosystems are dominated by human structures and activities, a defining characteristic. This dominance means that people play a large role in the functioning of urban ecosystems. The comparison between carbon cycling in Sunset and nearby forests illustrates this dominance and the large role played by people: most of the carbon in Sunset is in human structures and most of the exchange of carbon with the atmosphere is due to human activities. The human activities underlying this atmospheric carbon exchange in urban ecosystems, transportation and building heating, in part cause the Urban Heat Island Effect, another striking example of the outsized effects of people and their activities on ecosystem functioning. The Urban Heat Island Effect is also an excellent basis for an illustration of the interdependence of elements in ecosystems, an organizing principle of this book.

The Urban Heat Island Effect is a global pattern of higher temperatures in cities and suburbs than in surrounding rural areas. Climate Central, an independent organization of leading scientists and journalists, recently estimated that average temperatures in US cities are 5 to 9°F higher than in surrounding areas, with some neighborhoods in highly developed cities experiencing as much as a 20°F increase.[13] The major causes of warmer urban temperatures include the structures that define

Cities and suburbs around the world exhibit the Urban Heat Island Effect of higher temperatures compared to surrounding rural areas. The dominance of built structures and surfaces that generate, absorb, and retain heat is largely responsible.

cities and suburbs—buildings, roads, driveways, and parking lots—and the activities that define urban lives, such as driving, heating and cooling our buildings, and running our appliances. The latter generate waste heat, whereas the former absorb and store heat, and both factors are particularly potent where transportation and building densities are high.

The Urban Heat Island Effect is a clear example of people exerting a major influence on the physical environment where they live. It is also a very good example of the physical environment feeding back to influence people and thus, of the interdependence of people and the physical environment, and as I'll describe below, biological elements in urban ecosystems. The Urban Heat Island Effect influences people by affecting their health and well-being. As cities grow, they become hotter and the risk of heat-related illness and death increases. This is what David Hondula and his colleagues at Arizona State University reported for Maricopa County, the core county of the Phoenix-Mesa-Scottsdale metropolitan area, the third fastest growing metropolitan area in the United States.[14] By 2050, Hondula and his team projected that heat-related deaths could more than quadruple in their study area. And in nearly half of the twenty-seven urbanization and temperature scenarios they evaluated, heat-related deaths were projected to more than double. Higher temperatures in city centers and suburbs also affect residents' health and well-being by exacerbating ozone and particulate concentrations in the air, making it difficult, and potentially life-threatening, to breathe.

Just like humans, animals and plants are affected by higher temperatures in cities and suburbs. In some cases, species respond to increasing temperature by increasing their reproduction and becoming more numerous. If these species are associated with human health and well-being impacts, then this is likely to be unwelcome news to residents. As urban ecologists continue to study the Urban Heat Island Effect, focusing in particular on species that have negative effects on people, they are in fact finding that hotter cities and suburbs are ideal breeding grounds for a slew of species that most people would rather not have as neighbors. In Baltimore, Lewis Ziska, now at Columbia University, and his colleagues tested the impact of higher temperatures and increased CO_2 levels on the pollen production of ragweed, a major allergen in the eastern and central United States.[15] Ragweed in downtown Baltimore and its suburbs produced more total pollen and exhibited higher peak pollen production than ragweed at rural sites. City and suburban residents may also be exposed to allergenic pollen for longer during the year than their rural counterparts because growing seasons where they live are longer.[16] With respect to animal species, studies from the tropics are increasingly associating the occurrence of dengue fever, a mosquito-borne viral disease affecting half of the world's population, with urban temperature. For example, a multi-institutional team from São Paulo reported that temperature was the primary factor positively influencing the incidence of dengue among residents, over and above vegetation cover, the extent of slum-like areas, household income, land use, and population density.[17] Their laboratory analyses indicated that the mosquito carrier of dengue developed more rapidly and produced more eggs at the higher temperatures observed in the city. Back in the United States, another insect pest, this one contributing less directly to human health and well-being but causing significant impacts nonetheless, also increases in abundance in response to higher city temperatures. Adam Dale, a PhD student at the time under the supervision of Steven Frank at North Carolina State University, found that the gloomier scale insects he counted on Raleigh's street trees, the poorer the condition or health of the trees.[18] He estimated that warmer parts of the city had over 70 percent more trees in poor condition than cooler areas. Given that street trees have positive effects on everything from your state of mind to your body mass index to the crime rate in your neighborhood and that communities of color tend to live in warmer neighborhoods that already have fewer street trees to begin with, the gloomy scale insect is indeed a harbinger of the gloomy influence of the Urban Heat Island Effect on people.[19]

⋅⋅⋅

Notwithstanding the impacts of the Urban Heat Island Effect on human health and well-being, my explanation of urban ecosystems up to now has mostly focused on their physical and non-human living components, especially as they relate to people. This is only part of the story, however. If people are major components of urban ecosystems, then it follows that our social structures and processes are major players as well. The human structures and activities in urban ecosystems that I've focused on are motivated and shaped by the complex social fabric of our societies, which is itself altered and transformed by the physical and natural environment where we live. This interplay between the social and the ecological is at the heart of urban ecosystems.

In the early 2000s, three prominent urban ecologists put forth their versions of how they thought urban ecosystems were structured, each of which emphasized the social aspect of ecosystem functioning. Two were the founding directors of recently established urban long-term ecological research sites, the first urban sites to be included in the National Science Foundation's Long Term Ecological Research Network. Stewart Pickett, the director of the Baltimore Ecosystem Study, based his model of the Baltimore urban ecosystem on understanding from the field of human ecology, or the study of how humans relate to their natural, social, and built environments.[20] Baltimore's urban ecosystem was defined as the interplay between a human social system and a resource system. The institutions, cycles, and order of the social system influence natural, cultural, and socioeconomic resources and are influenced by them in turn. For example, my pre-pandemic daily commute by car (social cycle) to my university (institution) motivated by the social norm of working on campus (a form of social order) where I make use of and create socioeconomic and cultural resources (information that my students and I share in the cultural context of my organization and region) affected air quality and temperature (natural resources). When air quality becomes too poor, such as it is in New Delhi at the moment, daily commutes stop, with knock-on effects on other elements of the system in this example.[21]

Nancy Grimm, the founding director of the Central Arizona-Phoenix long-term ecological research site, took a different tack and described her focal desert urban ecosystem in terms of a cycle of changes in human perceptions and attitudes, societal patterns and processes, land use, ecological patterns and processes, changes in ecological conditions, and coarse-scale environmental context.[22] My recent research on bird likeability can serve to illustrate this framework.[23] Along with two of my former students, Lillian Collins and Grant Paton, I proposed the

Likeable, Therefore Abundant Hypothesis, which posits that birds with characteristics preferred by urban residents will be more abundant in suburbs in part because people add habitat and food resources to their yards to benefit the birds they like. In other words, human perceptions and attitudes in relation to birds change societal patterns and processes (homeowner behavior), which influences land use (gardening and landscaping practices), resulting in altered ecological patterns, processes, and conditions (different plant species and more birds that homeowners like). Coarse-scale environmental context (soil type, local climate) dictates the feasibility of specific gardening and landscaping practices, as well as the specific bird species the homeowner encounters in their yard. The altered ecological patterns, processes, and conditions can then feedback to influence human perceptions and attitudes, and the cycle begins again.

In parallel to these efforts to define and understand the social and ecological dimensions of urban ecosystems, Marina Alberti at the University of Washington used a complex adaptive systems approach to categorize patterns, processes, effects/changes, and drivers in cities and suburbs.[24] Complex adaptive systems are a good match for cities and suburbs because they involve inter-connectivity among a multitude of elements of various kinds. The most interesting characteristic of complex adaptive systems is the fact that there is no centralized agent of change that dictates what the system will do or look like. Instead, what the system does or looks like is unpredictable, the end result of so many different elements affecting and responding to each other. Think back to the Urban Heat Island Effect. It is caused primarily by the replacement of vegetation by built surfaces and human activities that emit waste heat into the atmosphere. Those two major causes are the products of innumerable factors, including your decision to crank the A/C overnight, the age and efficiency of your A/C unit, the type of car you drive, where you choose to live, the pattern of development in your city, your region's topography, the reflectivity of the window glass where you work and the materials used to make the building, the decisions of developers and city planners, zoning regulations, the design of your and other neighborhoods and streetscapes, the number, types, age, and condition of trees in your city, and the weather. None of these factors in and of themselves cause the

Urban Heat Island Effect, but their interconnectivity does. This complexity of inter-relationship is what urban ecosystems are all about.

— ⁓

The universe of urban ecosystems on Earth has expanded rapidly in the last century. So much so that in 2010, just over half of the world's population lived in urban areas. Over the coming decades, the urbanization of humankind will continue, particularly in developing regions of the world that include the globe's biodiversity hotspots. As a result, this century has been termed the Urban Century, during which more people and more non-human species will interact than ever before. Urban ecosystems will flourish in surprising and complex ways, presenting humankind with the opportunity and challenge of designing our habitats anew.

In this chapter, I described the urban ecosystem concept that is the basis for the structure of this book. Urban ecosystems are where many people and, as evidenced by the positive association between human population density and species richness reported by Gary Luck, many other species live. In the United States, urban ecosystems often occur in metropolitan areas that include city centers and their suburbs. Different types and sizes of places within metropolitan areas can be understood as urban ecosystems, from an individual homeowner's yard to an entire city. People play a large role in the relationships between the living and non-living elements in urban ecosystems by means of the structures they build and their day-to-day activities. The human social system, including our individual behaviors, attitudes, and preferences, and the social systems and structures that define our societies, are integral elements of urban ecosystems. Just like in any other ecosystem, people are part of reciprocal relationships in urban ecosystems, whereby they influence an aspect of their environment and it, in turn, influences them. The multitude of localized interconnections in urban ecosystems makes them particularly complex, especially with respect to the unexpected properties, like the Urban Heat Island Effect, that occur as a result.

Before I move on to explore the interdependent relationships between you and nature in the following chapters, I want to highlight the management implications of two of the characteristics of urban

Cooling off:
what you can do to mitigate
the Urban Heat Island Effect

Your choices and actions can help mitigate the Urban Heat Island Effect and reduce the likelihood of adverse impacts on your and your neighbors' health and well-being. You can

- **Maintain the trees on your property and add a few more.** Trees shade your home and increase local evapotranspiration, the process by which water is evaporated from plant leaves and other surfaces, absorbing ambient heat as it does so. An International Society of Arboriculture–certified arborist can help you keep your existing trees in good health for the long term (www.isa-arbor.com).

- **Walk, cycle, or take public transit** when possible to reduce the overall heat emitted from transportation where you live.

- **Choose a cool roof** that reflects more sunlight and heat than a traditional roof when it's time for a replacement.

- **Consider installing solar panels on your roof.** The shade from the panels will reduce the temperature of your home and decrease your air-conditioning needs.

- **Minimize the heat emissions from energy used in your home:** increase the thermostat in the summer and lower it in winter, use smart power strips to reduce phantom power used by your devices, change your bulbs to LED, choose energy efficient appliances, and upgrade your windows and home insulation if you can.

- **Help to map the Urban Heat Island in your city.** The National Oceanic and Atmospheric Administration's NIHHIS-CAPA Urban Heat Island Mapping Campaign is funding cities and their partners nationwide (https://nihhis.cpo.noaa.gov/Urban-Heat-Islands/Mapping-Campaigns/Campaign-Cities). Campaigns need volunteers of all ages to collect the data necessary to target mitigation strategies to those most in need.

Right: Trees help mitigate the Urban Heat Island Effect. A black tupelo sapling with a watering bag around its base.

ecosystems I have just enumerated. First, our outsized influence on other elements in urban ecosystems means that we can fundamentally change the way cities are conceptualized, designed, and planned to create healthy habitats for our and other species. Second, the multitude of localized interactions in urban ecosystems means that fundamental change will be extremely difficult to achieve and may be accompanied by positive and negative surprises to which we will need to adapt. Nonetheless, those same localized interactions imply that each one of us is critically involved in the functioning of the urban ecosystem where we live. No single person, agency, or institution can change the system. The system changes because of each and every one of our actions. Cranking your A/C unit has an effect on air temperature outside your home—a small one if your action is considered in isolation, but a very large one if one considers the resulting Urban Heat Island of your suburb or city. Our day-to-day choices can have big consequences on the physical environment and the other species in our urban ecosystem, whether we can immediately see or feel those consequences and whether the consequences manifest in our neighborhood or in a part of the city we've never been to (see the sidebar *Cooling off: what you can do to mitigate the Urban Heat Island Effect*). Let's now explore these consequences, as well as the ways that nature affects us. The planetarium's attendant has turned on the lights. It's now time to head home and consider your relationship with nature in your yard.

CHAPTER 3

YOUR YARD

I LOVE TO TAKE LONG WALKS. I DON'T WALK IN A LARGE PARK OR NATURE preserve; I simply start walking as soon as I step out the door. For me, there is nothing as freeing as leaving everything but your house keys behind and exploring the intricacies of the urban unknown. My perambulations take me along the sidewalks of my residential neighborhood and those adjacent to it. From this vantage point, I observe urban nature in front and side yards and as glimpsed behind houses. I notice the landscaping aesthetic of each property: neat as a pin with not a blade of grass out of place, filled with flowers and shrubs in carefully tended beds, or less managed with wild-looking jumbles of plants that catch my eye. I also look and listen for birds, never failing to marvel at the paradisiacal blue of eastern bluebird wings or the entitlement of American robins lounging on lawns at dusk.

It was on one of these walks that I came across Wing Haven Garden and Bird Sanctuary. The first time I passed it, I didn't really grasp what I had discovered. I was walking along a residential street I had never travelled before, admiring the large, old houses and their mature gardens. Looking ahead, I noticed an 8-foot brick wall edging the sidewalk and continuing on much farther than I would have expected had it been bordering the side yard of the house ahead of it. I tried peering into the space behind the wall without much luck, but noticed tall trees and lots of them enclosed within its boundary. After the wall, I came across a large white house and then another open space next to it, this time with a wide entrance to the street and a gate into a leafy dimness beyond. At the time,

Eastern bluebird at nest box.

I was really enjoying my brisk walk, so I chose not to stop to investigate what was clearly something a little different than the typical house and yard in that neighborhood.

I opened Google Maps when I got home, which named the special place I had come across. Wing Haven is actually nearly three acres of gardens and wooded areas. Nearly a hundred years earlier, Elizabeth and Edwin O. Clarkson, after purchasing the white house I had seen, soon decided to add eleven more adjacent lots to their property and to dedicate the space to birds. Since that time, Wing Haven has provided respite to 150 bird species, including bald eagles and woodland warblers, within what is now a highly developed urban landscape just three miles from the city center. A check of the Cornell Lab of Ornithology's eBird database tells me that in 2021 alone, visitors and staff observed fifty-five bird species in Wing Haven, including the declining redheaded woodpecker that is listed as Near Threatened by the International Union for Conservation of Nature, the body that maintains *the* list of imperiled species around the world, and the pine siskin, a common bird in steep decline according to

Looking across the street at Wing Haven Garden and Bird Sanctuary, the ultimate yard designed with birds in mind.

the Cornell Lab (to learn more about eBird, see the sidebar *eBird: birding in the twenty-first century*).

Soon after finding Wing Haven, I explored what was behind those brick walls and now visit regularly. I meander along paths marked only by trampled leaf litter and shaded by massive willow oaks, tall pines, and persimmons. Frog-filled ponds peek through the dense ground and shrub cover, ideal habitat for brown thrashers who flick piles of dead leaves skyward looking for insects. More than once, I've paused to find a barred owl peering down at me from on high. In other, more maintained areas, boxwood hedges line trim lawns, and northern cardinals sing from cherry trees, their bright red plumage complementing the pink flowers.

Needless to say, Wing Haven is not the typical residential yard in a large city. But it *is* a yard. It's easy to see the other houses surrounding the property, even if those houses are a little farther away than usual. Wing Haven is really a representation of what is possible if nature is welcomed into our yards. I use the word "welcomed" here with intention.

eBird:
birding in the twenty-first century

The Cornell Lab of Ornithology's eBird program is a global database of more than a billion bird sightings contributed by the public, and just like iNaturalist, is an example of citizen or community science. Download the eBird app to start contributing your sightings of birds where you live or farther afield. Once you do, you will benefit from lists of species expected to be in your region, based on their known ranges and the nearby sightings of other birders. The eBird app is also a great resource for finding rare and interesting birds and birding hotspots, especially when you travel. One of my favorite things to do in a new place is to open the app to see the species reported in the area. I often find an easy spot to visit, like a local park, and get to see birds that are new to me, with help from others online who already know what they are called. On more than one occasion during my travels, I've met real-life eBirders in the field and had the opportunity to benefit from their knowledge firsthand. Finally, your and others' ebird sightings are the basis for some pretty spectacular avian research coming out of the Cornell Lab. My favorites right now are the abundance animations. In shades of pale yellow-brown to deep purple, you can watch waves of American robins sweep across North America as the year unfolds. The animations depict the expected number of robins at any given time or place across their continental range, an extraordinary example of the enhanced understanding made possible by nearly seven hundred thousand eBird users.[1]

Your yard is your own personal outdoor space, to do with as you choose (within the limits of city ordinances or homeowner association regulations, of course). Your yard is where you have the most direct intentional effect on nature. In this chapter, I will show you that how you choose to manage nature in your yard can matter more to birds, including species of conservation concern, than whether there is public greenspace or undeveloped land nearby. I'll also show that small changes to your yard can have relatively big impacts on bird diversity, and I'll describe exactly what those changes are. And because your yard is where you experience nature most frequently, I'll explore the effects of exposure to that nature, including exposure to birds in particular, on your and your kids' attitudes and behaviors toward nature, which play an important role in addressing the pressing global environmental challenges of our day. I've chosen to focus on birds in this chapter for a pragmatic reason: There is much more research on the effects of human activities in yards on birds than on other animals. This research is a result of the special bond that people and birds enjoy, which also makes them the ideal organisms for thinking about the effects of exposure to nature on people.

How you manage nature in your yard matters just as much or more to birds than how much greenspace there is nearby

When we think of natural areas in cities and suburbs, yards are not front of mind. In our urban landscapes, natural areas are confined to public spaces, such as parks, nature preserves, and greenways. Our society's sharp distinction between humans and nature means that anywhere humans settle, including anywhere they plan to do so, does not include nature. I once contrasted the future land use map of a portion of my city with the United States Geological Survey's National Land Cover Database for the same area.[2] The city map was categorized into sixteen types of residential, institutional, retail, office, and industrial uses, whereas only a single category, not including water, represented anything one might consider as natural (this was labelled Greenway and is now labelled Open Space/Recreation). In comparison, the National Land Cover Database map was a mix of green and yellow shades, representing different types of forest and pastureland, including in areas that were already developed. To the city planning department, and I would argue most if not all residents, our urban landscapes are dichotomies of human uses in their various forms and nature. Even spaces claimed for future human use are not considered natural. After comparing the maps, I was surprised to find that when I drove past an undeveloped, private lot with relatively mature forest near my university, even I, who love and adore nature in all its forms, had a hard time labelling it as a natural area. For most of us, nature is only present in the spaces we designate for it.

Virginia opossum.

Intertwined with this dichotomous view of our urban and suburban spaces is the conception of what should be considered "real" nature. We are all familiar with racoons and opossums that live in our neighborhoods and other developed areas. But do they qualify as really "natural"? I doubt that most people would consider them adequate representatives of the pristine natural world that we hold in such high esteem and that only truly exists where humans do not, in nature preserves and in the unmanaged spaces in parks and greenways. Maybe we see these species too frequently or perhaps these and other species that we live in regular contact with are too tainted by their close association with us that we do not consider them really natural after all. These are pretty weighty issues to grapple with in this type of book, but they are worth pondering.

In fact, yards are major repositories of nature, including, as we'll see later, elements that we assume need and belong in nature preserves, such as threatened species. Estimates from cities in the United States and the United Kingdom indicate that at least a third of city greenspace is found in yards.[3] For example, in metro Boston, yards contain 37 percent of total canopy cover and in Sacramento, 54 percent of tree cover and 80 percent of grass cover is on residential land. Across urban and suburban areas in the United Kingdom, 50 percent of total greenspace—grass, bushes, and trees—occurs in domestic gardens, implying that 23 percent of total urban or suburban area, green or otherwise, is covered by garden greenspace.[4] Finally, in Leipzig, Germany, front and back yards contain more greenspace than public areas in a quarter of city districts.[5] All told, these statistics mean that a substantial portion of habitat for plant and animal species in cities, and in some cases even the majority, is in your and your neighbors' yards.

This astounding fact has prompted ecologists and conservation organizations to focus on the potential of residential yards to provide high-quality habitat for wildlife. For instance, Douglas Tallamy, a professor at the University of Delaware, recently initiated the Homegrown National Park movement. In his excellent book, *Nature's Best Hope: A New Approach to Conservation That Starts in Your Yard*, Tallamy argues that our existing national parks are too few and far between to adequately conserve nature. Instead, each of our yards, and other developed spaces such as office parks and school grounds, can add to a new and vast Homegrown National Park, urgently needed to restore biodiversity and the clean air and other benefits it provides. The largest cooperative conservation project ever attempted, the movement's goal is to replace approximately half of the privately owned lawns in the United States by native plantings by catalyzing the collective effort of homeowners and others nationwide. Find out how you can participate in the sidebar *You are nature's best hope: how to add your yard to the newest national park*.

Although we humans have a hard time thinking of our yards as wildlife habitat, and lots of it, birds do not. To the birds you see in your neighborhood, whether perched on your house or a tree branch in your yard or flying across the road, the habitat resources in your yard are just as or more important than those in nearby public greenspace and undeveloped areas. Think about this the next time you see a flutter of wing out of the corner of your eye or hear bird song in the morning or evening. The birds that you live amongst, your avian neighbors, critically depend on the habitat that you intentionally or unintentionally provide

You are nature's best hope: how to add your yard to the newest national park

Douglas Tallamy's Homegrown National Park movement is a response to the staggering loss of biodiversity over the last several decades. Instead of relying on national parks and other preserves to conserve nature, it calls on each one of us who owns or manages private property to add native plantings to these spaces. Our small effort, combined with those of others, can achieve the project's awesome goal of twenty million acres of native plantings across the country.

Contributing to Homegrown National Park

The beauty of Homegrown National Park is its simplicity. All you have to do to help achieve the project's goal is to plant one or more native plants in your yard (if you are unsure which species to plant in your region, visit homegrownnationalpark.org for helpful resources). Then, add your planting to The Map, which keeps track of the location and acreage of plantings across the country and the project's overall progress toward achieving the twenty-million-acre goal (as of this writing, the total stands at 23,650 acres across 11,770 sites). Your single plant or half acre will be plotted as a cute lightning bug, intended to light up the motivation of others visiting The Map. You can also follow the project's #onthemap and #startdigging hashtags to connect with other participants and see what they planted. Because of its simplicity, its focus on the spaces where we most directly influence nature, and its emphasis on community and cooperation, Homegrown National Park has enormous potential to mitigate biodiversity loss, as well as dramatically change the way we think about conserving nature in the future.

Douglas Tallamy's Homegrown National Park movement aims to replace half of the privately owned lawns in the United States with native plantings.

on your property. Whether you choose to replace your lawn with native plantings, as Douglas Tallamy suggests, or remove a tree to create space for other amenities, strongly influences the number and different types of birds where you live, perhaps even more than whether your neighborhood has a park, has tree-lined streets, or is near a tract of native habitat. And I'm not only talking about very common species like house sparrows and American robins. The birds that depend on you include specialists, like desert birds, and those that are threatened by human activities. To birds in the residential areas of cities and suburbs, your and your neighbors' yards are essential habitat.

Some of the evidence that your yard is important habitat for birds in residential areas comes from a former fellow student of mine, Adam Smith, who completed his PhD in the same lab that I did and is now at Environment and Climate Change Canada. During his studies, Smith created the Ottawa Bird Count, a volunteer-based effort to systematically monitor birds in the city. The project has led to the collection of more than a decade of valuable data on birds in Ottawa's neighborhoods and enabled Smith and his colleagues to address the question that interests us here: What are the relative effects of the amount of vegetation on residential land compared to non-residential land on bird species richness, or the number of different bird species?[6] Smith and his colleagues compared the amount of tree, shrub, and grass in the yards of houses and apartment buildings with that in parks and other large greenspaces within a third of a mile of 246 count locations along the sidewalks and paths of Ottawa's neighborhoods. They found that the total number of native bird species, the number of bird species who primarily depend on forest, and the number of threatened species were similarly as dependent on yard vegetation as on public greenspace. Smith's analysis predicted that increasing the amount of vegetation in yards or public greenspace areas by 10 percent would each add about a fifth more forest-dependent or threatened species to neighborhoods. Furthermore, by plotting vegetated area against human population density, Smith and his colleagues found that as more people move to an area, the vegetated area of non-residential land becomes constrained, whereas residential vegetated area does not.

The red-shouldered hawk (top) and ruby-crowned kinglet (bottom) are examples of species that primarily depend on forest, but also visit yards

This and Smith's other results tell us four vital lessons about the importance of vegetation in our yards to birds. First, birds rely just as much on the vegetation in our yards as they do on the vegetation in parks and other public greenspaces. Second, this includes species, like forest-dependent and threatened species, that may be otherwise declining or suffering from habitat loss and are therefore conservation priorities. Third, as our cities and suburbs continue to grow in human population, trees, shrubs, and grass will be increasingly found primarily in our yards, which, as a result, will become more and more critically important as habitat resources for birds. Finally, and happily, a small change in the amount of vegetation in yards in a neighborhood, just 10 percent, can result in a relatively large change, 20 percent, in the number of bird species you'll find there.

The other studies that compared the effects of vegetation and other habitat resources in yards to those in public greenspaces or undeveloped areas all show a larger effect of the resources in yards on birds. One of these was carried out at the Central Arizona-Phoenix urban long-term ecological research site I mentioned in chapter 2.[7] Just like Smith, Susannah Lerman and Paige Warren, now at the USDA Forest Service and the University of Massachusetts, Amherst, respectively, benefited from long-term monitoring sites for birds located in residential areas. They found that birds in neighborhoods responded twice as much to habitat features in front yards than to the distance to the nearest tract of desert habitat. The birds they observed included twenty-one primarily desert-dependent species, a third of the total. And, similar to Smith's results, they estimated that a relatively small change in the number of habitat features in front yards could make a big difference to desert birds: half of the desert species observed in the study were counted at monitoring sites if yards within 150 feet on either side collectively contained just ten desert tree species and twenty shrubs.

Results similar to Lerman's and Warren's from Phoenix have been reported in the Chicago area and in Hobart, Tasmania.[8] In the Chicago area, the number of bird species counted along residential streets is dependent to a greater extent on the wildlife resources in yards, such as trees, plants with fruit or berries, and birdfeeders, than on canopy cover

Five simple things you can do to create a bird-friendly yard

Ecological research on birds in residential yards suggests that implementing the following five recommendations will result in more birds of a greater variety in your yard and more species of conservation concern:

1. **Add more vegetation to your yard.**

2. **Choose plant species that attract birds.** The National Audubon Society's native plants database (https://www.audubon.org/native-plants) can help you identify the appropriate species for your region and find where to buy them.

3. **Diversify the type and structure of vegetation in your yard.** Add plant species that you don't already have and aim for a mix of

A welcoming yard for birds. This backyard is filled with plants of different species and forms: trees, shrubs, vines, and herbaceous plants. The resulting variety in habitat structure attracts a wide variety of bird species. Birdfeeders that offer different foods also help.

Slippers sporting his Birdsbesafe collar. The colorful collar is easily seen by songbirds, thus preventing Slippers from sneaking up on them unawares.

plants with different forms and of multiple heights, like a bit of lawn, a garden bed with multiple species, some shrubs, and a few trees of various heights.

4. **Provide supplemental food for birds** by planting fruit-bearing plants or adding a birdfeeder to your yard. Be sure to use safe bird-feeding practices that minimize the potential for birds attracted to your feeder to come to harm. See the Cornell Lab of Ornithology's Project FeederWatch guidelines at https://feederwatch.org/learn/feeding-birds/ to learn more.

5. **Keep your cat indoors,** use a leash to walk them outside, or equip them with a Birdsbesafe collar. A randomized trial found that cats wearing the collar killed three times fewer birds in the fall and nineteen times fewer birds in the spring than uncollared cats. The collars are widely available for purchase.[9]

or the area of open space, including forest preserves, within two-thirds of a mile. Again, small changes to yards were predicted to make a relatively big difference: increasing the proportion of yards that contained at least one plant with fruit or berries by just 10 percent would increase the bird count by nearly two species. In Hobart, distance to native vegetation had minimal influence on the number and different types of native birds observed in yards, as well as on the number of woodland birds. Instead, garden characteristics, such as shrub cover and whether supplementary food for birds was provided, played a large role. Hobart's yards were also home to six endemic species found only in Tasmania and one critically endangered species, the swift parrot.

The fact that birds in residential areas depend on vegetation and other habitat resources in yards is great news. It means that your gardening and landscaping choices can make a real difference to bird populations in your city or suburb. Further, the evidence suggests that you don't need to become a master gardener to have an impact. Even a small change, like adding a shrub or tree, will increase the likelihood that you will see a swift parrot or cactus wren, depending on where you live. So, what changes should you make? I've come up with five main recommendations distilled from the research in Ottawa, Phoenix, the Chicago area, and Hobart and a few other sources. Read on for more details and see the sidebar *Five simple things you can do to create a bird-friendly yard* for a distilled version that includes a few additional resources.

First, the Ottawa results suggest that simply adding vegetation to your yard has a positive effect on bird diversity. We all have that patch of bare earth or forgotten garden bed that could be home to a plant or two.

Second, when you do add vegetation to your yard, choose species that attract birds. The number of desert birds in Phoenix and the number of woodland birds in Hobart were positively associated with specific shrubs and trees in yards. Douglas Tallamy's own research suggests that suburban yards with more native plants have greater bird diversity and provide more caterpillar food for nesting birds, which translates into more young fledged from nests.[10] But it's important to keep in mind that non-native plant species may also provide important resources for birds where you live.[11] As long as the species you are planting is not invasive, whether it's native or non-native may not matter much.

Third, diversify the type and structure of vegetation in your yard. If you currently have a lot of lawn, replace some of it with a garden bed or add a shrub or tree species that you don't already have. Your aim is to increase the horizontal and vertical complexity of habitat in your yard so that it is attractive to a wide variety of bird species. In the Chicago area, more bird species were counted along streets with a higher ratio of evergreen—in other words, more vegetative diversity—and in Hobart, tall trees were important attractants of woodland birds.

Fourth, feed your avian neighbors by planting fruit-bearing plants or by adding a birdfeeder to your space. More bird species were counted along Chicago-area streets with yards with fruit-bearing plants and more native birds visited yards in Hobart where residents offered supplemental food. Birdfeeding, in particular, is associated with improved physiological condition, more fledglings, and larger populations of several native bird species.[12]

Finally, keep your pet cat indoors, use a leash to walk them outside, or equip them with a Birdsbesafe collar. The number of outdoor cats was negatively associated with the number of bird species counted along Chicago-area streets and, more broadly, cats are a primary cause of bird mortality nationwide. And yes, I've walked a pet cat on a leash. We both ended up enjoying the exercise!

Adding vegetation and food for birds to your yard and eliminating or minimizing avian predation by your pet cat will result in more birds of a wider variety on your property. If you implement these recommendations in your front yard, as many people do, then social theory and recent data suggest that your neighbors are likely to follow suit, magnifying the impact of your actions. Increasing vegetation and bird diversity in your yard also has broader impacts on the conservation of global biodiversity and the health of the planet through its reciprocal effect on you. I'll now turn to how nature, including birds, in your yard can help to reverse the extinction of experience, a lack of connection to nature that is threatening our best efforts to preserve it.

Experiencing nature in your yard leads to love and care for the environment

Birds and people have a special relationship. With the exception of domesticated species, birds are probably the animal group that we knowingly interact with the most. We're both active during the day, which means we encounter one another a lot. And birds on the whole aren't what you would call shy. They soar, swoop, flit, and flutter. They swing and jump from one feeder rail to another like Olympic gymnasts performing a routine. Or, my favorite, zoom around in a figure eight pattern at dusk above my garden—what I like to call the hummingbird happy dance, but is really the birds foraging for flying insects. Many birds are spectacularly colorful, like the Baltimore oriole I held in my hands while it received an identifying leg band—the most impressive sunset has nothing on the shades of orange and gold I saw reflected in the bird's plumage. And birds also make a lot of noise, much of it beautiful, but some less so, especially if it happens at 5 a.m. Birds also occur everywhere where humans do and in curious forms adapted to the local conditions—most famously in the Galapagos Islands, where they taught us about evolution. Because of their conspicuousness, we are privileged to witness just about every aspect of their life cycles, from the nest to finding a mate of their own. In sum, birds are easily visible, and very often beautiful, representatives of the natural world that just about anybody would say they like.

For all of the reasons above, bird feeding and bird watching are popular activities used to teach kids about nature. In schools, lesson plans about birds abound, but there isn't much evidence of their effectiveness. Rachel White at the University of Brighton in the United Kingdom was curious about the potential impact of these relatively simple activities on kids' environmental knowledge and attitudes, so she and her colleagues created and tested the Bird Buddies program to find out.[13] Eight classes of seven- to ten-year-olds at eight different suburban schools in Brighton participated in the program, none of which had watched or fed birds on school grounds before. Before starting Bird Buddies and without knowing anything about it, students filled out a survey that asked whether their family fed birds at home and how many nature activities they had done in the past year, and whether they liked birds, how they felt about

Two common species at birdfeeders in the eastern United States: the house finch (top) and the northern cardinal (bottom).

them, and their importance to humans. Students were also tasked with identifying common bird species from pictures in the survey. The same questions were asked again following six weeks of monitoring and feeding birds in school grounds.

By comparing pre- and post-program student responses to the survey, White and her colleagues found that Bird Buddies had a big impact on students' knowledge of and attitudes toward birds. After regularly watching and feeding birds for six weeks, students were able to identify about twice the number of bird species on average than before they started and reported liking birds a lot more. Their emotional responses to birds and the importance they attached to them also significantly changed. Ultimately, participation in Bird Buddies altered students', and teachers', behaviors in relation to the environment. During the six-week program period, nearly a quarter of students went birdwatching outside of school for the first time. Once the program ended, and despite a few grumbles about the cold and needing to keep still and silent while birdwatching, more than 80 percent of students wanted to continue watching and feeding birds in the school grounds and learning about wildlife in class, and at least half thought they would seek out birds outside of class as well. One year later, four classes were still watching and feeding birds and teachers observed that the original participants were generally more interested in and involved in environmental activities at school than other students.

What White and her colleagues discovered in Bird Buddies—improved environmental knowledge, a stronger and more positive emotional connection to nature, and pro-environmental behavior, all from directly engaging with the natural world—is a cure for a pernicious phenomenon termed the extinction of experience. Proposed in 1978 by Robert Pyle, a prominent nature writer, the extinction of experience is the disappearance of nature experiences, especially among children.[14] In his essay defining the term, Pyle reflects on the dramatically altered landscape near Denver, Colorado, where he roamed as a young naturalist in search of butterflies. What was once grassland, where he readily found butterflies aplenty, had been transformed into a matrix of housing, shopping centers, and roads where only a nature trail remained. Playing on the word extinction, Pyle's extinction of experience refers not only to the extinction of the human experience of nature but to its proximal cause, the local extinctions of wildlife in highly developed landscapes.

Although areas where human population density is high are also areas that contain a lot of species as I described in chapter 2, recall that this positive relationship only holds for spatial scales larger than two-thirds of a mile across. In these bigger landscapes, there is room for the habitats of humans and other species, allowing both to coexist in large numbers. However, in anything smaller than two-thirds of a mile across, the relationship between human population density and the number of other species is negative. In these smaller areas, like your neighborhood, built structures and lawns crowd out the native habitat that some species rely on. As a result, these species become locally extinct. You won't find them in your neighborhood any longer, but they still occur in the region. In other words, your child is less likely to come across the goatweed emperor butterfly, as a young Robert Pyle did, today than when there were fewer houses in your development or before your development was built. Recall that over 80 percent of Americans live in cities and suburbs, a proportion similar to those in other high-income countries, and you will have an idea of the pervasiveness of the extinction of local, everyday nature experience in our society.

Our urban population is not the only contributor to the extinction of experience. Today's children and youth spend more time indoors away from nature than they once did. Time diary data from the University of Michigan Panel Study of Income Dynamics, a long-term survey of households across the country, show that, between 1981 and 2003, the amount of time spent outdoors per week by kids and youth aged six to seventeen declined by 50 percent.[15] Between 1997 and 2003, the same data similarly show that the percentage of children aged six to twelve participating in outdoor activities at least once per week declined by 37 percent.[16] And a survey of over eight hundred mothers nationwide in the early aughts reported that, whereas 70 percent of mothers played outside every day when they were young, only 31 percent of their children did.[17] On average, American kids and youth spend twenty-two of twenty-four hours each day indoors or in vehicles.[18] And when they do go outside, very few—5.4 percent, according to the National Kids Survey—spend time wildlife watching, hiking, or camping.[19] One look at the comparison table in the latest National Survey of Fishing, Hunting, and Wildlife-Associated Recreation says it all. In 1985, 51 percent of young people aged six to fifteen watched wildlife that year, either at or away from home. By 2010, only 31 percent did. This trend in children spending less time outdoors interacting with nature is also playing out in the United Kingdom. In 2009, the Childhood and Nature Survey found that children there preferred playing indoors the most and spent less than 10 percent of their time playing in natural places such as woodlands.[20] In comparison, their parents and grandparents spent over 40 percent of their childhood playing in nature and outdoor activities were preferred over others.

I should note here that these statistics gloss over important variability among demographic groups in their ease of access to the outdoors and nature. People living in higher-income areas of cities and suburbs are surrounded by more vegetation and a greater diversity of plant and bird species than residents in lower-income areas.[21] All else being equal then, wealthier residents can more easily experience nature since it occurs where they live or close to it in a multitude of forms. Similarly, neighborhoods with larger Latinx or Black populations in cities across the United States have less tree cover along city streets and in public parks.[22] Parks in these neighborhoods are also smaller, have fewer facilities such as trails, are more poorly maintained, including having more physical environmental hazards, and are less safe in terms of crime than parks in neighborhoods with more White residents.[23] For people of color then, access to nearby nature is diminished since there is less of it but also because it may be too dangerous to experience it.

At this point, it is time to ask: What are the implications of this progressive extinction of experience among our children? We've already seen the immediate implications in the Bird Buddies results: Regular feeding and watching of birds lead to a greater knowledge of bird species and a stronger emotional connection to birds among students. Therefore, as the experience of nature declines in children, we can expect them to know less about nature and to care less about it. One Bird Buddies result that I didn't mention was the fact that 80 percent of students thought that the act of feeding birds increased the number of species visiting their school-yards. However, pre- and post-program monitoring of species showed that this was not the case—the number of bird species stayed the same. The effective invisibility of birds to students at the beginning of the Bird Buddies program is a stark example of what I imagine as a dimensionless and gray ecological worldview, in which the blues, reds, and yellows of common birds are not discernible because we don't know they exist. In my case, my ecological world got a lot more colorful and interesting as a PhD student when I first collected ground beetles, predators that live in soil, leaf litter, and lawn. One look under the microscope at the kaleidoscopic blues and magentas of their elytra, the hard casings that protect their wings like the spotted ones of ladybugs, pierced the gray fog of my ignorance. I now see ground beetles everywhere, crossing the sidewalk in front of me, when I garden, even in my building at the university. A similar thing happened when I learned the songs of over a hundred bird species for another dissertation project. I'm now surrounded by species-specific sound of an always startling variety wherever I go—sometimes much to the annoyance of my family members who don't care to be continually interrupted by bird identifications (see the sidebar *The magic of bird song: how to use the Merlin Bird ID app* to replicate this experience). For me, the participants of Bird Buddies, and anyone who has learned of and interacted with new species, it's like visiting a tropical island for the first time, except that the exotic-looking plants and animals go home with you. Once this happens, emotional connection with your colorful new ecological world is possible. You, and your child, need to be aware of the birds or other species surrounding you to care about and value them.

The extinction of experience among children has less immediate effects, as well. Childhood nature experiences, or their absence, influence how we feel about and value nature as adults. Masachi Soga at the University of Tokyo and his colleagues recently surveyed undergraduate students at nearby Tokyo Gakugei University to test for this effect.[24] They found that students' emotional connection to nature—measured using an established set of ranked items such as "I feel very connected to all livings things and the Earth"—was positively associated with the frequency of students' current contact with nature and the frequency with which

The magic of bird song: how to use the Merlin Bird ID app

The Cornell Lab of Ornithology's Merlin Bird ID app first came to my attention in one of Margaret Renkl's excellent essays in the *New York Times*.[25] Renkl described an experience like my own of having her ecological horizons broadened after letting the app listen to the bird sounds in her yard. Species names cascaded across her screen as the app's artificial intelligence software compared what it heard to a database of recordings. Although many of the birds were familiar to her by sight and sound, a few were not—species that she wasn't aware shared her property. As she described it, these species only existed for her as "undifferentiated sounds in the trees." That is, until Merlin made them magically appear on her phone's screen!

The Merlin Bird ID app uses several methods to help you identify birds and learn more about them. The Bird ID Wizard bases its suggestions on the date, your location, and your answers to three simple questions about size, color, and behavior. Sound ID and Photo ID compare real-time or recorded audio and your photographs, respectively, to the Macaulay Library database to populate a list of potential species. Each of these methods is powered by the observations of eBirders from near and far who have either recently seen or heard a similar bird in your area or contributed photographs and recordings to the Macaulay Library.

Next time you are in your yard, use Merlin to find out which birds are there too. You can also use the app to identify and keep track of the new birds that visit your yard once you've begun to take the steps listed in the sidebar *Five simple things you can do to create a bird-friendly yard*. Merlin might be a good choice for this type of monitoring since the observations you log in the app are not publicly shared.

they interacted with nature as children. The same relationships held for the degree to which students valued natural areas, birds, and butterflies for their aesthetic, well-being, and educational benefits. Students who interacted with nature to a greater extent as adults or as children valued natural areas and butterflies more strongly than those who interacted with nature less, whereas the value students placed on birds was only affected by current contact with nature. Setting these relationships aside for a moment, Soga's results are just as remarkable for the fact that the researchers controlled for the perceived overall greenness of students' childhood environments. Soga and his colleagues measured frequency of contact with nature by asking students how often they visited natural areas such as woodlands and how often they observed or touched animals and plants. Thus, contact with nature here is referring to an intentional and direct engagement with the natural world, not some general or passing exposure because you happened to grow up in a very green neighborhood. Just like the Bird Buddies program that emphasized regular, close-up contact with birds by feeding them, Soga's results indicate that a child's active engagement with nature is needed to develop a strong emotional connection with nature that lasts into adulthood.

In turn, this lasting effect influences our behavior in relation to nature and the environment. This relationship is frequently assessed as the association between connection to nature and pro-environmental behavior, the idea being that people who feel more strongly about nature are more likely to behave in ways that benefit or minimize potential harm to it and the environment more broadly. Connection to nature can be measured using any one of at least seventeen different scales, or series of questions, with pro-environmental behavior not far behind. In addition, pro-environmental behavior can be self-reported—I tell you that I recycle—or observed—you take the trouble to check for aluminum cans and plastic milk jugs in my recycling bin each week. Because of this variability, and the fact that studies investigating the behavioral consequences of connection to nature have done so using different numbers and types of people in different locations, all of which may influence study results, it's difficult to reliably conclude that a relationship exists. Luckily, Julie Whitburn and her colleagues at Victoria University of Wellington in New Zealand recently undertook a meta-analysis, a study of studies, to find out.[26] By synthesizing the results of twenty-six studies published in the last twenty years, they found that connection to nature does indeed positively influence both self-reported pro-environmental behavior, such as conserving energy and water, reducing consumption, using public transit, and supporting environmental movements, and observed pro-environmental behavior, such as signing up for a newsletter that includes practical tips on sustainable living. This overall relationship holds regardless of study location and whether study participants were children or adults, male or female.

Enter the pigeon paradox. The paradox, coined by Robert Dunn at North Carolina State University and his colleagues, is the notion that the conservation of nature worldwide depends on the lowly and abundant pigeon, probably the most familiar representative of urban nature.[27] Since most people on the planet live in urban areas and, as we've seen, pro-environmental behavior depends fundamentally on experiencing nature as a child by way of forming a lasting emotional connection with it, then the global conservation of species and habitats, and other planetary environmental challenges like climate change, depend critically on restoring and conserving urban nature. As Robert Pyle so eloquently put it, "What is the extinction of the condor to a child who has never seen a wren?"[28] In other words, why would it matter to a child who rarely goes outside and even more rarely interacts with wild plants and animals, and ultimately the adult they will become, if three billion birds disappear from North America, as they have over the last fifty years?[29] To this child, the loss of so many birds, even common ones, won't make much of a difference because the child has never or only rarely seen them. To the child, the birds are effectively grayed out, invisible, because they've had so few opportunities to get to know them, care about them, and value them. Worryingly, the relationships embodied in the pigeon paradox likely loop back on themselves in a worsening cycle, whereby the extinction of experience leads to an emotional disconnect from nature and, as a consequence, its degradation, which heightens the extinction of experience. If this is the case, we can expect a shifting baseline of diminished biodiversity and human quality of life that worsens from one generation to the next.

It seems to me that the easiest way to tackle the extinction of experience is to create nature experiences for your children in your yard. Since your yard is right outside your door, you won't need to travel far, saving you time and money. It's also likely to be a safe space where you can keep an eye on your child if you want to. I imagine that the familiarity of their own space will make your child comfortable to explore the intricacies of nature, letting their imagination and curiosity guide them. The regular contact they get with nature, it being so close to home, will also maximize the connection that your child develops with the natural world. I've already listed things you can do to improve habitat for birds in your yard (see the sidebar *Five simple things you can do to create a bird-friendly yard*) and involving your child in one or more of these would be an excellent way to start exposing them to the natural world. For example, tending the new plants or starting to feed birds in your yard with your child can help to reverse the extinction of experience. Or you could go outside with your child for a few minutes to identify and count birds using the Merlin app (see the sidebar *The magic of bird song: how to use the Merlin Bird ID app*). I've also created a list of easy and inexpensive nature-based activities and projects that can be done in your yard in the sidebar *Nature-based activities and projects for little house wrens aka your kids*. The point is to make accessing and engaging with nature as simple and enjoyable as possible for all concerned. I think your yard is the ideal place for this to happen.

I hope that after reading this chapter, you have a better idea of the truly special role that you and your yard play in the conservation of biodiversity in your city or suburb and globally. I really can't overstate the potential of your yard to provide critically needed habitat for animals like birds and to equip you and your children with the knowledge and perception needed to tackle the global environmental crises of species loss and climate change. The amazing thing about this potential is that it exists where you spend most of your time, just beyond your front and back doors, and that it can be realized by a few simple changes to how you manage and use your property. Douglas Tallamy envisions the realization of this potential as a Homegrown National Park. I prefer to imagine it as a hundred-year-old tree growing in your front or back yard, like those in Wing Haven Garden and Bird Sanctuary. The tree is far taller than your house and your hands don't even come close to meeting when you wrap your arms around the trunk. The majestic spread of its branches and gently waving leaves can be seen from down the block. The tree has grown up from the

Nature-based activities and projects for little house wrens aka your kids

I compiled this list from the many on the Internet that focus on outdoor, nature-based activities for kids, like the Appalachian Mountain Club's 10 Backyard Nature Activities for Kids. Here are my own favorite activities that don't require a lot of preparation, can be adapted for toddlers and primary school kids, and can be done in yards small or large and with lots or very little nature.

- **Start a nature diary.** Have your child record their observations of nature—the weather, the animals and plants they see, what they smell and hear—at different times of day and throughout the year. All they need to do is head outside for a few minutes on a regular basis. They can record their observations using pictures and/or words. Ask them what they observed and why they thought it was important to take note of. After a while, you can both look back over time at the daily and seasonal events that your child added to the diary.

- **Go on a nature scavenger hunt.** Pick five to ten nature elements in your yard, like an acorn, a tree, something red, or a flying insect, and write or draw them on a piece of paper. Leave room on the paper for your child to either place a sticker next to each element or tick mark that they found it. Provide them with a cloth bag and set them loose to find as many elements as possible. You can make this a friendly competition among siblings and friends too.

- **Make a nature bracelet.** This is a great one to inspire creativity. Make a bracelet around your and your child's wrists of inside-out masking tape. Then, explore your yard for flowers and leaves to stick to your bracelet.

- **Go bug hunting.** Kids love insects! Provide your child with a plastic magnifying glass, a collecting container (any plastic jar or glass Mason jar with holes punched into the lid will do), and a pair of large tweezers. Look under things, like a plant pot, to find insects, and in the grass, along twigs and branches, and on leaves and flowers. Take some time to notice these tiny animals. When you find something, discuss what it looks like and what it was doing when you found it with your child.

- **Go on a backyard safari.** Put on some vests or shirts with lots of pockets and pretend that you are exploring the wilds of your yard (which you really are). Ask your child to seek out wild animals and plants that you didn't intentionally add to your property. You will be surprised at what they find!

- **Celebrate nature's colors.** This is a simple activity that's great to do in different seasons. Ask your child to paint or draw a picture using a color they see in your yard. They can also decorate the driveway

To counter the extinction of experience, have your kids make nature bracelets using the flowers and leaves they find in your yard.

or sidewalk using chalk of the same color. Note the date and the season on the drawing and add it to a seasonal color journal that your child can look through on rainy days.

- **Explore a miniature ecosystem.** Spread an old white sheet, shirt, or towel below a tree or shrub. Have your child gently shake a few branches above the sheet to see what falls out. Touch and smell the leaves, bits of bark, and flowers and use a magnifying glass to inspect any creepy crawlies that you and your child have discovered. Try to figure out how each item on the sheet connects to the others in the miniature ecosystem of the plant.

- **Create nature art.** Provide your child with a frame made of colorful cardboard or construction paper, crayons, glue, and scissors, and ask them to create a work of art using bits of nature they find in the yard. They can create a collage or a mosaic, use blades of grass as paintbrushes, or press leaves and flowers within the frame.

- **Create a field guide to the nature in your yard.** Whenever your child discovers something new in your yard, have them add it to a field guide. Each entry could include a name for the discovery, what it looks like and what it was doing in pictures and in words, the date, time, and weather conditions when the discovery was made, and any noteworthy observations your child wants to make. A field guide is a great show-and-tell piece for friends.

- **Construct a fairy house.** Search for tiny construction materials like grass, twigs, and leaves for a fairy house or village. You and your child can add to the village over time and your child can play with their toys in the village again and again.

soil in your yard and the care you've provided it over the years and is now repaying the favor. Birds of every color and stripe flit among its branches and you and your children play in and under it year-round. The tree is so massive and captivating that people and animals are drawn to it like they are to any thing of beauty. What a special place your property would be with such a tree.

CHAPTER 4

YOUR STREET

In this era of online teaching, my Zoom sessions have been consistently enlivened by the photograph one of my students has chosen as her placeholder when her video camera is off. It's a shot of her in a formal dining room, in front of a mahogany buffet adorned with a silver candelabra and red candles, looking thrilled and bemused at the same time. Next to her, a barred owl is also looking straight into the camera, seemingly less thrilled but somehow bemused as well, as if to say, *At least it's a well-appointed room.*

The student in the photograph is Jennifer Bates, a PhD candidate in my lab. She had just attached a collar and radio transmitter to the owl's neck, which you can make out if you know it's there, using a generously offered dining room as a makeshift field station. The funny thing about the photograph, apart from the presence of an owl in a dining room, is the fact that a barred owl would be anywhere near a dining room to begin with. According to the Cornell Lab of Ornithology, barred owls occur in large blocks of mature forest. However, Jennifer, and the owl, were in a house in an inner suburb of Charlotte, North Carolina, a city of nearly a quarter of a million people at the time. In other words, nowhere near mature forest. Jennifer was there to track barred owls in the residential areas of the city to compare their behavior to rural counterparts. The barred owl was there for reasons of its own.

By the conclusion of Jennifer's research, she and her then-advisor, ornithologist Robert Bierregaard now at Drexel University, estimated that up to three hundred barred owl pairs could be breeding within ten miles of Charlotte's city center.[1] Despite being nominal poster birds for old-growth forests continent-wide, we now know that barred owls occur in older suburban and urban neighborhoods throughout the southeast north to Connecticut and as far west as Cincinnati, Ohio, in the United States and in the Vancouver metropolitan area in British Columbia, Canada.[2] The owls are attracted to these neighborhoods because, in several important ways, they replicate the habitat conditions of mature forest. Just like an old-growth forest, many older urban and suburban neighborhoods in the barred owl's range are graced with large trees and open understories—in the case of neighborhoods, understories are lawn and a few ornamental shrubs. Large, old trees provide barred owls with the roosting and nesting sites that they require and the open understories facilitate their sit-and-wait hunting strategy—it's easy to see a small bird or mammal below you when there aren't too many leaves and branches in the way. Combine these structural characteristics of older neighborhoods with the fact that barred owls are generalist predators and can capitalize on prey that are very abundant in urban and suburban environments, like songbirds and cottontail rabbits, and you've got pretty good barred owl habitat indeed.

The rub comes in the form of another typical characteristic of suburban and urban neighborhoods, namely roads and streets. Collisions with vehicles are a major, if not the dominant, source of mortality for owls as a group. Owls are particularly vulnerable to being hit by vehicles because they tend to travel long distances and are therefore more likely to encounter a road, are attracted to roadside perches like street trees, are low-flying, and are easily blinded by vehicle headlights at night. In the case of the barred owl inhabiting urban and suburban neighborhoods, collisions with vehicles pose a real risk due to the ubiquity of streets and cars. In fact, in Charlotte, barred owls are the most common bird of prey admitted to the local raptor rehabilitation center due to collisions with vehicles (most owls die of their injuries).[3]

The mortality suffered by barred owls in urban and suburban neighborhoods potentially turns what otherwise appears to the owls as prime habitat into what ecologists refer to as an ecological trap. Animals get

A high risk of mortality from collisions with vehicles transforms what is otherwise attractive habitat for barred owls—large, old trees and an open understory—into an ecological trap.

caught in ecological traps when they choose apparently high-quality habitat, but, due to recent alteration by human activities—recent here to be interpreted in evolutionary terms—suffer higher rates of mortality than would be the case elsewhere.[4] It's as if you visited the state fair every year to ride the roller coaster, something you'd enjoyed doing since you were a kid. However, unbeknownst to you, a new employee stopped making the required safety checks during the fair, greatly increasing the likelihood that your ride could become deadly.

Jennifer ended up focusing her research on raptor-vehicle collisions, with the aim of pinpointing why collisions with vehicles happen in some places and not others and if certain species, like barred owls or red-shouldered hawks, are more vulnerable than other species due to inherent aspects of their ecology. So far, for the barred owl, she's figured out that collisions with vehicles are far more likely on narrow roads, like local residential streets. This could be because narrow roads tend to be lined by utility poles and street trees where owls might perch in wait for their next meal, which may very well be across the road. Thus, local residential streets, perhaps like yours, embody the notion of an ecological trap. Their very attractiveness puts owls at risk.

More broadly, Jennifer's results point to the starkly positive and negative impacts of your street, and roads in general, on nature. Of all the spaces explored in this book, your street is where human use is paramount. We build streets and roads for the singular purpose of getting from one place to another by car. In all likelihood, you've never or rarely thought of your street in and of itself as a place where you interact with nature to a significant degree. But, as I'll show in this chapter, your street is where collisions between wildlife and your and other vehicles occur, taking a potentially large toll on local wildlife populations. At the same time, roads and streets are where an important source of the benefits that nature provides to people resides, in the form of street trees. These trees are not only habitat for many wild species in cities and suburbs, like the barred owl, but they also significantly enhance the quality of our living environment and, as a result, our physical health. In the coming pages, I'll explore how driving on your street and local and regional roads presents a risk to certain types of wildlife species because of where they occur and how they behave, and how some of these species have gone so far as to change their behavior in response. Getting back to Jennifer's results and those of other road ecologists, I'll discuss what you and municipal and state agencies can do to minimize roadkill. On the flipside, I'll show you how much the trees along your and other streets improve air quality and stormwater management, lower home energy costs and increase property values, and alter how often you walk or bike and the amount of crime in your neighborhood. Given these benefits, I'll suggest ways that you can help to increase and maintain the stock of street trees in your area. The next time you drive along your street, where on the face of it nature plays a very minor role, I hope that the interactions between you and nature in this chapter come to mind, and the realization that you interact with the natural elements in your urban ecosystem wherever you are.

Your street is where human use is paramount, but also where important interactions between people and nature occur.

Driving along your street risks wildlife becoming roadkill, which reduces population sizes and increases local extinction

I spent a lot of time driving around the outskirts of Ottawa, Canada, as a graduate student. I was really into amphibians at the time and collecting data for my first research project. Surprisingly, no one had yet compared the abundance of frog and toad species in agricultural and urban areas and how these stacked up against more natural forested areas, so I made it my job to find out. This meant driving all over the Ottawa metropolitan area between a half hour after sunset until midnight about every third night between April and June to listen to frogs and toads call. A lot of the driving was on country roads that cut through the fields, forest, and wetland that surround the city.

There are a lot of wetlands surrounding Ottawa (the city sits at a low point at the confluence of three major rivers). And as I soon found out, there are a lot of frogs and toads in those wetlands. On warm, humid, and cloud-covered nights, the country roads would be awash with hopping leopard frogs, spring peepers, and American toads on their way to wetland breeding sites from where they spent the winter. In some cases, it would be a frog or two, easily caught in the headlights and avoided, even at relatively high speed. But on other occasions, the road surface itself seemed to be heaving as hundreds of frogs and toads lustily jumped their way towards a wetland or pond on the other side. In those cases, there really wasn't much you could do. We drove over the frogs and toads, even though we were out there to count them in the first place.

This happened to my advisor, Lenore Fahrig at Carleton University in Ottawa, as well. But she noticed that there appeared to be far more frogs and toads on roads with little traffic compared to busier roads in the same area. If you're anything like me, when I see roadkill—and especially if you see a lot of it as I did as a graduate student—I think that there has got to be fewer individuals of the species in question in the area because so many of them are being killed by cars. Well, my advisor being the brilliant scientist she is thought the opposite. She hypothesized that the comparatively large number of dead frogs and toads on low-traffic roads was because there were lots of frogs and toads in the adjacent wetlands and forests to begin with. Lots of frogs and toads trying to cross a road translates into a large number being killed, even if passing vehicles are relatively rare. Using the same logic, high-traffic roads had few dead frogs and toads because the populations of the species in the forests and wetlands adjacent to the road were small. Heavy traffic meant that many of them had already been killed by passing vehicles.

By counting frogs and toads along high-traffic and low-traffic roads and by listening to frogs and toads call from nearby wetlands—a method to estimate their numbers, Fahrig and her colleagues did, indeed, find that frog and toad populations next to high-traffic roads were smaller.[5] They counted fewer live and dead frogs and toads on high-traffic roads, as Fahrig anecdotally observed prior to the study, but a greater proportion of these were dead compared to low-traffic roads. In other words, high traffic likely reduced the size of nearby frog and toad populations because of roadkill. Her results also confirmed that where you see a lot of roadkill of a particular species is where that species is locally abundant. Jennifer also reported this relationship for the barred owl: Collisions between owls and vehicles are more likely where roads and streets intersect high-quality habitat that presumably contains more owls.

Of course, animals other than frogs, toads, and owls are killed or injured on roads and streets. To give you an idea of the pervasiveness of the roadkill risk run by wildlife, I'll first provide a sense of the reach of the road network in the United States using a compelling analogy described by Kurt Riitters and James Wickham, research scientists with the United States Forest Service and the Environmental Protection Agency, respectively.[6] Imagine the conterminous United States being split up into 8.6 billion baseball fields and standing at home base in each one. In one out of every five cases, you'd find a road crossing the field, and in one out of every twenty-two cases, that road would be no further away than second base (the analogy also works with football fields with you standing at the goal line and the road in one out of every five cases crossing at midfield or closer). In other words, most land in the United States is near a road—82 percent within two-thirds of a mile according to Riitters and Wickham. Roads are a commonplace sight for people in most landscapes and a common structure that many types of animals come across in just about every part of the country.

Roadkilled eastern gray squirrels are common sights where the species is locally abundant.

As a result, wildlife-vehicle collisions occur between people and all sorts of different animal species. Studies from around the world have documented familiar species killed on roads, like white-tailed deer, elk, and moose, but also wild boars, bobcats, badgers, baboons, Asiatic cheetahs, impalas, wombats, koalas, badgers, red foxes, gray wolves, Florida scrub jays, Midland painted turtles, desert tortoises, black ratsnakes, eastern monarch butterflies, burrowing owls, and armadillos.[7] Even the Galápagos lava lizard is not immune to being roadkilled. And, although data on insects is rare as you can see from my list of species, there is evidence of roadkilled beetles, butterflies and moths, bees and wasps, grasshoppers, flies, dragonflies, mayflies, stoneflies, caddisflies, mantises, cockroaches and termites, and earwigs (all from a mile and a quarter stretch of two-lane highway in Ontario, Canada, over two years).[8] The same study estimated that fifty million butterflies and moths, 133 million bees and wasps, and a billion flies could be killed on roads in southern Ontario each year. The only other estimate of this kind that I am aware of is that for birds in the United States: Collisions with vehicles could account for 89 to 340 million deaths annually.[9] That's thirty-five to 135 birds killed per mile of road per year.

These are very large numbers. But do they translate into smaller population sizes of roadkilled species and an increased risk of local extinction? After all, there are probably many billions of bees and wasps buzzing around southern Ontario, so losing 133 million, a small proportion, to collisions with vehicles may not really matter much to their persistence. In my opinion, these numbers do matter, especially for certain types of species, as I'll show later. I base my opinion on four lines of evidence. First, while we don't have hard data on roadkills reducing population sizes for many species, we do have it for some. I've already described how roadkill reduces the population sizes of frogs and toads around Ottawa. Roadkill also contributes to smaller numbers of Florida scrub jays, black ratsnakes, Galapagos lava lizards, red foxes, gray wolves, hedgehogs, and most likely other species.[10] Second, road mortality can dramatically increase the likelihood of local extinction. Two spotted turtle populations in Maryland have an over 90 percent chance of going extinct in 150 years in large part due to roadkill, and another turtle population, that of diamondback terrapins inhabiting a salt marsh peninsula in Georgia, have only a one in two chance of still being around in fifty years also because of roadkill.[11] A similar fate may await populations of 124 mammal species around the world that have been classified as vulnerable to roadkill in that 20 percent or less of their numbers need to be killed by vehicles for their risk of extinction in fifty years to go up by 10 percent, including North America's very own black bear, grizzly bear, and bighorn sheep.[12] Third, roadkill is a threat to rare and threatened species. Because populations of these species are small and/or declining, any source of mortality matters to their persistence. A recent study in Taiwan calculated that 19 percent of 496 species and 13 percent of all animals found dead on the nation's roads were nationally protected.[13] This included the majority of Taiwan's protected non-marine turtles, snakes, lizards, and mammals.

Finally, roadkill is one of several anthropogenic stressors that may be causing the large declines in biodiversity documented over the last several decades. David Wagner and his colleagues at the University of Connecticut described the effects of these stressors on insect populations as "death by a thousand cuts."[14] Because many stressors, such as roadkill, pesticide use, and invasive species, are likely to be involved in biodiversity loss, either directly or indirectly, it's difficult to know when and where any given source of mortality will be important. The precautionary principle, then, dictates that we reduce the intensity of all stressors, including roadkill, to the extent that we feasibly can (see the sidebar *Death by a thousand cuts: strategies to minimize the stress you place on biodiversity*).

Although many different animal species are killed or injured on roads, some are more vulnerable than others based on their characteristics and life cycle needs.[15] I've already shown you that more abundant species are more liable to be roadkilled. Three other characteristics that put a species at risk increase its exposure to the road network, either because it tends to wander over long distances or because it lives for a long time. Large mammal and bird species that tend to move over greater distances are more likely to encounter roads during their peregrinations, especially in or near cities, and are thus at a greater risk of being roadkilled than smaller species. This is partly why large mammals like the gray wolf and

Death by a thousand cuts: strategies to minimize the stress you place on biodiversity

Biodiversity loss is likely caused by several interacting anthropogenic stressors, or human activities that lead to wildlife mortality and/or reduce reproduction. Major stressors include climate change and its effects, such as increasing fire and storm frequency; agricultural intensification; the accumulation of nitrogen compounds in soil and water; pesticide use; chemical, light, and sound pollution; invasive species and novel pathogens; the loss of forests and other habitats; dams and water management; overharvesting; cat predation; and collisions with vehicles and buildings.

This list may seem overwhelming and too big to do anything about, but there *are* feasible actions that you can take to reduce the stress you place on biodiversity. I've listed here what currently appear to be the most impactful, many of which tackle multiple stressors at once (see also the sidebar *Five simple things you can do to create a bird-friendly yard* in chapter 3). Note that in my list, I'm emphasizing doing less, not eliminating activities entirely. This is for pragmatic reasons—many of us don't have access to public transit for our daily transportation needs— and because your needs and preferences may sometimes trump the negative effect of an activity on biodiversity.

- **Drive less and stay under the speed limit when you do drive.** Traffic volume and vehicle speed are major factors underlying the likelihood of wildlife-vehicle collisions. You can reduce the chance you kill or injure wildlife with your car by choosing to walk, cycle, or use public transit when possible and by staying under the speed limit when you do drive. If this sounds simplistic, consider that the 70 percent reduction in driving in four states locked down at the beginning of the pandemic in the spring of 2020 reduced wildlife-vehicle collisions by 34 percent on average and by 58 percent for the mountain lion.[16]

   Driving less will also reduce the greenhouse gas emissions and pollution your car produces. Passenger cars and light-duty trucks account for 58 percent of greenhouse gas emissions from the transportation sector, itself the largest source of emissions in the United States.[17] And the pollution you generate when you drive impacts wildlife populations. For example, the products of passenger vehicle exhaust, nitrogen oxides and ozone, interfere with the ability of pollinators (bees, flies, moths, and butterflies) to find flowers and ultimately the health of their and plant populations.[18]

- **Consume less.** The production and transport of the food and material goods that we buy involve the loss of habitat and the generation of greenhouse gas emissions and pollution. Each year on average, your consumption of things like coffee, beef, soy, rubber, and lumber is responsible for the loss of five, often tropical forest, trees that are the habitat for many animal and plant species (think about this the next time you're at a meeting or at dinner with friends and family—each of you is responsible for the loss of five trees year after year).[19] This loss of forest and the agricultural activities that replace it are the second largest source of greenhouse gas emissions globally.[20] Your consumption of plastic, directly in products and indirectly as packaging and in the manufacture of products (including foods), is considered one of the most pervasive and long-lasting sources of pollution to atmospheric, terrestrial, freshwater, and marine systems on the planet. For example, a recent study estimated that, by 2050, 99 percent of all seabird species on Earth will be ingesting plastic.[21] That's not just the herring gulls you're used to seeing at garbage dumps, but penguins in Antarctica too.

You can reduce the impacts of your consumption by buying fewer things, using what you have for longer, buying used items like clothing, reducing food waste—21 percent of food in the United States is wasted by consumers, or 0.8 pounds per person per day[22]—using less plastic, conserving water, composting, and recycling. You can also reduce your consumption of foods and products that are associated with high water use and greenhouse gas emissions, like beef.

- **Reduce your use of fertilizers and pesticides.** Fertilizer use leads to the accumulation of nitrogen in soil and water—like plastic, a widespread pollutant of terrestrial and aquatic systems. Nitrogen pollution is linked to the declines of seventy-eight federally listed at-risk species, including snails, mussels, a salamander, a toad, a butterfly, corals, a beetle, fish, and turtles, by means of its direct toxicity, eutrophication or the creation of aquatic dead zones, and the spread of nitrogen-loving plants.[23] In Ohio, even very common butterfly species like the cabbage white—the small white butterfly with dark spots on its wings that you've most likely seen in your backyard or garden—are declining due to nitrogen pollution, as well as the use of pesticides that are toxic to the animals or the plants upon which they depend.[24] Pesticide toxicity to non-target organisms in the United States, such as aquatic invertebrates, insect pollinators like butterflies and bumblebees, and terrestrial plants, has doubled since the early 1990s.[25]

  To reduce your use of fertilizers and pesticides, choose foods from small-scale farms that use fertilizers and pesticides responsibly, or grow some of your own. At home, reduce the amount of fertilizer you use on your lawn and garden and avoid pesticides if you can. Lawn fertilizer is the largest source of nitrogen pollution in urban waterways, in some cases more than any other source combined.[26] You can replace your use of synthetic fertilizer altogether by taking advantage of the natural fertilizer provided by leaving grass clippings on your lawn and mulching with fallen leaves in the fall. You'll save time, bags, money, and the greenhouse gases emitted from maintenance or waste vehicles and leaf blowers. Finally, a pesticide-free yard is one in which plants and animals will thrive. You'll be surprised at the various critters that colonize your space and help you control pest species, like spiders, ground beetles, bats, chimney swifts and swallows, frogs and toads, and non-venomous snakes that politely keep to themselves.

- **Minimize the chance that birds collide with the building where you live.** Collisions with building windows kill between 398 and 988 million birds in the United States each year, the largest human-mediated source of mortality after cat predation.[27] Nearly half (44 percent) of collisions are with one- to three-story buildings, including single-family homes, and most of the remainder are with low-rise buildings of four to eleven stories. One of the factors that increases a building's collision risk is indoor or outdoor lighting at night. Migratory bird species that travel at night can become confused by our artificial lights. If those same species call for help to their flockmates, as many do, then large numbers of birds can become ensnared in the light traps that are our buildings and end up colliding with them.[28]

  You can reduce the chance that birds collide with the building where you live by turning off outdoor lighting or using timers and motion sensors to limit it and using window shades, shutters, or curtains at night. Reducing the light pollution coming from your building will also limit the ways in which artificial light at night interferes with plant and animal development, physiology, and behavior that lead to population declines. In the United Kingdom, nighttime light pollution is partly responsible for the declines of 178 moth species over the last forty years, 93 percent of which are nocturnal.[29]

  Daytime collisions of birds with windows often occur because birds can't tell that the sky or vegetation they see in the window is a reflection on glass. To prevent this from happening, close your shades or curtains in rooms not in use and install screens or parachute cord curtains on your windows or dress up your exterior window glass with DIY patterns or decorative films (check the National Audubon Society or your local chapter for the correct spacing). These measures are especially important during the spring and fall migration periods, so make using them a reason to decorate for the season. And if you live in an apartment building, ask your building manager about the possibility of motion sensor indoor and outdoor lighting in common areas and making your building's windows more visible to birds.

brown bear and large birds like owls are particularly vulnerable to dying on roads. Species that need to move among different habitat types to complete their life cycle and therefore are more likely to encounter roads are also in the vulnerable category, regardless of their size. This includes frogs, toads, salamanders, and turtles that move among two or more different kinds of habitat each season, from spring aquatic breeding sites to summer foraging areas to terrestrial overwintering sites depending on the species. Long-lived species like turtles—the common snapping turtle has a lifespan on the scale of humans—are also vulnerable to being killed on roads simply because they are more likely to encounter them at some point during their lengthy lives.

The way a species behaves when it finds itself on or near a road also plays a big role in whether it will be struck by a vehicle. Birds and dragonflies that fly low to the ground seem to be more vulnerable than their high-flying counterparts, as are birds that fly only a short distance away when disturbed, which increases their risk of being run over by a fast-moving car or truck.[30] Solitary bird species may also be at risk compared to their flocking counterparts because they can't benefit from the vigilance of the many eyes in a flock to get out of the way of an oncoming vehicle in time. And some species are attracted to roads and roadsides, putting them directly in the line of fire as it were. In Lake Jackson bisected by Highway 27 in northwestern Florida, females of three turtle species, the Florida scooter, yellow-bellied slider, and common musk turtle, nest along the mowed grassy shoulder of the highway and experience high road mortality as a result—so much so that the populations of these species in the lake are male-skewed.[31] Roads and roadsides also attract moose to the minerals in deicing compounds that supplement their winter diets, scavenging raptors such as black vultures that can detect the presence of road-killed carcasses more rapidly, kestrels and owls that use fences, utility lines, and trees as perches, the globally threatened Florida scrub jay for the open scrubby habitat that is in short supply elsewhere, reptiles for the warm road surface itself, and cliff swallows that hang their mud nests under highway bridges and overpasses.[32]

For all of these types of species especially vulnerable to being hit by vehicles, the big question is whether they avoid roads and/or traffic

Black vultures may be vulnerable to being hit by vehicles due to their attraction to roadkilled carcasses.

when they encounter them. The answer is that some species do and some do not, with the latter being at high risk of being hit by a vehicle. For instance, in central Massachusetts, female black bears minimize their roadkill risk by choosing to cross smaller roads with less traffic and lower speed limits rather than larger, busier roads.[33] These bears have clearly learned, either from direct experience or from a parent, to avoid roads with high traffic volumes. Learning also appears to be an important factor in birds. During eight years of driving around Norway, Arild Husby and Magne Husby of Uppsala University and the Norwegian University of Science and Technology, respectively, recorded the avoidance behavior of birds sitting on the road when their car approached, as well as the type of road they were driving on, their speed, and the type of roadside vegetation on both sides of the road.[34] They found that after controlling for all of these factors, bird species with larger brains for their body size, like the carrion crow, were more likely to avoid their car by flying directly away from the road rather than across it, like the redwing and other smaller-brained species did. Husby and Husby suggested that this was because larger-brained species might more readily judge the speed and direction of an approaching vehicle or because they were better able to learn the best means of avoiding the threat. The Florida scrub jay and many owl species also appear to learn to avoid traffic. Inexperienced jays that occupy roadside breeding territories have twice the risk of getting hit by a vehicle when they first arrive than four years later.[35] And in Charlotte, Jennifer found that young barred owls less than two years old make up the majority of owl-vehicle collisions in the city.

As for those species that do not avoid roads or traffic, I return to frogs and toads, and salamanders, in Canada as the ultimate examples. As I've described, amphibians crossing roads on warm and wet spring nights in the countryside surrounding Ottawa are common sights, with many animals being run over by vehicles in the process. Given this continued exposure to roads and traffic season after season and year after year, amphibians might be prompted to learn to avoid roads and traffic to reduce their risk of mortality, as some birds in Norway have. Using unconventional field methods like pushing a Radio Flyer wagon equipped with Mag Lite flashlights along a deserted road in a national park in New Brunswick at 2 a.m., two creative ecologists have provided evidence that these animals indeed don't avoid cars and traffic and even behave in a way that puts them more at risk when facing an approaching vehicle. Julie Bouchard, then a PhD student in Lenore Fahrig's lab, tracked northern leopard frogs moved to points thirty feet from high-traffic or low-traffic roads or to roadless control sites from a nearby river where they had spent the winter.[36] Using a flashlight with a red filter that wouldn't disturb the frogs, she and her colleagues noted the direction and speed of every hop once the frogs were released at each site. All of the frogs kept moving in the direction they had been going prior to being captured at the river—that is, in the direction of the road—and all of them crossed or attempted to cross the road when they got to it. Bouchard also observed that as frogs approached the road, especially those with higher traffic, they started to hop more slowly and in a more haphazard way, behavior that they also exhibited when hopping across the high-traffic road itself. A few years before, Marc Mazerolle in New Brunswick, and now with the United States Geological Survey, had collected data that supported this finding.[37] Like Husby and Husby in Norway, Mazerolle noted the behavior of each frog, toad, or salamander he came across during four years of nighttime driving surveys along a two-lane highway through Kouchibouguac National Park. Only 18 percent of the 2,767 amphibians he approached with his car moved out of the way—the rest were frozen in their tracks and therefore certain to get run over if Mazerolle hadn't driven aside. The Radio Flyer surveys were used to test whether it was the sound of the car's motor, its headlights, or both that caused amphibians to stop dead, finding that the silent wagon with headlights and the running car without lights both had an effect.

If the image of a poor little spring peeper blinded by oncoming headlights in the middle of a road has your heart wrenching, you might well be asking what can I, or us humans, do to minimize the risk that our driving poses to wildlife? In the case of migrating amphibians that must cross a road inconveniently located between terrestrial and aquatic habitats, we can construct a culvert under the road and use barrier fencing to direct amphibians to it. This strategy has generally proven effective at reducing amphibian deaths on roads—by over 50 percent in Whistler, Canada, for example—but culverts may not be used by all species and some species, such as toads, may avoid culverts of certain sizes and in particular locations.[38] For mammals, wildlife over- and underpasses and associated fencing have proven extremely effective—just search for "Banff wildlife overpass" on YouTube and you'll be treated to grizzly bear cubs safely crossing the TransCanada highway.[39] The success of over- and underpasses is wonderful, but their widespread use is limited by major construction and maintenance costs and we do not yet have evidence that they benefit animals other than mammals. Transportation planners could consider the location of new roads and streets so they avoid the habitats of rare species or bisecting wildlife movement corridors. Yet again, funding to assess the locational effects of roads and streets on wildlife is very limited. And for existing roads and streets, changing road width and removing roadside structures and vegetation that attract wildlife like utility poles and street trees is just impractical, has negative consequences for wildlife in other ways, may not be effective, and may simply not be feasible given the costs of vegetation maintenance on a large scale.

In the sidebar *Death by a thousand cuts: strategies to minimize the stress you place on biodiversity*, I recommend simply driving less, to the extent that we can, as a very pragmatic way to reduce wildlife roadkill deaths and in recognition that traffic volume is probably the single biggest factor influencing the likelihood of wildlife-vehicle collisions. I also recommend going the speed limit when you do drive, speed also being a major factor underlying collision likelihood. Another way to reduce our speed, since I know that we're not always looking at the speedometer when we drive, especially on well-known or empty streets, is to use wildlife crossing signs to signal the threat to drivers at roadkill hotspots where extra attention and slow driving are needed. Given the limitations of the mitigation measures I outlined in the previous paragraph to reduce widespread roadkill and assuming you are driving the least you can, reducing speed voluntarily and advocating for relatively low-cost wildlife crossing signs seem like the most efficient actions we can each take to reduce wildlife mortality on our roads and streets.

To be effective, wildlife crossing signs need to be placed where road-kills are highest and be specific as to time of year or day when animals are most likely to cross the road or street in the greatest numbers.[40] Without this information, the signs don't appear to reduce collisions with wild-life, although they do result in reduced vehicle speed. The effectiveness of wildlife crossing signs is also enhanced by an advisory or mandatory speed limit reduction indicated on the sign, which substantially adds to the decrease in vehicle speed. Once a sign has proven effective, in that roadkill has declined along the stretch of road, it should be removed. Otherwise, drivers may end up thinking the sign, and others like it, are not reliable since they don't see many roadkilled animals where signs are installed. If roadkill picks up again, signs can be reinstalled.

The information needed to implement useful wildlife crossing signs—location, timing, and amount of roadkill—is information that you can provide to scientists and local and state governments. Without it, wildlife crossing signs and the other mitigation measures I've described like culverts for migrating amphibians can't be justified in terms of their

If deployed correctly, wildlife crossing signs are an efficient means of reducing wildlife mortality on our roads and streets.

cost and effectiveness. A comprehensive report on wildlife-vehicle collisions commissioned by the United States Department of Transportation stated that the lack of consistent and precise data on roadkill was a major impediment to the systematic reduction of wildlife-vehicle collisions across the nation.[41] Close to home, collecting roadkill data will help to identify mortality hotspots for species that aren't typically thought of when we think of wildlife-vehicle collisions and for which we have very little data despite the large threat, like the barred owl. It can also help scientists identify areas where rare species or species of concern are being hit by cars and trucks, and therefore mitigation is critically needed even if roadkilled animals aren't that common. The best way to collect roadkill data is to contribute to an existing roadkill project on iNaturalist (see the sidebar *How to help identify roadkill hotspots*). Although the main purpose of these projects is to pinpoint the best locations for mitigation measures, they are also helping to track the spread of invasive species, like the eastern fox squirrel in California, and have even turned up species new to science, such as the Nechisar nightjar in Ethiopia.[42] Most importantly, however, the data collected by untrained observers, possibly such as yourself, have been shown to be just as accurate and useful in identifying high-risk areas as those collected by trained experts.[43] By participating in a citizen science project, you can help create very large and useful datasets that can make a difference to the fate of wildlife. Just think of the two thousand citizen scientists who collected nearly fifty thousand roadkill observations in six years in Flanders, Belgium, one of the largest roadkill datasets in the world.[44]

The trees along your street make you healthier, safer, and richer

If roadkill is your street's vice, then street trees are its virtue. Originally planted to beautify America's new city streets in the late nineteenth century, street trees now represent an important resource that improves the quality of our living environment and our physical health. As defined by municipalities and in some cases enshrined in tree ordinances, street trees are trees located within the right-of-way of any publicly maintained street or road. If you aren't an urban planner or property rights expert, every street and road in a municipality is located within a right-of-way

How to help identify roadkill hotspots

There are several roadkill projects in iNaturalist (see the sidebar *How to use iNaturalist* in chapter 2 for more information about the platform). Nonprofits such as nature preserves, university scientists, concerned citizens, and state agencies have all created projects to collect data for specific road segments of concern or more widely. One of the largest projects is GLOBAL Roadkill Observations, a worldwide incarnation of the California Roadkill Observation System developed by Fraser Schilling, director of the Road Ecology Center at the University of California, Davis. The California Roadkill Observation System has been a leader in the collection of citizen science roadkill data and is 97 percent accurate in terms of species identification with locational accuracy of around 40 feet.[45] To contribute to GLOBAL Roadkill Observations or another project, all you have to do is search for the project when you make a new observation. Like with other iNaturalist observations, photographs are very useful and help others verify your species identification. But don't take unnecessary risks to record roadkill. Always stay safe so you can make more observations at a later date!

that typically also includes space for sidewalks, utilities, and landscaping. It's called a right-of-way because the municipality has been granted the right to use the land for transportation even though they do not own it—the adjacent property owners do. In the United States, the paved portion of the right-of-way for local residential streets is anywhere between 18 and 38 feet wide, whereas the right-of-way itself is on average 55 feet wide.[46] That leaves an estimated 17 to 37 feet for sidewalks, utility poles, and landscaping on both sides of America's paved streets. For example, my street is approximately 26 feet wide, including the curbs and gutters, and the first 16 feet of my property adjacent to it are part of the right-of-way. There are two willow oaks within this 16 feet, so those are street trees according to Charlotte's tree ordinance. Transportation rights-of-way exist wherever there are streets and roads in a municipality, large or

Street trees are trees located within the right-of-way of any publicly maintained street or road.

small, so any tree located within those spaces is a street tree, whether it's on the side of the road, in the median, or in a traffic island. Apart from agreeing that street trees are located within transportation rights-of-way, municipalities across the country differ in the types of vegetation that qualify as street trees—in some cases, any woody vegetation, tree or shrub, is a street "tree," whereas in others only single-stemmed trees of a certain size are considered street trees. Municipalities also differ in their allocation of maintenance responsibility. In Charlotte, the city is responsible for maintenance. In other locations, the property owners are.

The street tree population of a city or town is also idiosyncratic, depending on the climate and soils of the area, the size, age, and wealth of the municipality, and the values and preferences of residents. Recent statewide street tree inventories can give us an idea of this variability in terms of the number of trees in cities and towns and their sizes and species. In California, street tree density is between eleven and ninety-one trees per mile of roadway depending on the region, averaging seventy-five trees per mile across the state.[47] In some regions, there is one street tree for every two people whereas in others one for every ten. Regions also vary in the age of their street trees. Some have very young populations with more than half of trees small enough for your fingers to meet when you wrap your hands around their trunks. Others are dominated by larger trees at least as wide as dinner plates. Statewide, the California street tree population is very speciose. One hundred and seventy-five different tree species are planted in Californian rights-of-way, with no single species or genus accounting for more than 11 percent of trees. Eight of the ten most abundant street tree species in the state are non-native, like the London plane tree, the Southern magnolia, and the Callery pear.

The street tree picture is very different in other states. Some states, like New York, also have a high density of street trees, but most others (Massachusetts, Maryland, and Missouri) hover around fifty trees per street mile.[48] Street tree populations tend to be more mature than in California: very young trees represent approximately 20 percent of all street trees in New York, Maryland, and Massachusetts. In New York, Massachusetts, Maryland, Indiana, and Wisconsin, nearly half of street trees are maples, especially the Norway maple, which accounts for about a third of street trees in Wisconsin and Massachusetts.[49] Although Indiana streets are lined by a whopping 243 different tree species, the street tree populations of the other states include a modest sixty-six to eighty-eight species. Of the top ten tree species along the streets of these states, the majority are native species.

The one characteristic that states across the country share is their low stocking level of street trees. The assessments for California, Maryland, Massachusetts, and Missouri included estimates of the proportion of right-of-way space "stocked" with a street tree. In just two of the statewide, regionwide, or municipal estimates were stocking levels greater than 60 percent—both were in Missouri: the St. Louis suburbs and in communities with twenty to fifty thousand residents. Therefore, in these states, there exists the potential for street trees to double, or more, in number.

Another way that street tree populations vary is among residential communities of different races or ethnicities, household incomes, ownership statuses, and education levels. In Tampa, Florida, neighborhoods with more tree cover in residential rights-of-way are those where household incomes are higher, where more people own their homes, or where fewer Black or Latinx people live.[50] In New York City, neighborhoods with wealthier households, more homeowners, more residents with at least a high school diploma, and fewer Latinx residents have more street tree cover, whereas neighborhoods with more Black or Asian residents, although not lacking for street tree cover, have fewer street tree species.[51] There aren't many studies of this kind so it's difficult to state with assurance that street tree cover varies in a particular way in neighborhoods with particular demographic and socioeconomic characteristics, especially since street tree cover in general varies so much among cities. However, we do know that differences among communities exist, and we can speculate on the possible reasons for the differences. Street tree cover might vary among neighborhoods because public funding and service provision related to tree planting and maintenance are inequitably distributed or have been in the past. Street tree populations might differ also because people of different races, ethnicities, or education or income levels prefer different amounts of street tree cover and different numbers of tree species. These preferences may be realized by differential levels of tree planting requests and maintenance by residents or by people moving to neighborhoods with the amount and diversity of street tree cover they find most pleasing.

I mentioned earlier that street trees are an important source of nature's benefits in towns and cities. For example, each year one of the towering seventy-five-year-old willow oaks in the right-of-way in my front yard sequesters 752 pounds of carbon dioxide and removes 55 ounces of ozone from the air. Its roots take up 938 gallons of water that would otherwise run into the gutters along my street and its broad, leafy canopy intercepts nearly 5,400 gallons of rain. The shade it bathes my house in saves me 60 kWh of energy I would otherwise use to air

Street tree populations include individual trees of varying ages and sizes (above) and of several species (right: pignut hickory in the foreground and red maple in the background).

condition my house in the summer. In total, these benefits amount to a value of $34.13 per year and, for the carbon storage alone, $633.35 over the lifetime of the tree.

I estimated these benefits and their dollar amounts using the US Forest Service's MyTree app (see the sidebar *Money does grow on trees: using MyTree to estimate the value of your street tree*). As a comparison, I also estimated the value of and benefits provided by an average-sized Norway maple where I used to live in Madison, Wisconsin—recall that the Norway maple is a common street tree in Wisconsin and other states in the Midwest and in the Northeast—and a small London planetree in Eureka in northern California—the most common street tree size and species in that region of the state. The Norway maple with a trunk diameter of dinner plate proportions removes 21 percent of the carbon dioxide and 8 percent of the ozone from the air that my willow oak does, takes up or intercepts 7 percent of the runoff or rain that my oak soaks up, and saves 15 percent of the energy I save for air-conditioning. The benefits of the Norway maple add up to $11.16 per year, a third of the value of my oak. The London planetree, just big enough for a pair of hands to not quite meet on either side of the trunk, is worth about half as much as the maple.

Greg McPherson, an emeritus scientist with the Forest Service's Pacific Northwest Research Station, used models similar to those embedded in the MyTree app to estimate the street tree benefits and their dollar value for California as a whole based on the inventory data I described earlier.[52] On average, each street tree in the state sequesters enough carbon dioxide, absorbs enough air pollution, takes up or intercepts enough stormwater, saves building occupants enough energy, and adds enough to home sales prices each year that it is worth $110.63. Summing across all street trees in California yields $1 billion of benefits each year. That is net of the carbon dioxide emissions generated by maintenance vehicles and the decomposition of pruned limbs and dead trees, and the emission of biogenic volatile organic compounds by trees that stimulate ground-level ozone production. Taking into account the average management cost per municipal tree in California of $19, the state's street trees generate nearly $6 of benefits for every dollar spent on their upkeep.

Money does grow on trees: using MyTree to estimate the value of your street tree

The US Forest Service developed the MyTree app (available online at *https://mytree.itreetools.org/#/*) as a user-friendly version of its more complex suite of iTree tools, which planners, managers, and scientists use to estimate the benefits and values of trees and forests around the world.

The MyTree app is intended to estimate the benefits and values of a single tree, although you can create a project to compare several individual trees. To use MyTree, you'll need the tree's location, species, general condition, and size; whether the tree is in full sun, part shade, or shade; and the tree's approximate distance from a building, as well as the age of the building. You can also add optional information on the apparent health of the tree, such as the transparency of its crown, and any signs of pest damage. The benefits and values calculated by MyTree are summarized as a nutrition label—perhaps as a nod to the Forest Service's home within the US Department of Agriculture—with the amounts of each nutrient, like ozone, listed under categories, like Air Pollution Removed Each Year, that have dollar amounts. Use the MyTree app to find out what your street tree is worth or what a particularly beautiful or large tree in your neighborhood does for your community.

Most of a California street tree's value (83 percent) is accrued by the tree's positive effect on home sales price, followed by the home energy savings it produces (10 percent). In other states, the mix of values is different. For instance, in Missouri, the worth of an average street tree each year ($102.48) is split evenly among an increase in home sales price (33 percent), stormwater benefits (29 percent), and home energy savings (32 percent).[53]

McPherson also calculated the total replacement value of all street trees in the state as if the trees were considered just another type of urban infrastructure, like roads or the pipes beneath them. If all of the street trees of varying species and sizes in California were lost, it would cost $2.49 billion to replace them, or $2,667 per tree.

In my opinion, McPherson's infrastructure analogy is apt, and really more than just an analogy. In fact, street trees *are* a kind of urban infrastructure. The modest valuation of the benefits or services provided by an individual street tree in one year—$110 for the average street tree in California—adds up over time and across trees to amounts that are on the same scale as other infrastructure types. The closest I can find to a replacement cost for California's roads is $137 billion, the amount needed according to the American Society of Civil Engineers to bring the state's roads back into good repair.[54] Of course, one hundred and thirty-seven billion is far larger than the $2.49 billion replacement cost of the state's street trees—fifty-five times larger to be exact—but the fact that the two amounts could reasonably be line items in the same budget, and considering the vastly larger road network, supports the contention that street trees in California can be thought of as urban infrastructure. In Missouri, the numbers tell a similar story: the net present value of street trees in Missouri is $2.7 billion, equivalent to the amount you'd need in the bank to generate the $148 million in annual benefits provided by the trees, assuming a conservative interest rate of 5.47 percent, whereas the replacement value of the state's entire transportation network—roads, bridges, rail, public transit, aviation, and waterways—is $125 billion.[55]

The replacement values of California's and Missouri's street tree populations are certainly underestimates. Street trees provide a wealth of benefits to people that aren't as easily translated into economic terms as home energy savings or even amount of absorbed carbon dioxide, and so aren't included in the valuations I've described so far. Research on street trees in particular isn't yet very common—studies tend to lump street trees in with private trees in their analyses—so we don't have hard evidence for all of the possible benefits they might provide, like fostering a sense of community or a sense of place among residents, embodying cultural heritage and history, providing spiritual and educational opportunities, and altering our behavior. For this last, recent studies of street trees in Milwaukee and Green Bay, Wisconsin; Phoenix, Arizona; and Portland, Oregon, lend some interesting insight.

In Wisconsin, Wei-Lun Tsai at the US Environmental Protection Agency and her colleagues found that more tree cover along Milwaukee's and Green Bay's sidewalks increased the likelihood that residents would choose to walk or bike at least once a week to get to work or school or to run errands.[56] Specifically, a 10 percent increase in sidewalk tree cover within neighborhoods increased the probability of walking or biking by a third. And this was regardless of the season, how long residents had lived in their homes, their demographic characteristics like their age and sex, or their perceived sense of safety along city streets. Tsai hypothesized that sidewalks with more tree cover were shadier and therefore more inviting to the potential pedestrian or cyclist, but I think that aesthetics must also play a role. Some of the streets with sidewalks in Tsai's analysis were wide, split-lane roadways with speed limits up to 55 mph where the presence of trees might make a walk or bike ride a much more pleasant prospect.

By encouraging people to be more active, that 10 percent increase in tree cover along sidewalks influences people's health. In Phoenix and Portland, Tsai and her colleagues used the heights and weights listed in driver's license databases to calculate resident body mass indices and tested whether more tree cover along sidewalks and in front yards was associated with lower indices, controlling for resident age, gender, income and race, neighborhood walkability, and park proximity.[57] In both cities, a 10 percent increase in street and front yard tree cover lowered the odds of residents being overweight or obese by 18 percent. Put another way, a resident's odds of being overweight or obese decreased by 22 percent in the most compared to the least treed neighborhoods in Phoenix, and by 39 percent in Portland.

Portland was the stage for another street tree study carried out by Blair Burley, a doctoral candidate at Florida State University.[58] Burley took advantage of a recent street tree planting in the city, part of Portland's Grey to Green Initiative, to investigate whether the presence of the trees reduced violent crime in neighborhoods. Although it may seem counterintuitive, previous research has found that trees and other vegetation reduce crime, most notably in a landmark study in Chicago that reported fewer property and violent crimes in apartment buildings surrounded by more vegetation.[59] Experts have hypothesized that this may be because more natural surroundings encourage people to spend more time outdoors. When people spend more time outdoors, they are more likely to notice the goings-on in their neighborhood, including crime, which may deter potential criminals. More people spending more time outdoors also means that neighbors are more likely to encounter each other and engage in positive interactions, leading to a greater sense of community and social cohesion, which in and of themselves are known to reduce crime. Or, the positive effect of nature on mental health, specifically as a reliever of mental fatigue—I'll describe the restoration power of nature in more detail in the next chapter—may reduce anger and other negative emotions that prompt people to commit violent crimes.

The reason that the above may seem counterintuitive is that we typically associate densely vegetated areas with a higher likelihood of crime. Shrubby and tangled brush is not a place most of us would want to spend much time in and it's easy to imagine potential criminals lurking in the undergrowth. The difference here is the type and degree of maintenance of vegetation. Dense, overgrown shrubs may indeed be associated with a higher likelihood of crime, but so far, the evidence suggests that well-maintained, treed areas are not.[60] In fact, just the opposite. Because of this, Burley chose to focus her study on the 19,497 well-maintained street trees planted throughout Portland's neighborhoods between 2011 and 2015. For every one hundred new street trees planted in any given neighborhood, there were twenty-four fewer violent crimes committed the following year. Burley also found that the crime-fighting powers of street trees were significantly greater in lower-income neighborhoods where violent crime was more common to begin with. And, as with the other street tree studies I've described, these effects occurred regardless of a neighborhood's sociodemographic characteristics, including the number of residents, homeownership status, and race and ethnicity, or total crime count.

Given that street trees are so valuable—they clean our environment, save us money on home energy costs, and reduce violence in our communities, among other benefits—it's worthwhile to check in on the health and resilience of their populations, or their ability to keep providing the benefits that we currently enjoy. Data on the change in street

You are more likely to walk or bike to get where you're going if your sidewalk is lined with trees.

tree populations over time in cities and towns in the United States are rare because many places don't keep track of what happens to trees from year to year. Nevertheless, there is some evidence that street tree populations are declining, or at risk of declining. About half (46 percent) of 667 American municipal forestry programs surveyed in 2014 reported removing more public trees—along streets, in parks, and in other public spaces—than they planted.[61] Also, about half (47 percent) of municipalities in the same survey reported that their public tree budgets were inadequate to cover needs, with the shortfall being an average of 55 percent of necessary funds. In California, where long-term data do exist on street trees in particular, street tree density in 2014 was approximately 30 percent lower than in 1988.[62]

I can think of three reasons why street tree populations are declining in some places. First, street tree planting may not be keeping up with the rapid pace of development, especially in municipalities with small tree budgets. Second, street trees in many cities are nearing the end of their lifespans and are more susceptible to disease, insect outbreaks, and storm damage as a result. Even though large, mature trees provide residents with more benefits—as evidenced by the higher valuation of my willow oak compared to the smaller Norway maple and London planetree— best practice in urban forestry advocates for 40 percent of all trees in a population to be small, young trees so that at any given time, there are enough rapidly growing recruits to make up for the loss of the relatively few old trees that inevitably die. In parts of California, in Missouri and Massachusetts, and for the dominant Norway maple in Wisconsin, there are too many old trees and often not enough young trees in the street tree population. In these places, municipal tree budgets may not be sufficient to maintain many aging trees, remove old trees, and plant new trees in their stead. For example, in Missouri, average street tree condition deteriorated substantially between 1989, when two-thirds of trees were in good or excellent condition, and 2010, when only 19 percent were.[63] This trend suggests an aging and inadequately maintained street tree population that is likely to decline, as are the benefits it provides to people.

The third reason that street tree populations are declining compounds the first and second reasons. A surprisingly large number of

Newly planted street trees experience high mortality, like this struggling tulip poplar.

newly planted street trees don't survive and therefore don't play any part in replenishing the population. For example, in New York City, slightly more than a quarter of new street trees were dead or missing eight to nine years after being planted in the early 2000s.[64] The unexpectedly high mortality of new street trees undermines planting efforts and results in what may be assumed to be a one to one replacement of removed trees, budgets allowing, falling short of the mark.

Even if your city or town's street tree population has enough young, healthy trees and not too many old ones, and the municipal tree budget is adequate to plant and maintain trees, it may still be at risk of decline. Santamour's rule dictates that no single tree species should represent more than 10 percent of individuals and no single genus should represent more than 20 percent in order for an urban tree population to be resilient to disturbances. In New York state, 21 percent of all street trees are Norway maples, and 44 percent of trees are different kinds of maple, including Norway, sugar, and silver. Maples are particularly prone to the devastation wrought by the Asian longhorned beetle, a wood-boring invasive pest first reported in 1996 in New York City and thought to have arrived in the United States in packing material. The beetle is now known to be in New York, New Jersey, Massachusetts, Illinois, Ohio, and South Carolina. A street tree population with many maples is especially at risk of decline due to the beetle, which kills the trees it feeds on. Reducing the prevalence of maples by planting other species in New York and other areas with low street tree diversity will help limit the spread of the Asian longhorned beetle and other current and future invasive pests.

There are several concrete ways that you can help to ensure the long-term health of the street trees along your street and in your city and town. Check your municipality's parks and recreation or landscape management departments to find information on urban or community forestry initiatives that you can participate in. Your city or town may also have one or more non-governmental partners that help it fulfill its tree goals. Depending on where you live, you could improve knowledge of your municipality's street tree population and its resilience by helping to inventory trees and monitor their health over time, or by collecting data on the occurrence of tree insect pests and diseases. You could fill vacant street tree sites by volunteering to plant trees or help to increase the persistence of new and old trees alike by maintaining trees. If you have one or more street trees on your property or in front of your workplace, I've included a list of best practices for tree maintenance that you can begin right now, especially if your tree is young (see the sidebar *Give a little, get a lot: caring for your street tree*). Consistent maintenance over time can make a big difference to the survival and growth of a street tree—in New York City, it increased the survival of new trees by up to 40 percent. In exchange, your healthy street tree will provide you and your neighbors increasing returns on your own health and well-being for many years to come.

This chapter focused on your street and, by extension, the other streets and roads in your city or town. These spaces occupy relatively small footprints in the urban matrix and serve a narrow purpose. Nonetheless, your relationship with nature along your street is as deep and meaningful as ever. Driving along your and other streets and roads involves the potential of collision with a wide variety of animals, for which roadkill is an important cause of population decline and increased risk of extinction. This is especially true of common species, those raccoons, opossums, and squirrels that we often see killed on the side of the road, and species that move a lot or live a long time. Also vulnerable are species that are attracted to roads like nesting turtles and cliff swallows and those that do not avoid roads or cars and don't seem to exhibit any ability to learn to do so, like the spring peeper caught in the glare of flashlights strapped to a Radio Flyer wagon slowly rumbling its way. At the same time, your and other streets and roads are where street trees, an important natural element in the built environment, reside. Whether mostly young or old, one species or many, the street tree populations of American cities and towns provide residents with services, like cleaning the air and diverting stormwater, on the order of other types of urban infrastructure. Street trees also benefit our health and well-being by influencing our behavior, encouraging us to walk or cycle more and creating the conditions in which fewer of us commit violent crimes. However, despite their importance to urban quality of life, street tree populations across the country are declining or are at risk of declining due to inadequate budgets, aging canopies, the low survival of newly planted trees, and low species diversity.

Give a little, get a lot:
caring for your street tree

Newly planted street trees, as well as older, mature trees, need tender loving care to thrive in the tough conditions of the built environment. New street trees need particular attention to establish a strong root system so that they survive and grow, whereas older trees benefit from pruning to limit insect attacks, disease, and safety risks from falling limbs. Many municipalities or tree advocacy organizations provide tree care workshops or training in recognition of the precarious survival of new trees, an aging canopy, and the significant benefits that healthy trees provide residents. Below is a list of best practices distilled from several sources, including the Arbor Day Foundation, NYC Parks, and San Francisco Public Works. You can also download the Nature Conservancy's Healthy Trees, Healthy Cities app for tree-specific guidance.

Best Practices for Street Tree Care

- **Watering** is at the top of this list because it is the single most important thing you can do to help a new street tree survive and become established. The amount of water your street tree needs depends on the species and the climate where you live. A general recommendation is to water once a week during the summer for the first two years after planting. The soil around the tree should be moist but not soggy between waterings.

- **Mulching** reduces soil compaction, adds nutrients to the soil, and maintains soil moisture. Use natural mulch, like wood chips or bark pieces, rather than synthetic or dyed mulch, which pollutes the environment. Keep mulch away from the tree's trunk to avoid rot.

- **Weeding** at the base of the tree removes plants that compete with the tree for water and nutrients. Avoid planting ornamental plants around the tree for the same reason. Keeping the ground around the tree clear is particularly important when the tree is young.

- **Pruning** helps young trees develop good growth habits that will last into old age. New trees typically don't need pruning until they become established, after two or three years. Pruning at any age is a delicate operation that, if done improperly, can damage the tree. If you are responsible for the maintenance of your street tree, consult the excellent pruning resources on the Arbor Day Foundation's website (arborday.org) or call an arborist certified by the International Society of Arboriculture (ISA). Otherwise, submit a request for maintenance to your city or town's tree care department.

I've noticed a lot more roadkill during my daily commute since I began writing this chapter. I've also started taking stock of the street trees in my neighborhood, in some cases noticing for the first time trees that I had assumed were on private property but are in fact within public rights-of-way. I hope that reading this chapter has similarly heightened your awareness of the connections that exist between you and nature along your street. In a way, these connections are exemplary of the harshness of the urban environment for animals and plants. Streets and roads are a risky place whether you're a barred owl perched in a roadside tree or a young street tree struggling to survive tough growing conditions. To soften this inhospitableness, some of the recommendations in this chapter suggest ways to live in better harmony with wildlife, like driving less, using less fertilizer and pesticides, and taking good care of street trees. Let our streets also be then a reminder of and inspiration for the possibility of a better balance between people and nature where we live.

CHAPTER 5

YOUR PARK

My son and I love to visit our neighborhood park. He races to the playground as soon as it's in sight to use the swings, slides, and jungle gym in turn. It's a small park tucked between a residential street and a middle school, but it has just about everything you'd expect. From a central pavilion shading picnic tables, paths loop outward to skirt the play structures and lead into the lawn beyond, where they circle cherry trees, flowering plant beds, benches, and self-serve grills. Once my son is done swinging, sliding, and climbing, which never really lasts for long, he heads out to the wooded area beyond the lawn to play in the little stream that runs there. A small bridge crosses the stream into a bit of floodplain forest at the back of the park, where you can just hear the shouts of children through the loblolly pines, tulip trees, and river birches.

So far in this book, I've shown you how you are connected to nature in places where you might not, like your yard, and certainly don't, like your street, think nature exists in any real sense. Even though a yard may contain a garden and some lawn, we don't tend to think of it as harboring habitat for wild animals and plants. And your street and the network of roads in your city and town are typically assumed to be devoid of life, or, if nature is present, it's trying to avoid being killed or persisting as dusty, scraggly vegetation in the verge. Your park is fundamentally different from these spaces. Public parks are the places where we are supposed to find nature in cities and towns. You can't expect grass, flowers, trees, and shrubs in yards and along streets and roads—they may or may not be found in these places—but you'd be safe to assume that in just about every urban area in the United States, you'll find at least a bit of some, if not all, of these elements of nature in a park. What's more, you'd probably assume that nature has been left to its own devices in at least some small way in a park, where you wouldn't be surprised to find a flock of migrating birds, frogs calling from a pond, or maybe even deer grazing at dusk. Parks, and greenways that are the subject of the next chapter, are the two spaces explored in this book where wild nature is intended to reside.

This function of parks, a place to harbor nature in the city, was the purpose of public parks from their very beginning.[1] Starting in the mid-nineteenth century, some of the first municipal parks were created at the edges of rapidly growing American cities, like San Francisco, New York, and Chicago. The parks were large, idealized pastoral landscapes intended to provide a bucolic respite to the inhabitants. New York's Central Park and San Francisco's Golden Gate Park offered an escape from the crush of industrialization, especially for the wealthy, White upper classes. In these so-called pleasure grounds, visitors were encouraged to stroll along paths winding through carefully designed and highly manicured surroundings that idealized and attempted to perfect nature. Even though wild nature was not welcome in these first parks, they were nonetheless some of the first spaces to be designed and planned in cities to explicitly include it—the others being their precursors, the grand, canopied cemeteries, such as Mount Auburn Cemetery near Boston.[2]

Despite this auspicious beginning, the decades of the twentieth century saw nature take a second place to the social functions that parks were intended to fulfill. Initially, parks moved into the city proper with the intent being to provide the restorative effects of nature to the poor and immigrants in dense neighborhoods (but not Blacks). Although some parks still contained small remnants of the pleasure ground aesthetic—winding paths among trees, shrubs, and ponds—and neighborhood beautification was a goal of park designers, the primary purpose of parks was to provide space for civic programming and organized sports and as a place for children to play off the street (thus was born the playground). Trees and other vegetation were typically limited to the immediate peripheries of sports and play areas. In the postwar years of the 1950s,

parks with recreational facilities proliferated in the new inner-city housing projects and suburbs and provided patrons with the chance to swim,
play tennis or baseball, or attend a dance. During this time, parks were
often created next to new schools, which is how my neighborhood park
was born. The budgets of parks departments at the time were slim and all
but the minimum of lawn and trees were included in new parks to keep
maintenance low. On old aerial photos, my baby neighborhood park is
an open area with a baseball diamond and a handful of trees lining the
stream. By the 1970s, the seeming irrelevance of parks to suburbanites
with large yards and ongoing budgetary constraints resulted in deserted
and unkempt parks that were considered unsafe. Vegetation continued to
be removed in parks in the inner city to facilitate police surveillance and
minimize maintenance. Some parks also suffered from overuse by large
crowds, resulting in damage to vegetation and soil erosion.

At the same time, however, a movement to preserve nature in parks
began to blossom. Starting in the 1990s, parks became spaces where
ecological health was paramount.[3] Humans were no longer the only
beneficiaries of public parks. Parks were intended to provide habitat for
wildlife and an opportunity for unfettered ecological function. Accordingly, parks became sites for the restoration of nature. Exotic vegetation
maintained with large amounts of water, fertilizer and pesticides that
was characteristic of park landscaping in the past was replaced by native
plantings requiring minimal external inputs. It was during this period
that my neighborhood park underwent a transformation. In the early
2000s, the stream, up until then a straightened and eroded canal, was
restored to its current meandering incarnation. Native trees were planted
in the stream's new floodplain—the loblolly pines and river birches that I
see today. New paths were drawn, linking the playground to the grilling
areas and extending into the newly treed back half of the park. Later, in
the 2010s, the annual flowerbeds were dug up and replanted with native
plants that attract pollinators. It was at about this time when I first took a
top-down look at my park on Google Maps and realized that the looping
paths trace the shape of a butterfly. The play structures fill its lower wings,
the central pavilion is its body, and the grilling areas are the circular ends
of its antennae.

Wild nature is celebrated in today's public parks.

Public parks, then, have come full circle over the course of their history in the United States. They started as places where inhabitants overburdened by the noise and pollution of dense, industrializing neighborhoods could find respite in the peace, calm, and beauty of nature, albeit a highly refined and artificial version. After decades of neglect, nature has returned to dominate public parks, helped along by restoration projects, native plantings, and maintenance and management that promote wild nature. These two endpoints in the history of parks illustrate the relationships between you and nature in your park that I'll explore in this chapter. Inspired by my park's design, I'll first describe how the wild spaces in parks benefit butterfly populations and increase their diversity. I'll show you how you can help maintain the quality of these spaces so that their value to butterflies, and other wildlife, is enhanced. Since butterflies don't restrict themselves to parks in their search for nectar and resources for their caterpillar young, I'll also explore how patches of habitat in built-up areas are necessary for healthy butterfly populations in parks. Then, in deference to the original intent of parks as a restorative antidote to urban life, I'll describe Attention Restoration Theory and other ideas of how nature, and especially the wild bits, helps to relieve the stress and mental fatigue inherent in urban living and improve your mood. The Japanese practice of forest bathing, adapted for an urban setting, is one way that you can take advantage of the soothing properties of nature in your park. In the end, your park is one of the few places in your city or town where wild nature can thrive. Taking care of the little bit of wooded area or unimproved grassland in your park will ensure that the benefits of wild nature, for you and for butterflies and other species, can always be found close to home.

Maintaining wild nature in your park enhances the number and types of butterflies you find there

If I were to find myself on a hike in a Malaysian jungle, I might come across the chocolate albatross butterfly, its bright yellow wings edged with brown. Chocolate albatrosses are frequently spotted mudpuddling in clearings, where they crowd around puddles or moist patches of ground to imbibe precious nutrients. At other times, the chocolate albatross would be flying low to the ground among the surrounding trees, or, as a caterpillar, enjoying the nice green leaves of trees, shrubs, and woody vines in the caper family, like the sacred garlic pear tree.

If, during this tropical expedition, I wandered to the edge of the jungle where the trees and shrubs are less closely spaced and tall grasses thrive in the open conditions, I might spot a dark grass-brown butterfly, conspicuous by its five eyespots underlined in white. The dark grass-brown would be keeping to the undergrowth where it might bask in the sun or its caterpillars feed on the grasses.

Then, emerging from the trees completely into an adjoining ornamental garden, I'd probably see a third species of butterfly, the common rose, sipping nectar in a manicured flowerbed. The common rose is a swallowtail butterfly with wide black forewings and red, white, and black elongated hindwings. The bright red and white patches on its tails signal to predators that it would make a noxious meal, having spent its youth munching on the poisonous Dutchman's pipe vine in the adjacent forest. As dusk approached and the common rose had its fill of nectar from the

Public parks often include a diversity of butterfly habitats, from forested to open areas.

zinnias and cosmos lining the paths of the garden, it would flutter away into the trees to roost for the night on a twig or branch.

The park I've been exploring on this imaginary expedition is actually in Kuala Lumpur, a city of nearly two million people in Malaysia, and the butterflies are three of the species that John-James Wilson, now a curator of vertebrate zoology at the World Museum in Liverpool, and his colleagues found in their survey of ten municipal parks there.[4] I've selected these three species because they exemplify the three ways that wild nature increases the diversity of butterflies in public parks by increasing habitat diversity.

The positive association between habitat diversity and number of species is a ubiquitous pattern in ecology. It was first formally quantified by Robert MacArthur, a dominant figure in ecology in the middle of the twentieth century who helped to transform the field into an experimental, hypothesis-testing science and one of the founders of landscape ecology, my particular specialty. During the summers of 1956 and 1957 in the spruce forests of Maine and Vermont, MacArthur painstakingly tracked the movements and behaviors of five warbler species, small insectivorous forest birds, in order to figure out how all five species could co-exist on the same tree without one species outcompeting the others.[5] He went so far as to count the seconds each species spent at different heights in a tree and different distances from the trunk, keeping track of the time by saying "thousand and one, thousand and two, . . . " because he didn't have a stopwatch. He noted how often each bird moved, how far they moved and in what direction, and how they captured their insect prey. He discovered that each warbler species occupied a different zone of the tree where they ate different kinds of food. Blackburnian warblers, a small black-and-white warbler with a flame-colored throat, kept close to the trunk of spruce trees where it could find beetles, its preferred prey. In contrast, black-throated green warblers occurred at the periphery of trees where spiders, its meal of choice, could be found. By plotting the density of the bird species in relation to the volume of foliage at different heights, an index of the number of different warbler habitat zones, MacArthur discovered that the greater the amount of foliage, the greater the total density of birds and the more warbler species. Since then, the pattern of more species where there are more habitat types has been reported for just about every kind of organism, from soil mites to mollusks to mammals.[6]

In Kuala Lumpur, Wilson and his colleagues observed butterflies in four microhabitats in each park: unmanaged areas, hedges, flower-beds, and groves of trees. These four habitat types could be reasonably assumed to differ in nectar and host plant species, the plants that adults and caterpillars rely on for food, respectively, and thus be home to different butterfly species. Just like in Maine, where more spruce foliage at a certain height would attract warbler species adapted to feed in that zone, unmanaged areas in the parks of Kuala Lumpur attracted their own complement of butterfly species, like the chocolate albatross that is dependent on trees, shrubs, and vine species that grow in forests. The chocolate albatross was one of ten species found only in unmanaged areas in parks. Thus, these areas of wild nature added to the butterfly diversity of parks by providing specialized habitat that wasn't available in other microhabitat types.

In fact, the presence of unmanaged areas in parks added two different types of specialized habitat for butterflies. The first was the dense forest conditions and the plant species that thrive there that forest specialists like the chocolate albatross depend on. The second was at the edge of unmanaged areas and other areas. For some species, edges or ecotones where one habitat type transitions into another and conditions are therefore intermediate between the two are a habitat type in and of themselves. That's why the dark grass-brown that is adapted to brushy open conditions with scattered trees was one of those ten species that Wilson and his colleagues found only in unmanaged areas. Without unmanaged area, there would be no edge between it and more managed microhabitats in parks, and therefore no habitat for the dark grass-brown.

Finally, the presence of unmanaged wild areas in parks benefited a third kind of species, epitomized by the common rose butterfly. Wilson and his colleagues observed the common rose in two microhabitats, unmanaged areas and flowerbeds. This is because the butterfly needs both types of areas to complete its life cycle. Adult common roses depend upon the nectar in ornamental flowers planted in managed beds, but their caterpillars need the leaves of forest plants, like the Dutchman's pipe vine, to grow. Species like the common rose will only occur in parks that have flowerbeds *and* unmanaged areas, so the latter are necessary for these types of species too.

In sum, unmanaged areas in parks attract a different complement of butterfly species than do other habitat types. This is the reason that public parks that include wild forest remnants or un- or rarely managed grassland, as well as other types of butterfly habitat, have more butterfly species. For example, in Hannover, Germany, parks that are mown less frequently have on average twice the number of butterfly species as frequently mown parks, in part because less managed parks have a greater diversity of nectar plants and a greater number of habitats for butterflies.[7] In Halle in eastern Germany, parks that contain more forest or woodland also have more butterfly species.[8] In Malmö, Sweden, parks that contain un-mowed areas or tall grass that is only infrequently mowed have higher butterfly diversity on average than parks with well-mowed lawns and flower beds.[9] And in Singapore, public parks adjacent to patches of forest

Some butterfly species rely on edge habitat in parks, like this edge between a forested area and an open area.

Parks with more types of butterfly habitat have more butterfly species, like the eastern tiger swallowtail (left), which frequents woodlands as well as fields and flower gardens, and the sachem skipper (right), a butterfly of lawns and other open areas.

have more butterfly species, including over three times more rare species, than isolated parks.[10]

An increase in habitat diversity is not the only reason that wild nature in parks increases the number of butterfly species. Wild nature also acts as a refuge for butterflies when conditions in managed areas become unsuitable, or even hostile. As I described in this chapter's introduction, nature in parks can change dramatically over time in response to variation in maintenance budgets, the amount and type of park use, aesthetic preferences, and the priorities of park managers. It's not uncommon to see flowerbeds and shrubbery removed or existing plants entirely replaced with new species. To a butterfly, these changes translate into the sudden disappearance of important nectar and host plants and the loss of habitat that was there just a moment ago. Regular park maintenance activities

Wild nature is a refuge for some butterfly species when conditions in managed parks areas become unsuitable, as seen here when a flowerbed was replanted.

like mowing and the application of pesticides also affect butterflies in the managed areas of parks by eliminating "weedy" plant species that adults and caterpillars rely on or by killing adults and caterpillars outright. A wild area that is excluded from intensive maintenance and generally left to its own devices then becomes a retreat and refuge for species that would once have fluttered among flowerbeds, to wait until the remainder of the park again becomes suitable for them.

The study that best illustrates the refuge function of wild areas in parks was carried out in Tsukuba, a city thirty miles northeast of Tokyo, Japan, with just over 127,000 people at the time.[11] Masahiko Kitahara and Koichi Fujii at the University of Tsukuba compared the number and kind of butterfly species in two public parks, Doho Park where planted trees and lawns were maintained by pruning, mowing, and the use of insecticide and Akatsuka Park that was similar in these respects to Doho

Park but also contained some patches of remnant forest. Kitahara and Fujii counted thirty-six species of butterfly in Akatsuka Park and twenty in Doho, a difference partly explained by the presence of specialist species closely associated with remnant forest habitat, like the chocolate albatross or the dark grass-brown in Kuala Lumpur, but also due to the presence of generalist species that weren't found in Doho Park. These generalists whose caterpillars fed on a wide variety of host plant species, including plants characteristic of nearby residential gardens, were likely only found in Akatsuka Park because the park contained patches of unmanaged remnant forest refuge.

At this point, I should note that my use of the adjective "unmanaged" in reference to areas of forest or grassland in parks is misleading. I should really be using the relative terms "less managed" or "extensively managed" to distinguish wilder bits of nature in parks from intensively managed areas that are regularly mowed, raked, mulched, and treated with pesticides. In reality, wilder areas of nature in parks also need tending. Because of their location within human-dominated urban and suburban landscapes, natural areas in parks are subject to multiple stressors that, left unchecked, deteriorate their quality as wildlife habitat over time. High human use, even if it's only at the periphery of natural areas, is accompanied by litter accumulation, soil compaction, and damage to vegetation. Large volumes of runoff from surrounding development also add litter and erode soil. These factors, as well as air pollution and elevated temperatures, make for harsh growing conditions for many plants, the exception being invasive species that thrive in the unkempt interstices of the urban fabric where they can overwhelm natives.

Probably the most famous example of this process of deterioration is New York City's Central Park. Following the tenure of the influential Parks Commissioner Robert Moses, who revitalized Central Park after years of neglect during the first few decades of the twentieth century, the park again fell into decline in the 1960s and 1970s. Lampposts were damaged and didn't work, benches and buildings were covered with graffiti and/or boarded up, and germane to this book, wooded areas that the original designers Frederick Law Olmstead and Calvert Vaux intended as sylvan respites from city life were pale shadows of their former glory.

If left untended, the quality of wild nature in parks can become compromised by climbing vines and other stressors common in urban and suburban landscapes.

In particular, the four-acre Hallett Nature Sanctuary that Moses fenced off in 1934 as a bird sanctuary to be untouched by human hands was choked with climbing Japanese wisteria, Norway maples, and Japanese knotgrass, allowed to run rampant for decades to the detriment of the original plantings.[12]

Today, the Hallett sanctuary is once again open to the public. In 2001, the Central Park Conservancy began a restoration of the woods after sixty-seven years of abandonment by removing invasives, improving soils, planting natives, and installing irrigation. The sanctuary is now home to a lush and diverse native plant community that supports wildlife of all kinds—three hundred and sixty-eight species to be exact according to iNaturalist, including adults and caterpillars of the monarch and eleven other butterfly species.

The Hallett Nature Sanctuary story is emblematic of the challenges facing natural areas in parks across the country. City budgets are simply not up to the task of maintaining areas in parks not intended for intensive human use. As a result, invasives and trash quickly take over and the quality of woodland or grassland as wildlife habitat, and, as I'll show later in this chapter, as a restorative balm for the stress of urban living, are significantly diminished. In 1980, the Central Park Conservancy was created to address this shortcoming and to restore the other areas of Central Park that had been overused, damaged, or abandoned. Since then, park conservancies with similar goals have been created in cities across the country. These private, nonprofit organizations, as well as "Friends of the Park" groups, rely on thousands of volunteers to fulfill their missions, which, in some cases, include the majority of park maintenance activities. You can help tend the wild area in your local or regional park to ensure that it remains valuable wildlife habitat by participating in one of the many volunteer activities these organizations offer (see the sidebar *Join the Green Team!*). Today's parks are intended to benefit people and nature and what better way to forge this partnership then to get involved at the ground level.

Even though their bobbing flight is a little awkward-looking, butterflies move relatively long distances, up to 0.4 miles or about 2,100

Join the Green Team!

Under pressure from invasive species, the build-up of trash, and generally difficult growing conditions in the urban environment, the wild areas in public parks are in dire need of a little tender loving care. There are several ways you can help with their maintenance. Check for volunteer opportunities advertised by your local Parks and Recreation Department, by a park conservancy in your city, or by a "Friends of the Park" group in your area. Your time and energy will help to restore and maintain the wild bits of nature in your park that are so important to butterflies and other wildlife.

I've listed the types of volunteer activities below that will likely be on offer. They span a range of gardening and horticultural levels of expertise, time commitments, and target ages. You should be able to find an activity that fits your personal goals and needs.

- **Weekend Green Teams or Day in the Dirt** volunteers meet one morning a week to mulch, pull weeds, remove invasives, and plant native species. You can participate just once or for as many weeks as you like.

- **A Walk in the Park or Pick-up and Pitch-in litter clean-ups** occur weekly or on special days of the year, depending on your park. This activity is typically self-guided so it's great to do with your family or a friend. Gloves, trash pickers, and bags are usually provided.

- **Urban Ecostewards** maintain a specific area of the park, either on their own time or with a landscape management team during regular weekly hours. Ecostewards invest in their section of the park and really getting to know the plant and animal species that live there.

- **Seasonal projects** focus on specific tasks that need doing at key points during the year, like cutting and pruning, cutting back or removing invasive species at certain points in their life cycle, and raking and composting.

- **Other volunteer activities** that occur regularly include maintaining walking trails, repairing, cleaning, and painting benches, and planting and watering trees.

feet in a day depending on the species and the distance between habitat patches.[13] Given that the median acreage of public parks in American cities is six acres, roughly equivalent to a square area with 500-foot sides, this means that butterflies are more than likely leaving their neighborhood park and wandering into the surrounding development in search of nectar and host plants.[14] Accordingly, many studies of butterfly diversity in public parks have reported a positive effect of the amount and diversity of greenspace surrounding parks on the number of species found in them. For example, the number of butterfly species in public parks in Marseille, France, depends in part on the number of trees and the amount of grassland surrounding the parks, up to 800 feet away.[15] The same is true for parks in Malmö, Sweden, where the number of species in parks is a positive function of the area of backyard gardens, cemeteries, other parks, and nature preserves within two-thirds of a mile. And in Halle, Germany, the number of different kinds of greenspace, from forests to grasslands to trees and hedges, within a third of a mile had a positive effect on park butterfly diversity.

In other words, the value of your local neighborhood park for butterflies depends not only on the amount of natural area in the park but also on the greenspace in its developed surroundings, such as the flowers and trees in your yard. This is especially true for habitat specialist species with low or intermediate mobility that need frequent breaks as they meander through neighborhoods, including species that depend on forested areas in parks for their survival.[16] It's also especially true if your yard is within the butterfly daily movement range of a park, about 0.4 miles, which is the case for about 70 percent of American city residents. You can increase the number of butterfly species in your local park by planting a diverse garden of flowering plants in your yard (see the sidebar *Adding a stop on the Butterfly Highway*) and by more generally increasing the amount and complexity of vegetation in your yard as I described in the sidebar *Five simple things you can do to create a bird-friendly yard* in chapter 3. Either way, you will be creating a place where weary butterflies can take a break from their travels and a chance for you to get to know them better so you can easily find them again during your next visit to your park.

Adding a stop on the Butterfly Highway

The Butterfly Highway is a pollinator conservation program administered by the North Carolina Wildlife Federation. The program originated as the dissertation project of a recent PhD graduate from my department, Angel Hjarding. Hjarding was intent on fostering grassroots conservation in underserved communities that typically lack capacity for environmental education and advocacy by encouraging residents to plant butterfly gardens in their yards and in public spaces. The Butterfly Highway has since spread across North Carolina with more than two thousand pollinator pitstops protecting thirty thousand acres of pollinator habitat. You can create a pollinator pitstop in your yard to benefit the butterflies in your local park by following the simple guidelines below from the Butterfly Highway program and the North American Butterfly Association's (NABA) Butterfly Garden Certification Program. Be sure to register your pitstop on the Highway at https://ncwf.org/habitat/butterfly-highway/ if you live in North Carolina, or register with NABA's program at http://nababutterfly.com/butterfly-garden-certification-program-home/ otherwise.

Guidelines to create a pollinator pitstop in your yard

- **Start small.** A balcony planter or small corner of your yard dedicated to flowering plants will benefit butterflies in your neighborhood.

- **Plant a diversity of species that attract pollinators.** NABA recommends at least three species of nectar plant and three species of caterpillar food plant, each represented by more than one plant. The ideal is to create a garden that feeds both adult and young butterflies to help increase population sizes. Consult NABA's Regional Garden Guides at https://www.nababutterfly.com/guide_index.html for lists of butterfly-friendly species native to your area. Each recommended plant attracts specific butterflies, so you can create a custom butterfly experience based on the butterfly species you like most.

- **When you select plants, choose a variety** of flower colors, flower shapes, and bloom times to attract the greatest diversity of butterfly species.

- **Find a spot for the garden where it will receive at least six hours of direct sunlight a day.** Butterflies also need a place to warm up in the morning so try to locate the garden next to bare ground or even pavement that receives early light.

A front yard stop on the Butterfly Highway.

- **Add a puddling dish** to an open sunny spot near flowering plants to provide butterflies with nutrients. You can easily make a puddling dish by filling a shallow flower pot saucer with landscape sand and soil or compost and keeping it moist. Include a few small decorative rocks for butterflies to bask on.

- **Consider adding some height** using flowering vines, trees, and/or shrubs that attract butterflies. These elements attract a different complement of species than shorter vegetation and protect the rest of the garden from strong winds, making it easier for butterflies to feed. Taller vegetation also provides a place for butterflies to roost at night and to hide from predators.

- **Last but not least, avoid pesticide use!**

Wild nature in your park relieves stress and mental fatigue and improves your mood

So far, I've shown you how different habitats in parks influence the diversity of wildlife that call parks home. But what about the primary beneficiary of parks, the people that visit them? Do they benefit from a diversity of natural elements in parks such as areas of wild nature in addition to managed lawns and flowerbeds and the variety of animal and plant species that go along with them? And if they do, how? These are important questions for two reasons. First, the answers deepen our understanding of our relationship with untended or extensively managed nature, something we know relatively little about, especially in cities and suburbs. Second, if the answer to the first question is "yes"—that is, the diversity of nature provides us with something that we need or desire—then we have a strong utilitarian reason to conserve it. In the mid-2000s, in the wake of the United Nations' Millennium Ecosystem Assessment that described the extensive loss and degradation of ecosystems worldwide and the myriad benefits or services that they provide, ecologists were keen to provide empirical evidence of nature's benefits to aid in its conservation. In Sheffield, England, Richard Fuller, now a professor at the University of Queensland in Australia, focused on a benefit from nature that was little understood at the time and that we are only really beginning to grasp in the present day—its positive effect on our mental well-being.[17]

Fuller and his colleagues knew that nature had been associated with mental health benefits in recent studies. What they wondered was whether the quality of the natural environment, in terms of its diversity of species and habitats, had an effect on the strength of this relationship. To find out, they interviewed 312 visitors to fifteen public parks in Sheffield, home to half a million people at the time. The parks they chose varied from small lawn-dominated public greens to larger parks with a mix of sports fields, woodlands, and grasslands. They asked visitors about how connected they felt to the nature in their park, the extent to which they felt they could gain perspective on their life or easily think about personal matters when visiting the park, and whether visiting the park cleared their head. At the same time, they counted the number of different types of habitat in each park, including lawns, grasslands, ornamental plantings, and woodland, and the number of herbaceous and woody plant species. After controlling for the park area, Fuller and his colleagues discovered that the more habitats and the more plant species a park contained, the more strongly visitors felt they were able to reflect on matters important to them. And just to check that it was indeed the diversity of habitats and plant species that were driving these relationships, Fuller also asked visitors how many plant species they thought their park contained. The number of plant species perceived by visitors was highly correlated with the actual number of plant species, which was highly correlated with the number of habitats. So, visitors' experience of a diverse natural environment matched the reality, lending support to the conclusion that habitat and species diversity in parks positively influenced visitors' capacity for reflection.

What Fuller and his colleagues had provided robust empirical evidence of is called Attention Restoration Theory (ART), proposed by Rachel and Stephen Kaplan in the late 1980s.[18] According to ART, nature improves mental well-being by restoring our capacity for directed attention. Directed attention is the brain's ability to focus or concentrate on a given task, and its ability to tune out competing stimuli in order to do so. Things like driving to work, planning your day, reading emails, budgeting, serving customers, and getting your kids to bed on time all require directed attention. As I'm sure you know from experience, your capacity to focus on your to-do list, your goals, and your responsibilities starts to wane when you've been at it for too long or you have too much on your plate. When this happens, it becomes difficult to concentrate and you may even become irritable. What you are experiencing is called mental fatigue, and it occurs because the brain's ability to focus or concentrate is finite—at some point, that ability becomes exhausted, and we need to take a break. The fact that directed attention is needed to not only focus on a task but to actively ignore everything else around you as you do so is why some people wear noise-cancelling headphones at their workplace, why living in a large city packed with people and traffic can be so draining, and why, in my estimation, the pandemic has taken such a mental toll on all of us—it takes effort to keep track of where and when to wear a mask, but also to tune out the daily news of rising infections and emerging variants, and this on top of all the usual activities vying for attention.

Rachel and Stephen Kaplan proposed that spending time in nature alleviates mental fatigue by allowing the brain's directed attention center to rest. This is because in nature all four of the essential characteristics of a restorative environment occur in abundance: being away, extent, fascination, and compatibility.[19] When I teach Attention Restoration Theory, I explain these characteristics by first asking students to think of the activity they usually do when they need a break from studying and the reason that the activity "works," that they feel rested or restored when they get back to the books. Common responses are exercising, playing guitar, listening to loud music, and working on a hobby. The students tell me that these activities are effective because they are so different from studying, they can really get into them, and they are enjoyable. These characteristics are those of a restorative experience, which nature offers to all of us. Being in nature gives us a sense of *being away*, of being in a very different place than we just were. Contrast the physical space of your office or workplace with the experience of walking on uneven ground under a canopy of leaves. The magnitude of the difference here, between white walls and tree trunks say, allows for a deep or immersive experience, one that the Kaplans termed had *extent*. Nature also has the ability to *fascinate* us, to draw our attention effortlessly to the sound of the crunching leaves under our feet, the flutter of a butterfly, or the call of a bird. We don't need to exert effort to notice these things; we just do. Finally, nature is *compatible* with our intent to relax and is an environment that we instinctively enjoy—we don't need to put any effort into finding pleasure in the experience. A variety of settings and experiences will be restorative to some degree to different people, but nature, as Attention Restoration Theory posits, is the one environment that people in general find the most beneficial.

Attention Restoration Theory is not the only explanation for the positive effect of nature on mental well-being. A few years before the Kaplans elaborated their theory, Roger Ulrich proposed his own explanation emphasizing the psychological, rather than cognitive, benefits of nature.[20] Ulrich suggested that humans automatically experience positive emotions when viewing nature because we have evolved to associate nature with an abundance of resources and a high probability of survival. For instance, parkland-like landscapes with scattered trees, long vistas, and even ground elicit positive reactions because in our species' history, places like these were easy to navigate and contained lots of resources. But even the simple presence of vegetation or water can make people feel good. For example, in an early experiment, Ulrich had two groups of students view a variety of natural and urban scenes in windowless rooms immediately after sitting an introductory geography exam.[21] The natural and urban scenes were chosen such that the nature scenes were generally views of scruffy vegetation that would be generally considered unappealing, whereas the urban scenes were views of neat and orderly commercial development lacking people, cars, litter, and graffiti. Compared to the urban group, the students who viewed scenes of nature felt significantly more warmhearted, friendly, pleased, and carefree than the students who viewed the urban scenes. In contrast, the urban students experienced significantly more sadness following their experience. Several years later, Ulrich and his colleagues reported that people who watched videos of nature following a stressful movie experienced much faster and more complete recovery from stress, measured as lower blood pressure, less muscle tension, less anger and aggression, less fear, and more positive emotions, than people who watched commercial street scenes.[22] This result highlights that Stress Reduction Theory, as it has come to be known, is especially relevant to people experiencing stress, just as Attention Restoration Theory is particularly relevant to people suffering from mental fatigue.

In reality, the ways that nature improves mental well-being suggested by these theories are intertwined. If nature improves your mood, you are likely to also experience improved cognitive functioning, and conversely, better cognitive functioning improves your mood. Finally, the simple fact of physically distancing yourself from stressors by visiting a quieter natural environment with fewer people can also diminish stress and improve mental well-being.

In the years since the publication of the Kaplan and Kaplan and Ulrich theories, many studies have demonstrated the restorative and stress-reducing capacity of nature. Within the realm of public parks, two large studies are particularly convincing. Patrick Grahn at the Swedish University of Agricultural Sciences and Ulrika Stigsdotter, now at the University of Copenhagen, analyzed close to one thousand responses from a representative sample of Swedes living in the most populous part of the country near the cities of Stockholm, Malmö, and Gothenburg.[23] They found that Swedes that visited public parks more often or spent more time in public parks on a yearly basis reported lower levels of stress, irritation, and fatigue. This relationship held whether the respondent was three years old or seventy-five, male or female, rich or poor, lived in the city center or a suburb, did or did not have a private garden at home, and lived near or far from a park.

In England, Matthew White and his colleagues at the European Center for Environment and Human Health at the University of Exeter took advantage of long-term survey data to examine the effect of amount of greenspace near respondents' homes with indices of mental distress and life satisfaction.[24] The strength of White's study lies in the use of a survey of a large number of people (about ten thousand) over eighteen years. Tracking the mental health and well-being of the same people over time as they naturally moved to new houses and neighborhoods enabled White to rule out the effect of personality and the possibility that a positive association of greenspace with life satisfaction, for example, was due to happier people choosing to live in greener neighborhoods rather than greener neighborhoods making the people who already lived there happier. The amount of public greenspace in respondents' neighborhoods did indeed predict lower levels of mental distress, an indicator of anxiety and depression, and greater life satisfaction. When White compared the magnitude of these effects to those of the other significant predictors of mental health and well-being of total, public and private, greenspace, he found that the positive effect of nature was about a third the size of that of being married compared to being unmarried and 10 to 20 percent of that of being employed compared to unemployed.

Let's now get back to the specific contribution of wild nature in parks. Additional research in England and research in Italy and Denmark show that wild nature in parks enhances restoration and mood, especially for people experiencing high levels of stress.[25] In England, visitors to large parks and botanical gardens across the country rated walks through the most natural areas of the sites—those with trees, shrubs, and herbaceous plants mixed together without any indication of intentional design—as the most restorative, in that walkers were able to mentally escape from mundane routines and work, felt relaxed and comfortable, and considered their surroundings special and unique. In Italy, visitors to public parks in the cities of Rome, Bari, Padua, and Florence with high biodiversity and complex, more natural vegetation structure experienced greater well-being and restoration than visitors to less biodiverse and more managed parks. This positive effect was particularly pronounced for parks in the city centers compared to the suburbs, indicating that stressed-out city dwellers benefited more from wild nature in their parks than their suburban counterparts. Finally, in Denmark, public squares in Copenhagen perceived to contain wild and untouched nature, free-growing lawns, few people, and that felt safe were preferred by the most stressed visitors—those ranking in the top 25 percent of reported stress levels. These aspects of squares contributed to stressed visitors' sense of being away, of being in an utterly different world than is usually the case and thus away from routine demands and obligations, one of the essential characteristics of a restorative environment as defined in Attention Restoration Theory.

There may be a limit to the wildness of nature that elicits restoration and stress relief, however. Dörte Martens and his colleagues at the University of Zurich and the Swiss Federal Research Institute compared the effects of walking along a path through a tended part of a forested area in Zurich and a wild part of the same forest.[26] In the tended part of the forest, recently cut logs were piled next to the path and the space between trees was fairly open. In comparison, nothing had been cut in the wild part of the forest for the last six years and the vegetation looked brushy and unkempt. The people who participated in the study were randomly assigned to the two forest conditions and on the whole did not differ in age, level of education, where they lived, and how often they typically visited greenspaces. Martens found that those who walked through the tended part of the forest reported being calmer and in a generally better mood and experiencing less anger and depression than those who walked

Wild nature in parks offers mental restoration and a chance to improve your mood, especially when you are experiencing stress.

on the wild side, as it were. The positive effect of maintenance wasn't due to a greater sense of safety because the two groups of walkers didn't differ in this respect or in the degree of fear or threat they felt prior to their walks. It also wasn't due to a greater aesthetic appeal of the tended walk compared to the wild walk because the two groups rated the walks as equally attractive. As it stands, it seems that in the wildest settings, such as a heavily forested area, some indicators of human presence and care are necessary to trigger positive, stress-relieving emotions, possibly because we have evolved to associate these indicators with human success: signs of recent human industry tell us that people are thriving in the area. In other words, it could be that we feel at home where nature is in abundance, as Stress Reduction Theory suggests, but also where other humans are present.

Given the wealth of evidence that nature in parks positively impacts our mental well-being, the question to ask now is how often do you need to visit your park to experience restoration and stress relief and how long should you stay when you get there? Part of the answer to the first half of the question is simply visit nature in your park as often as you can. Fascinating research out of my alma mater, Carleton University in Canada, suggests that not visiting nature results in a negative feedback loop whereby the less you visit, the less connected you feel to nature, the more you underestimate its benefits, and the less you want to visit.[27] Like other universities, hospitals, and even shopping malls in Canada, Carleton has a network of underground tunnels that link academic buildings, student residence halls, and other facilities so that, as my husband, a proud Carleton graduate, boasted soon after we met, students can stay warm and dry on their way to class in the winter, and even keep their pajamas on if they're running late. Elizabeth Nisbet, a PhD candidate at the time, and her advisor in the Department of Psychology, John Zelenski, noticed that students chose to use the tunnels to get around campus even when it was sunny and mild when they could have walked through Carleton's treed, parklike campus next to the Rideau River instead. Nisbet and Zelenski hypothesized that the students' urban lifestyles of many hours spent indoors and limited access to greenspace had resulted in their disconnection from nature and consequently, their underestimation of the benefits of walking outdoors instead of through the tunnels. To test their hypothesis, Nisbet and Zelenski randomly assigned 150 students to a tunnel or outdoor walk of the same duration and to be either forecasters, who predicted how they would feel after the different walks but didn't actually take them, or experiencers, who went on the walks and reported how they felt afterwards. Experiencers reported more positive emotions, fewer negative emotions, more relaxation, and a greater sense of fascination after walking outdoors than through the tunnels. The predictions of forecasters didn't differ between the two types of walk, but, as expected, forecasters predicted that the tunnel walk would be more pleasant than it turned out to be for experiencers and the outdoor walk less pleasant.

Nisbet and Zelenski also reported that students who experienced the outdoor walk identified themselves more closely with nature than the students who used the tunnels, and that this closeness was the result of the positive emotions the outdoor walk elicited. Getting back to the question of how often you should visit your park, these and Nisbet and Zelenski's other results indicate that each visit will make you feel good and more connected to nature and eager to visit again. Conversely, not visiting your park will heighten your disconnection from nature, causing you to underestimate its benefits and ultimately, to choose to do something other than to go to the park. My advice then is even if you don't feel like going to the park, go to the park!

For those who need specific goals, and I confess I am one of them, two recent findings suggest a minimum dose of nature needed to realize health and well-being benefits. In England, people who spent at least 120 minutes, or two hours, per week in parks, nature preserves, or the countryside were much more likely to report being in good health and to have high life satisfaction than people who did not spend any time in nature.[28] The bump in health and life satisfaction from spending two hours in nature per week occurred regardless of the number of visits and was comparable in size to the increase from meeting physical activity guidelines of 150 minutes of exercise per week. And in Michigan, spending twenty to thirty minutes three times per week in nature most effectively reduced stress levels—spending less or more time didn't lower stress nearly as much.[29] It didn't matter exactly where people encountered nature and it didn't matter when during the week the visits occurred. In summary, it seems that we should all aim for a nature pill of at least an hour and a half per week. The evidence suggests that it doesn't really matter where you get your pill from, the type of natural setting you visit, although we do know that wild nature, with a bit of tending, is particularly potent. Lately, I've taken to visiting my neighborhood park or one of the nature preserves in my city to practice forest bathing, a Japanese custom of connecting with trees using the senses, to get the most out of my nature experience. If you're new to visiting nature for nature's sake, my quick guide to forest bathing might help you get used to simply being in wild nature (see the sidebar *Connecting to nature using your senses: how to practice forest bathing*). Remember that even a short visit counts towards your weekly dose of nature and that the trick is to just make that first visit. Once you do, you'll want to go again, and again, and again.

Connecting to nature using your senses: how to practice forest bathing

Forest bathing, or Shinrin-Yoku, is the Japanese custom of soaking up the atmosphere of a forest through the senses. This short guide, adapted from Qing Li's *Forest Bathing: How Trees Can Help You Find Health and Happiness*, is a good starting point if you're unfamiliar with the practice.

You can practice forest bathing wherever there are trees, like in your local or regional park or even in your yard. If you're new to the idea of spending time in nature just to appreciate it, choose a location where you feel most comfortable, maybe a park you've been to before with a bench or path among scattered trees, a treed spot in your yard, or a place that brings up happy memories. Leave your phone at home, or silence it if you prefer to keep it with you. When you're ready, take a seat or walk slowly around the site, without a specific destination in mind. Use all your senses to connect with the forest or trees around you in the following ways:

- **See** the light falling between the trees; notice the different shades of green beside, above, and below you; look at the networks of branches and roots.

- **Sniff** the air; inhale the fragrant phytoncides emitted by the trees, which Qing Li's research has shown reduce blood pressure and boost immune function.[30]

- **Hear** the wind moving among the leaves, the twitter or sharp call of a bird, and the scamper of a squirrel up a trunk.

- **Touch** the bark of different kinds of trees; feel the roughness or smoothness of the bark, the pattern of its groves or patches; handle some soil or dead leaves.

- **Taste** the air as it moves into and out of your lungs; do this at different points along your route or at different times to check for any difference in flavor.

- **Be aware** of the thoughts and emotions moving across your mind; identify the type of thought or emotion as it arises, then gently let it drift away; enjoy the happiness and peace of being with nature.

Forest bathing, the Japanese practice of soaking up the atmosphere of a forest through the senses, can help you reap the mental health benefits of wild nature in your park.

If there is one thing I hope you take away from this chapter, it is the importance of helping to tend the wild spaces in your neighborhood park, or in a regional park if your neighborhood park doesn't have any. The act of tending wild nature close to where you live is an opportunity to engage all of your senses in developing a stronger connection with nature and to bathe in the relaxation, happiness, life satisfaction, and relief from anxiety, irritation, and fatigue that nature offers. As you tend a patch of wild nature in your park, take the time to reflect on the habitat and refuge you are creating for specialist and generalist butterflies alike, a respite from city living for you *and* for monarchs, summer azures, red admirals, eastern tailed-blues, and spicebush swallowtails. And remember, these and other butterflies are present in your park in part because of the garden pitstops in the yards, office parks, and cemeteries in the surrounding landscape. I hope you make a point of visiting the little bit of woodland, forest, or grassland in your park soon, even if you don't feel like it (because you may not realize what you're missing) and especially when you feel most stressed and fatigued (to get the biggest mental well-being boost from your visit). Think of it as a whole new part of your neighborhood to explore!

CHAPTER 6

YOUR GREENWAY

ONE OF THE MOST ENJOYABLE AND SATISFYING ASPECTS OF MY JOB AS A professor is mentoring student research. This is especially true when the research in question stems from a student's passionate interest in the urban environment and if their interest is in something I don't know much about. When that happens, I have the privilege of helping a student develop the skills they need to expand their knowledge, and I get to learn something new about urban ecology along the way.

Exactly this situation presented itself to me when Johnny Peterson, a recent graduate of the BA Environmental Studies program in my department, walked into my office in the fall of 2019. Johnny was curious about the otter den he had discovered kayaking one day in a wildlife refuge just north of the city. He wanted to know more about the otter family's comings and goings, and wanted to learn how to use an infrared video camera to monitor their activity. I had not studied otters before, nor had I ever used infrared cameras to track wildlife, but I was gung-ho to help him out.

What followed was a semester-long project on the otter family in the wildlife refuge that turned into ongoing funded research on otters throughout the city. In between kayak trips to change the SD card and batteries in the camera at the refuge, Johnny explored the web of streams that interlace Charlotte, finding otter tracks along the wide, sandy, and canopied banks of streams that bisected residential neighborhoods, ran alongside industrial parks, and meandered at the corner of an interstate interchange. Johnny wanted to know whether the otters living in these more or less urban streams had different diets, due to urbanization affecting the availability of fish, crayfish, and other foods, and whether they were active at different times of day—some mammals in cities are active at night rather than at dusk in order to avoid humans. So, I bought more cameras and we enlisted the help of a molecular biologist on campus, Adam Reitzel, to sequence the DNA in otter feces, so-called spraints, Johnny collected at the streams. Luckily, I didn't have to do any spraint collecting. Instead, my inbox was filled with close-ups of flattened, whiskered faces; otters rolling and rubbing themselves on sandbanks, like cats marking their territory; and an otter family loping up a grassy, streetlamp-lit slope, mom doubling back to make sure the slowpoke wasn't left behind.

Johnny's cameras also captured bobcats, coyotes, wild turkeys, raccoons, opossums, chipmunks, squirrels, deer, muskrats, wood ducks, and great blue herons. Data like these are increasingly being used by ecologists to study the distribution of species over large areas. The attractiveness of camera-trapping, as it is called, lies in the set-it-and-forget-it approach, notwithstanding the need to change out batteries and SD cards every once in a while. Using camera traps, ecologists now have the capability of tracking species that are otherwise difficult to find at more, and more remote, sites than is typically the case. The drawback, from a professional ecologist's point of view, is the sheer amount of footage that must be watched to check if and when the one or more species of interest has made an appearance. However, if you're not a professional ecologist and you want to experience the thrill of seeing a bobcat slink into the frame or of a bear cub playing with its mom, then you can help out with this task (see the sidebar *People-powered research: a Zooniverse of possibilities*). Johnny's otter project is one of the most popular research projects I've participated in, and I think it's because it affords a glimpse into the hidden lives of the creatures with which we share our yards, streets, parks, and greenways.

One of the sites where Johnny set up his cameras was where I would not have expected otters to be: in a stream as close as an aboveground stream can get to Uptown Charlotte. The section of Little Sugar Creek where Johnny monitored otters flows just outside the elevated highway

People-powered research: a Zooniverse of possibilities

I first heard about Zooniverse (www.zooniverse.org) as the platform that hosts the Snapshot Wisconsin project, a camera-trapping effort by the Wisconsin Department of Natural Resources to monitor wildlife populations across the state. On Zooniverse, Snapshot Wisconsin volunteers identify the elk, pileated woodpeckers, bears, and other animals that trigger the more than three thousand camera traps in the state. It's a fascinating way to spend a few minutes, or more, on your laptop or mobile phone. There are also discussion boards for identification help, to talk about the research or educational outreach part of the project, and to post animal selfies, photos of unusual species interactions, and captures of impromptu yoga poses—my favorite being a sandhill crane captured in a Karate Kid crane kick pose. Snapshot Wisconsin volunteers have helped to identify animals over eight million times and these data are being used to improve the efficiency of annual winter wolf tracking and territory mapping, to help predict where and when human-bear conflicts will occur, and to map the statewide occurrence of coyotes, opossums, and other species that are not currently being monitored by any other method.

Zooniverse also hosts the Wildlife of Los Angeles project, The Indy Wildlife Watch, which is collecting data on where and when animals occur in Indianapolis, and the SquirrelMapper project intent on understanding why black and gray morphs of the eastern gray squirrel occur in different neighborhoods. Or, if you need a break from the urban wild for a moment, indulge in counting penguins, documenting the behaviors of burrowing owl families in California, classifying clouds for NASA, or listening to manatee calls. I have to say there is nothing better than checking your phone for the latest coyote photo from Indianapolis!

that rings the city center and is flanked by a busy street and shopping mall on one side and apartment buildings and offices on the other. Less than twenty years ago, the section, like its tributaries and other watercourses close to and in Uptown Charlotte, flowed underground—in Little Sugar Creek's case, below the parking lot of what was once the first indoor mall in the Southeast.[1] In 2002, the stream was daylighted, or uncovered, and the restoration of its channel and banks began. Now, instead of a ditch filled with brown water, the urban section of Little Sugar is a vibrant stream flowing over shallow riffles into deep pools and meandering across its newly revived floodplain replete with wetlands and banks ripe with swamp hibiscus and alder. A public paved path was incorporated into the restoration design so that residents and visitors can now walk, run, or cycle along the stream and take in the sound of the bubbling water or the sight of frolicking otters as they pass—county maintenance staff who regularly remove invasive plants from the floodplain have even seen the otters playing in a decorative waterfall that links a tributary to the stream.

The creation of the Little Sugar Creek greenway in Charlotte is emblematic of urban stream restoration projects in cities across the United States. As of the last comprehensive count in 2004, more than thirty-seven thousand river or stream restoration projects had occurred in twenty-four states, most of them implemented along less than a mile of watercourse length.[2] In cities, many of these projects are initiated to improve the health of neglected streams that have been built over and/or suffer from the Urban Stream Syndrome, an illness with symptoms that include steep, eroded banks, polluted water, and little aquatic and terrestrial life. Public paths are often an integral part of these projects and act to link the site to surrounding neighborhoods, increasing access to greenspace and potentially spurring economic activity, as well. For example, the restoration of a 1.2-mile segment of the Tujunga Wash near North Hollywood in Los Angeles transformed the barren and inaccessible banks of the wash into a public greenway that meanders among native western sycamores and other plantings and can divert and clean up to 325,000 gallons of stormwater runoff a day.[3] In Cincinnati, the recently completed Lick Run Greenway replaced the underground sewer of the same name with paths, a playground, a basketball court, and the capacity to divert millions of gallons of stormwater a year, thereby reducing the sewage overflows that plague the Ohio River.[4] And in Baltimore, the Stony Run Trail now edges a meandering rocky brook that once cut deep into the earth and funneled polluted stormwater into Baltimore Harbor and Chesapeake Bay.

The urban section of Little Sugar Creek in Charlotte, North Carolina, which was restored in 2002 and where North American river otters have recently been observed.

This chapter will explore greenways like these that are becoming more and more common in American cities. Along such a greenway, nature is intentionally designed and engineered to restore stream and floodplain functions, such as providing habitat, cleaning water, and reducing flooding. However, despite the popularity of the practice, it's currently a point of contention whether restoration achieves the goals it has set for itself, notwithstanding the presence of otters in a restored urban stream in Charlotte. I'll describe how stream restoration is intended to cure the Urban Stream Syndrome and then describe the current evidence of its effectiveness in relation to water quality, biodiversity, and frequently sky-high project costs. A symptom of the Urban Stream Syndrome that isn't cured by restoration is the input of large amounts of polluted stormwater from yards and other developed spaces, so I'll also list a few practices that you can do at home to help out your restored greenway. Refurbished nature in greenways does have one unequivocal benefit, however, in the form of green exercise. Like spending time in nature in your park, walking, running, or cycling along your greenway has cognitive and psychological benefits, as well as physical benefits that go beyond those resulting from the exercise alone. I'll show you that outdoor exercise seems less strenuous and more enjoyable and satisfying, making you more likely to get back out there and do it again. Being relatively new additions to American urban and suburban landscapes, streamside greenways are still a work in progress. I like to think of them as our hope of what cities will look like in the future when the balance between people and nature is a little more even than it is today.

The success of urban stream restoration in your greenway depends on how you manage stormwater in your yard

For the earth and environmental science field methods course that I teach in my department, my students and I used to make our way down to the creek that bisects campus to take the measurements, like water velocity and channel depth, that are needed to calculate discharge, or the volume of water flowing through the creek per second that day. To get to the creek, we'd have to negotiate the floodplain forest along its banks, stepping carefully to avoid fallen trees and the leaf litter–filled holes they left behind and pushing the branches of shrubs and saplings out of our way. Walking in a forest is a new and intimidating experience for many of the students who take this second-year course, but it pales in comparison to the prospect of climbing down into the creek bed ten feet below. Inevitably, the most adventurous or experienced of the students would take up the challenge and scramble down the scoured red clay banks to stand in the shallow ribbon of water at the bottom, the roots of the overhanging trees coming through the clay assisting their descent.

I haven't used that creek for the field hydrology part of the course in a few years because the creek channel as it was no longer exists. The forest edging the stream on both sides is also gone, removed to make room for excavators, loaders, and dump trucks. In a now-wide-open area, this heavy machinery reshaped the floodplain, filling in the deep creek bed where we once worked and redirecting the flow of water into a new, meandering channel. The new channel is much shallower and contains rocks and logs placed in such a way as to create riffles of bubbling water perfect for aquatic insects and deeper pools for fish. Its stabilized and vegetated banks gently rise to ground level. Although trees will be planted in the floodplain, I still miss the old sycamore that hosted a nesting pair of white-breasted nuthatches, the first nuthatches most of my students had ever seen.

What I have just described is the restoration of my campus creek, which undeniably had been suffering from the Urban Stream Syndrome. If you've never taken my or a similar field methods course or aren't a professional hydrologist, you'd probably think the original creek on campus, flowing as it did within a heavily forested valley, looked pretty good as is. But creeks are not supposed to flow 10 plus feet below ground level in between steep, eroded banks. In non-mountainous areas, streams and rivers naturally meander, or loop back and forth, within their floodplains. Think of the squiggly line of the Mississippi River as the ultimate example. Along a meandering stream, erosion is concentrated at the outer edge of each bend where water flows faster. This creates a slightly steeper bank and deep pools of water. On the inside of bends, water moves more slowly and eroded sediment is deposited, forming a little beach called a point bar. And in between bends where the stream straightens out a bit, there are riffles, the shallow rocky parts of streams. Over time, the loop of a meander will get pinched off from the main channel as the cutbank erodes away and sediment piles up in the point bar. When this happens, the stream begins to meander in the other direction so that if you watched the stream over decades, it would look like a snake moving across sand. Importantly, a meandering stream is never too far from the surface of its floodplain, so-called because the flow of water in the channel regularly overwhelms its shallow banks and spreads into the surrounding landscape.

Streams suffering from the Urban Stream Syndrome are a wholly different type of hydrological beast.[5] First, many streams in cities and suburbs have been channelized, or straightened and deepened. This can occur some decades in the past before any houses have been built and when the land is being farmed. Farmers channelize streams to direct water where they need it, to reduce the natural tendency of a meandering stream to flood, and to claim as much of the floodplain for planting as possible. Streams may also be channelized during the development process, again to reduce the chance of flooding. Second, streams in urban watersheds, the upland catchment areas that feed overland runoff and groundwater to streams, receive very large inputs of runoff in short periods of time. Urban watersheds are typified by their impervious surfaces, the concrete and asphalt that are used to make our streets and roads, driveways, parking lots, and buildings. Where rainwater once fell on soil and pooled and evaporated or slowly infiltrated into the ground to make its way eventually to a stream now lies an impermeable surface designed to efficiently funnel rainwater into gutters, storm drains, and pipes that lead directly to waterways—the fish symbols stamped on some storm drain covers alerting residents to this fact.

In addition to sealing soil, the impervious surfaces in urban watersheds replace vegetation. Trees, shrubs, and other plants reduce the amount of water flowing to streams in two ways. First, plant leaves, branches, twigs, stems, and trunks are a three-dimensional surface from which rain droplets evaporate into the atmosphere instead of making their way to a stream. Second, plants themselves absorb rainwater from the soil for use in photosynthesis, again circumventing the transport

On this storm drain are stamped a fish symbol and the words "flows to river" to indicate that the drain is connected directly to the local waterway.

of rainwater to waterways. Over and above the cover of impervious surfaces and even if vegetation is present, a last reason why urban watersheds direct so much runoff so quickly to their streams is that developed terrain is designed to slope smoothly toward gutters and drains or directly toward streams. This leaves very little uneven ground where rainwater can pool and evaporate and accelerates the flow of water downslope.

As a result of the changes to their channels and watersheds, urban streams fill up very quickly during storms with fast-moving, polluted water. Since people generally do not go out for a stroll or a run along a greenway when it rains, few of us have actually seen the torrent that is an urban stream in inclement weather. What we do see is the aftermath: plastic bags and bottles caught in the branches of a streamside tree—there's no way the water got that high, is there?—or the appearance of a large tree limb in the channel or floodplain—the water can't have carried that here, right? The answer to these questions is unfortunately yes. The characteristically high discharge of urban streams following

This "litter gitter" traps plastic bottles, coffee cups, and other debris carried by runoff into urban streams.

storms—recall that discharge is the volume of water per second flowing in a stream at a given moment—means that urban streams often flood—ironically, given the original intent of the straightened channel. It also means that urban stream channels are regularly subject to the powerful erosive force of all of that water, which over time downcuts the channel deeper and deeper, eventually leading to the 10-foot high crumbling banks of my campus creek.

Enter urban stream restoration. The aim of urban stream restoration is to restore the ecological structure and function of non-urban streams, including their natural variability in structure and function across space and time.[6] As I described above, streams in natural settings meander across their floodplains, eroding a bit of bank here and depositing the eroded sediment there—the balance of these two processes creating a stable system that has evolved to handle the water coming from the watershed in which the stream finds itself. Streams in natural settings are also home to a variety of plants and animals that live largely as those on land do: growing, eating each other, dying, decomposing, and generally

Large amounts of fast-moving runoff erode urban streams so that their beds often lie well below the surrounding landscape.

cycling nutrients like nitrogen and carbon among the different living and non-living components of the system, just like in the forest ecosystem I described in chapter 2. The goals of urban stream restoration projects include some or all these characteristics, depending on the specific stream and its context. In some cases, boulders and root wads, the root ball of a large tree with the underside facing the stream, are used to reinforce a rapidly eroding segment of the bank. In others, habitat rehabilitation is the overarching purpose and native plants are added to the banks and the land immediately adjacent to the stream. And in many cases, a stream reach is created anew, like in the case of my campus creek, often using the principles and methods of Natural Channel Design.

Natural Channel Design (NCD) is an approach to restoration that relies on stream classification based on watershed and channel morphologies, comparison to a reference reach as a model for restoration, and the use of in-stream structures to maintain the new, restored condition.[7] NCD practitioners first classify the impaired stream as one of ninety-four natural types using watershed drainage area, valley form, and on-site measurements of the stream's longitudinal profile, the pattern of meanders (if any), channel depth, width, and cross-sectional area, bankfull elevation (the point in the channel above which flooding occurs), and discharge. They then seek out a reference reach of the same type, but with stable, gently sloping, and vegetated banks—in other words, a healthy version of the impaired stream. The form of the reference reach's channel and meanders are measured and used as a template for the design of the restored stream. The most favored design approach is to move the stream channel to a new location so that it can most closely resemble the reference reach. But channels can also be re-designed in situ by widening them to create a new floodplain at a lower elevation or by simply stabilizing the existing banks. Once construction of the channel is complete, in-stream structures are added to support the banks, to direct the flow of water away from the banks to minimize erosion, and to create aquatic habitats. For example, cross vanes, U-shaped structures made of rocks that straddle the stream, force water to flow in the center of the channel and create upstream scour pools for fish. Finally, the banks and floodplain of the stream are revegetated with native plants, and the job of the NCD

A stream being restored using the Natural Channel Design approach.

practitioner becomes one of monitoring discharge, erosion, and biodiversity to determine the effectiveness of the project.

If you've ever seen a large-scale NCD stream restoration project in progress, with bulldozers pushing around mountains of earth, roots, and branches and excavators carving out a new stream channel, you may very well have asked yourself whether restoration is worth all the effort. Put another way, does urban stream restoration accomplish its goal of restoring the ecological structure and function of a degraded stream to levels characteristic of a non-urban stream? Or, simply, does urban stream restoration work?

As a first attempt at answering this question, examples of the failure of urban stream restoration are not hard to find. A pair of studies led by Christy Violin and Elizabeth Sudduth, doctoral candidates at the time at the University of North Carolina at Chapel Hill and Duke University, respectively, illustrate the inadequacy of urban stream restoration at replicating the habitat structure and biodiversity of non-urban reference sites and questions the frequently stated restoration goal of improving

A cross vane in a restored stream.

water quality.[8] The studies compared three types of sites in the Raleigh-Durham area: urban stream reaches restored using the NCD approach, unrestored urban reaches in parks or nature preserves that resembled the pre-restoration condition of the restored streams, and reference reaches in forested watersheds. Violin discovered that the urban reaches, whether restored or not, were deeper and had lower in-stream habitat diversity than the forested sites. The urban reaches also had very similar aquatic macroinvertebrate communities—a group of animals that are large enough to see with the naked eye and include insects and other organisms without a backbone, from snails to dragonfly larvae—that differed substantially from the communities in forested watersheds, including in having fewer animals sensitive to pollution and habitat disturbance. Sudduth, for her part, reported that none of the sites, forested or urban, restored or not, differed in measurements of stream primary productivity, ecosystem respiration, or the uptake of nitrogen, a common urban pollutant, with one exception: Restored reaches had a higher nitrogen uptake in the summer months. However, this effect was likely due to the removal of the canopy along restored reaches, thereby increasing the amount of light reaching the streams and water temperature, rather than the channel restorations themselves.

The results of two reviews and one meta-analysis of the effects of urban stream restoration corroborate these anecdotal findings.[9] Because of the scarcity of published studies on the outcomes of urban stream restoration, these syntheses include projects of very different scopes, from small-scale bank stabilization projects to large-scale channel and floodplain re-designs to stream daylighting. In general, restored urban streams have similar aquatic macroinvertebrate and fish diversity as upstream, unrestored reaches or prior to restoration. Only three of twelve reviewed studies reported more than a slight increase in macroinvertebrate diversity following restoration: in a daylighted stream, as a result of floodplain replanting, and in comparison to pre-restoration, but not reference sites. Of the four reviewed studies on fish diversity, two reported no or a modest increase following restoration and two reported that some structures were attracting fish, in one case of a similar species composition as a reference site. In addition, a meta-analysis of the effects of urban channel and floodplain restoration on aquatic macroinvertebrate diversity reported no significant change in abundance and species richness in comparison to unrestored urban reaches or reference sites. Finally, of ten studies of the effects of urban stream restoration on indicators of water quality, half reported no difference between restored sites and unrestored reaches or prior to restoration, three reported equivocal results of improvement in some metrics but not others, and two reported overall positive effects of restoration in comparison to unrestored reaches or reference sites, namely increased nitrogen removal from the water column by microbial communities that colonized in-stream structures like riffles and cross vanes.

The major reason that urban stream restoration apparently does not work is that it seeks to alleviate the symptoms of the Urban Stream Syndrome but ignores the cause. Locally restoring stream channels and floodplains—recall that most stream restoration projects are less than a mile long—does not change the fact that restored reaches are part of a stream network draining a developed watershed and still receive large amounts of fast-moving, polluted stormwater. Case in point, the in-stream restoration structures in one of the projects I came across in the reviews I described above were damaged three times by unexpectedly high flow.[10] In fact, urban restoration projects may be hamstrung from the get-go because reference sites upon which design parameters are based are often stream reaches in non-urban watersheds and therefore don't account for the hydrological stresses facing urban streams.[11] As a result, in-stream structures and habitats created during restoration are not likely to persist over time and will continue to be subjected to pollution carried from upstream.

Given all of this, what can we do to help our suffering urban streams? If you're a restoration practitioner, a good place to start may be to focus on out-of-channel interventions. In recognition of the apparent ineffectiveness of traditional in-channel restoration, Nathan Smucker and Naomi Detenbeck of the United States Environmental Protection Agency set out to assess whether out-of-channel restoration practices along urban streams and in their watersheds performed any differently.[12] They summarized the results of projects that included floodplain replanting, the creation of wetlands or stormwater ponds adjacent to streams or else-where in watersheds, upgraded wastewater infrastructure, disconnected stormwater outfalls, out-of-stream erosion controls, and reconnected floodplains. They found that the ecological structure and function, such as the diversity of macroinvertebrates and other aquatic species, and hab-itat structure, such as bank stability and sediment size, in urban streams restored using these out-of-channel methods were significantly improved compared to non-restored urban streams, but that water quality, such as the concentration of heavy metals in sediment and the total amount of nitrogen and phosphorus in water, was not. Of thirty-three restored streams in their analysis, none resembled the conditions in their respec-tive reference sites. In sum, out-of-channel restoration practices do one better than in-stream methods by substantially improving ecological conditions in urban streams, but they don't replicate non-urban stream systems.

A second approach that has promise is the widespread use of green stormwater infrastructure in developed watersheds. Green stormwater infrastructure includes things like disconnected downspouts, permeable pavement, rain gardens, and vegetated swales that treat rainfall where it lands rather than funneling it into the drains and pipes of conventional or gray infrastructure. Green stormwater infrastructure thus circumvents the transport of stormwater to urban streams and can make a big difference in stream health. For example, in Connecticut, runoff and the flow of pol-lutants to a stream draining a low-impact residential development with green stormwater infrastructure were unchanged from pre-development levels, whereas runoff and pollutant levels were more than 100 times higher than pre-development levels in a stream draining a traditional subdivision.[13] The amounts of nitrogen and phosphorus coming from the low-impact development were even similar to levels typical of a forested watershed. I'll describe green stormwater infrastructure in more detail in the next chapter. For now, if your neighborhood was not designed with green stormwater management in mind, there are some easy changes you can make to your property to minimize runoff impacts to your local stream (see the sidebar *Stormwater management in your backyard*).

Stormwater management in your backyard

If you have a yard where you live, then you can use it to manage the stormwater coming from your roof, driveway, and lawn. The goal here is to slow down the flow of water so that it has a chance to infiltrate into the soil on your property before making it to the storm drain and your local stream. Below, I've listed several doable changes you can make to your house and yard, depending on the amount of time and money at your disposal, based on suggestions by the New Jersey Agricultural Experiment Station at Rutgers University, the United States Environmental Protection Agency, and the Homeowner's Guide to Stormwater by the Little Conestoga Partnership in Pennsylvania, which you can also use to create a comprehensive stormwater management plan for your property (see stormwaterguide.org for the online tool).

Backyard Stormwater Best Practices

- **Disconnect your downspouts** by directing the flow of water onto your lawn, into a garden bed, or into a rain barrel rather than having it flow directly onto your driveway or into a linked sewer or storm drain system. Flexible black tubing should do the trick. Use at least 2 feet if you have a crawl space or 6 feet if you have a basement and be conscious of where the water will end up (hopefully not in your neighbor's yard).

- **Use rain barrels to collect water from your downspouts** that you can then use to water your lawn and garden, flush toilets, wash clothing, or wash your car. Be aware that rain barrels need regular maintenance to prevent mosquitoes breeding.

- **Use permeable pavement for a new project or when you need to repave your driveway.** Permeable pavement includes porous asphalt, pervious concrete, and different types of pavers, all of which allow water to soak into the ground below.

- **Plant a rain garden in a depression in your yard** downslope of runoff coming from your house, garage, or driveway. The soil, mulch, and plants in the garden will slow down and absorb the water, ideally within twenty-four hours of a storm event. Rain gardens should be at least 10 feet from building foundations and shouldn't be located above septic systems or wells. A low-cost alternative is simply to mow wet areas in your yard less frequently or not at all.

Two practices that reduce runoff from your yard: a disconnected down-spout (left) and rain barrels (right).

- **Plant one or more trees on your property.** Trees do a fantastic job of intercepting and absorbing rainwater that would otherwise flow into gutters and drains. See the sidebar *Give a little, get a lot: caring for your street tree* in chapter 4 for tips on caring for newly planted trees.

- **Remove pavement in your yard and replace it with soil and plants.** New Orleans residents who participated in the Front Yard Initiative to replace impervious with pervious surfaces have helped to divert two million gallons of stormwater per year from city pumping systems.[14] Their new gardens are less costly to maintain, although they require more of residents' time, and the original plantings in most are thriving. Seventy percent of participants have reported less flooding in their yards and 15% have noticed fewer mosquitoes.

Nature along your greenway boosts the mental and physical health benefits of exercise

At the beginning of this chapter, I promised that I would discuss the effectiveness of urban stream restoration as it relates to the high cost of projects. It may come as no surprise after having read of the lack of strong evidence for restoration success that the monetary value of water quality benefits from restoration are far below costs. However, restoration may still be justified based on the aesthetic improvement and recreational opportunities it provides. Melissa Kenney at the University of Minnesota and her colleagues assigned a dollar value to these benefits, as well as to the removal of nitrogen and bank stabilization, of a typical 0.25-mile urban stream restoration project in Baltimore, Maryland, a city federally mandated to remove nitrogen and other pollutants from surface waters before they reach Chesapeake Bay and a state with more than twice the number of stream restoration projects as any other state as of the last official count in 2005.[15] Based on the costs of recent projects in Baltimore, Kenney assigned a cost estimate for stream restoration of $500–$1,200 per foot of stream (in 2008 dollars here and in the rest of this paragraph). This compares to $33–$70 per foot for alternative methods, such as detention ponds, of removing the same amount of nitrogen that city officials assume the typical restoration project removes and up to $120 per foot of lining the banks of an unrestored stream with riprap, the large rocks that are sometimes used to stabilize streambanks. In other words, Kenney estimated that the water quality and bank stabilization benefits of urban stream restoration in Baltimore were, at the most, 38 percent of costs. Since restoration projects often also include efforts at beautification and recreational opportunities, Kenney also surveyed Baltimore residents to estimate the amount of tax money they would be willing to pay to restore a stream so that it provided these benefits. The amount for surveyed households as a whole came out to $560–$1,100 per foot. Adding this to the monetary benefits of water quality and bank stabilization brings the benefits of urban stream restoration in Baltimore to 49–150% of project costs and, at least for less costly projects, tips the scale in the favor of restoration.

The recreational benefits of urban stream restoration can be sizeable.

Kenney and her colleagues concluded their study by stating that the aesthetic and recreational benefits of urban stream restoration should be explicitly included as project goals given their oversized benefits to residents. Her study estimated what is called the passive use value of aesthetics and recreation, or the economic value that can be assigned to something that is not in any way associated with its use by people. It's the dollar value you might assign to knowing that tigers exist in Asia, that deep sea anglerfish call the ocean depths home, or that, in the case of Kenney's study, a stream was being restored in a part of your city far from your home and that you never had any intention of visiting. That being said, the aesthetic and recreational benefits calculated by Kenney are likely to be underestimates because they do not account for the actual use of greenways along restored urban streams and, specific to this chapter, the mental and physical health benefits that green exercise, or being physically active in nature, bestows.

Many studies of the effects of green exercise on mental and physical health aren't carried out outdoors but in laboratories where researchers can more accurately control the type, intensity, and duration of exercise. A classic study by Jules Pretty and his colleagues at the University of Exeter in the United Kingdom, the research team who coined the term "green exercise," used this approach.[16] Pretty recruited students and colleagues from his institution and members of the surrounding community to participate in a controlled trial of the effects of viewing urban or rural, pleasant or unpleasant scenes while jogging on a treadmill for twenty minutes at a light intensity. Rural and urban pleasant scenes were those of trees and other vegetation, blue sky, and water, with the major difference being the presence of well-kept buildings. Rural unpleasant scenes were also predominantly natural, but included damaged trees, broken machinery, and abandoned buildings, whereas urban unpleasant scenes were views of buildings in disrepair, graffiti, scaffolding, and trash. The control group were joggers who stared at a blank white screen. Across all groups, jogging on a treadmill lowered mean arterial blood pressure and systolic and diastolic blood pressure and increased feelings of self-esteem. Joggers who viewed pleasant scenes, especially the rural variety, generally had lower measures of blood pressure still, whereas those looking at urban unpleasant scenes had higher mean arterial pressure. Pleasant scenes also boosted joggers' sense of self-esteem, whereas unpleasant scenes depressed it relative to the exercise-only control. These results led Pretty and his colleagues to conclude that exercise in pleasant green environments has physical and mental health benefits over and above exercise alone that should be considered in public health policy.

Since Pretty's study, several reviews of available evidence have confirmed that green exercise confers mental health benefits.[17] When you walk, run, or do other types of recreational activities in parks or gardens, on college campuses, or in wilderness areas compared to more built-up areas or indoors, you are likely to feel more revitalized and restored, have more energy, and experience a greater sense of enjoyment and satisfaction. You will also likely be less tense, angry, anxious, and stressed. For example, an analysis of over two thousand responses to the national Outdoor Recreation and Demand Survey in Finland found a positive effect of physical activity in nature on respondents' emotional well-being, controlling for how active respondents typically were, how stressed they reported feeling in the recent past, and their age, income, and disability status.[18] The more frequently participating Finns engaged in physical activity that broke a sweat for at least twenty minutes in urban parks and forests near their homes or further afield, the calmer, more peaceful, and happier, and the less nervous and downhearted they reported feeling. The frequency of physical activity of the same duration and intensity level outdoors in built environments, like along streets, or indoors at the gym or at home did not have this effect.

It's more difficult to say whether green exercise improves physical health. In general, exercise in nature compared to indoors or in a built environment doesn't seem to be of much benefit to your blood pressure, cortisol concentration, body mass index, or general physical well-being.[19] However, the number of studies explicitly looking at the effects of green exercise on physical activity is still very small, so the conclusion that there is no effect is provisional.

On the other hand, a series of laboratory and field studies of the effects of walking while forest bathing have shown interesting physical health outcomes. Inspired by previous research, Qing Li, the author of *Forest Bathing: How Trees Can Help You Find Health and Happiness* and a leader in the field of forest medicine, led a laboratory study to test whether phytoncides affect human immune function.[20] Phytoncides are aromatic compounds produced by trees that help them fight off insects and disease and that you'd notice as the smell of cedar, pine, or citrus. Sure enough, natural killer cells, a kind of white blood cell that produces tumor- and virus-fighting proteins, amped up their activity when cultured in the presence of phytoncides from Japanese cedar and other local forest species.

No one had taken the next step of investigating whether people exposed to real-world levels of phytoncides in a forest might experience a similar boost in immune function, so Li and his colleagues conducted field experiments to find out. His first test subjects were twelve healthy middle-aged men from Tokyo who had not taken a forest bathing trip for at least three months and refrained from alcohol, recreational drugs, and hot spring baths, a common practice in Japan, that may have affected their immune function.[21] The men walked for two hours morning and afternoon over the same distances and at similar intensities in a forest northwest of the city on a three-day, two-night forest bathing trip. When Li tested their blood taken on the first and second days of the trip, he found that the number of natural killer cells and levels of tumor- and virus-fighting proteins increased over time and were substantially higher than before the trip. Inhaling the phytoncides produced by the oaks, beeches, and cedars in the forest appeared to have strengthened the mens' immune systems.

In follow-up field tests, Li and his colleagues corroborated their initial findings by showing that the enhanced immune function from a forest bathing trip does not occur in the same subjects walking for the same duration and at the same intensity in treeless areas of a nearby city.[22] They observed the same effects in women as they had in men and found that effects for both sexes lasted for at least a week post-trip.[23] They confirmed that phytoncides were present in the air at forest sites but undetectable at city sites.[24] They even went so far as to outfit hotel rooms with humidifiers that vaporized cedar oil to more directly test whether inhalation of phytoncides by subjects increased natural killer cell activity, which it did.[25] Walking while forest bathing also decreased blood adrenaline levels and blood pressure, whereas city walks did not, indicating lower levels of stress among subjects and matching the mental health benefits reported by other studies.[26] Other physical health benefits of walking while forest bathing reported by Li's research group include increased blood adiponectin and DHEA-S levels, compounds associated with cardiovascular health, a healthy body weight, and a low risk of diabetes.

Green exercise may also impact physical health indirectly by increasing our desire to exercise again and, if this is acted upon, our activity levels. I've already mentioned that green exercisers experience more enjoyment and satisfaction than exercisers in built or indoor settings, and that green exercisers feel more energetic after their workouts. These differential outcomes could influence green exercisers to exercise more frequently because they perceive their experience as more positive or beneficial. Moreover, evidence shows that green exercisers rate their workouts as less strenuous, another possible impetus for repeat behavior.[27] In fact, several studies have demonstrated that green exercisers report a greater intent to exercise again, and actually do exercise more frequently, than their peers in indoor settings.[28] In Norway, middle-aged men and women who cycled and did strength training in a natural area were more intent on exercising in the future and, in fact, engaged in more weekly exercise two to ten weeks later, than men and women who performed the same exercises in an indoor gym.[29] In addition, participants who exercised in both settings reported having more fun and feeling better when they exercised in nature, feelings that made them more motivated to exercise again. In another study, women in their fifties and sixties who did aerobic and resistance training once a week outdoors increased their overall physical activity levels, whereas a comparable group of women who performed the same exercises indoors did not.[30] And in Zurich, a survey of more than 250 exercisers of similar physical and mental health at indoor fitness centers and in urban forests found that forest exercisers were less eager to leave and were looking forward to exercising again more than indoor exercisers.[31]

As it stands then in relation to the physical health benefits of green exercise, it appears that if you exercise in a forest with phytoncide-producing trees, you will experience enhanced immune activity and increased levels of cardioprotective, anti-diabetic, and anti-obesity compounds in your blood. And if you exercise outdoors in a natural setting, forested or not, you will most likely increase your overall level of physical activity and enjoy the benefits of enhanced physical fitness as a result.

Getting back to the idea of running, walking, or cycling along a streamside greenway, new research has shown that blue exercise, or physical activity near bodies of water, has distinct mental health benefits. Anna Kajosaari and Tytti Pasanen at Aalto University and Tampere University in Finland, respectively, undertook a large survey of Helsinki residents to determine the locations where they were most likely to engage in leisure time physical activity.[32] Kajosaari and Pasanen were specifically interested in identifying what they termed the "environmental settings" of green or blue exercise, the types of natural areas and their size, the travel distances, and modes of transportation, most strongly associated with perceived

"Blue exercise" along greenways relieves stress and improves mood.

restoration among residents. These environmental settings could then be used by Helsinki planners to fine tune the availability and accessibility of green or blue exercise locations for maximum mental health benefit.

Seven hundred and sixty residents provided responses to Kajosaari and Pasanen's online survey by mapping the outdoor locations where they regularly engaged in physical activity and indicating the typical frequency of their visits, the intensity of physical activity they undertook while there, how they got there, and whether they perceived the location as relaxing, stress-relieving, or as a place to enjoy nature. Kajosaari and Pasanen then categorized each mapped location as a particular natural area type and size and calculated its distance from the respondent's home. Of nearly one thousand outdoor locations mapped by respondents, blue spaces, outdoor exercise locations near rivers, lakes, or the seaside, and large forests either near development or further away were rated as the most relaxing and stress-relieving, whereas built environments, maintained urban green spaces like parks and public gardens, and small urban forests were rated as the least. Large and small forests also rated highly as places to enjoy nature. Most respondents walked or biked less than a mile and a quarter from their home to get to a mapped location that they typically visited a couple of times a week and engaged in moderate intensity exercise when they got there. Most also visited locations closer to their homes more often than locations farther away. Along a continuum of exercise location types, Kajosaari and Pasanen's results point to locations near water and large forests, in or outside of developed areas, as providing the most substantial mental health benefits. Their results also suggest that the proximity of locations to where residents live positively influences visiting frequency and the magnitude of green or blue exercise benefits they gain.

What is striking about these results from Finland is the degree to which they corroborate past findings from Jules Pretty's lab in two important respects. Jo Barton, also at the University of Essex in the United Kingdom, and Pretty collated data from ten local studies of the effects of green exercise on mood and self-esteem to test whether mental health benefits differed among types of natural area.[33] Although mood and self-esteem were not statistically different among natural area types, they were most positive in locations near water, just as blue spaces were some of the most relaxing and stress-relieving in Helsinki. What's more, urban natural areas were as similar in their mental health benefits as non-urban natural areas. Just like in Helsinki where forests far from developed areas were reported to provide similar levels of relaxation, stress-relief, and nature enjoyment as forests near development, Barton and Pretty showed that urban natural areas were just as valuable in terms of mood and self-esteem as what most of us would think of as more pristine natural areas in rural surroundings. This means that, even though you might unconsciously deem the path along your local stream as second-rate in comparison to "real" nature outside of your city or suburb, it's not. It and paths through parks and other natural areas where you live have the same power to restore and recharge your mind and spirit when you exercise along them as trails through forests and fields far away.

Using the data from the ten studies, Barton and Pretty also calculated the duration and intensity of green or blue exercise needed to experience the best mood and highest self-esteem. They found that just five minutes of exercise in a natural setting produced the largest mental health benefits. Longer bouts were still beneficial but produced declining returns until the duration of exercise reached an entire day, at which point benefits ticked up again. With respect to exercise intensity, a light intensity was best for self-esteem, whereas light and vigorous exercise improved mood more than moderate exercise. In essence, Barton and Pretty's and Kajosaari and Pasanen's results imply that a short walk along your local stream is all you need to boost the way you feel about yourself and the world.

~ ~

Greenways along restored urban streams demonstrate just how much we are willing to invest in bringing nature and its functions back to cities and suburbs. In one sense, we've gotten it right in creating locations even in the densest parts of cities where residents can come into contact with nature and get some exercise at the same time. The value of the mental and physical health benefits from green exercise along restored streams, in addition to the aesthetic, educational, and potential economic impacts of greenways, outweigh the costs of creating them. For these benefits alone, greenways and their restored streams are worth it. What we need to do now is learn how to treat the Urban Stream Syndrome wholistically at the watershed scale. Out-of-channel restoration practices, such as the creation of streamside wetlands, disconnecting stormwater outflows to streams, and upgrading wastewater infrastructure take us part of the way there—they significantly improve aquatic biodiversity in streams. However, water quality is not improved by these methods, or by in-channel restoration epitomized by natural channel design. Little Sugar Creek near Uptown Charlotte is a case in point. Although otters flock to the site, the reach is still listed on the state's latest impaired watercourses list for high levels of copper and my recent check of local monitoring data online showed that turbidity in the creek still jumps to 100 times the water quality threshold level when it rains.

To address this shortcoming, we need to expand the scope of our care for urban streams to beyond the channel and floodplain and into the watershed, namely your yard and the other properties around you with permeable surfaces that can absorb stormwater. There are simple and effective changes that each of us can make to redirect stormwater away from the drains and pipes that connect to local watercourses and back into the ground where it belongs. Think of the lawns, gardens, and trees in your neighborhood just as you now do of street trees: they are a valuable type of urban infrastructure that is severely underutilized. I'll now turn to your neighborhood, the perfect setting to describe green stormwater infrastructure in more detail. But first, let me tell you about coyotes.

CHAPTER 7

YOUR NEIGHBORHOOD

I saw my first coyote soon after I moved to my neighborhood. It was about 10 p.m., and my family and I were walking home after dinner at a nearby restaurant. The street we were on intersects a powerline right-of-way and I looked into it as we passed, probably half curious about my new surroundings and half apprehensive about what could be lurking in the brushy depths. Lit by parking lot lighting from the next street over, the coyote paused for a second in the center of the right-of-way to return my glance before moving off into the next backyard. It felt like I'd glimpsed something secret, the wild workings of where I lived, thrilling for an urban ecologist but also a little unnerving when I considered that my house was only a block away.

I live in an older neighborhood close to the city center. In the late 1930s, the land was at the edge of the developing city and still being farmed. Soon after, the family who owned the farm decided to subdivide it and thus began my community of single-family homes, low-rise apartment buildings, small shopping centers, a small park, and elementary and middle schools. It's certainly more urban than suburban and getting denser by the day. I was surprised that a coyote was among my neighbors given how developed the area is, and even more surprised a few years later when several deer bounded across my front lawn and down the street. I've also seen a red fox sauntering along the sidewalk across from my house.

These wildlife encounters in my dense urban neighborhood are not unusual. I suspect that you, too, have unexpectedly seen deer, foxes, and perhaps even coyotes or bears where you live, whether it's downtown or in a suburb further away. Coyotes, in particular, are increasingly common sights in cities and suburbs, even in highly developed areas. I'm writing this on the last day of May in 2022 and I just checked the coyote observations logged on iNaturalist since the start of the year across the country (for more on iNaturalist, see the sidebar *How to use iNaturalist* in chapter 2). My search returned just over five thousand results, including sightings of coyotes strolling along sidewalks, in front and back yards, and in parks and other green spaces throughout American cities small and large. The most striking was a coyote standing over a dead white-tailed deer in the middle of North Sacramento Boulevard near West Carroll Avenue in the East Garfield Park neighborhood of Chicago, five miles west of Grant Park along Lake Michigan. On iNaturalist, I saw a coyote crossing the street in Long Beach, California; in a front yard in the Wallingford neighborhood of Seattle; in a yard three miles from the center of Houston; in Music Row in Nashville; in the Sky Lake neighborhood of Orlando; in Central Park in New York City; near Fenway Park in Boston; in downtown Omaha; in the Reynoldstown neighborhood of central Atlanta; and in just about every city and town in between. As a reminder, the five thousand observations I perused were from the first five months of a single year and thus, just a glimpse of where coyotes occur in urban and suburban places across the country.

My point here is that coyotes, and the other animal and plant species that live among us, are part of the character of our neighborhoods. We typically associate neighborhood character with things like housing type, how wide the streets are and whether they have sidewalks, the restaurants, shopping, parks, and schools in the area, and the lifestyles and habits of the people that live there. We don't automatically think of the deer browsing in our gardens, the coyote traversing the power line right-of-way, the wrens nesting in the cable box, the treefrog suction-cupped to a front window, or the native wildflowers growing on the side of the road. But these elements of our neighborhoods are all around us and, as I've shown you so far in this book, shape how we live our lives and how we see and feel about the world, just like our housing, schools, and coffee shops do.

Based on my research in Charlotte and sightings of coyotes across the country on iNaturalist, I'm beginning to suspect that coyotes occur just about everywhere that we live, in every type of neighborhood. In some places, they are numerous and bold, walking down the street in broad daylight. In others, there might just be one or two, or a young male just passing through. Whether we see them once or seemingly all the time, coyotes are a reminder of the wild animals and plants that we share our neighborhoods with. Coyotes grab our attention, but there are so many other species that have been our neighbors all along, most of them unnoticed. During the initial lockdown of the pandemic, my parents, who live on the densely developed island of Montreal in Canada, sent me a picture of wild turkeys exploring their manicured backyard. The turkeys didn't decide all of a sudden to move to my parents' neighborhood for the narrow streets and mature trees. They had been there all along, minding their own business among the houses and in parks, keeping their distance even though their human neighbors were mostly unaware of their existence. Think of wild turkeys next time you walk or drive through your neighborhood. They're there, as are coyotes, otters, beetles, moths, flycatchers, and many other creatures; you just can't see them (unless you look). Some of these neighbors have lived in your neighborhood for a long time, but others, like coyotes and wild turkeys, have just arrived. As the human population grows and our living spaces spread into and replace other habitats, we'll meet more and more of these new neighbors in unexpected ways. The coyote can teach us how to prepare for these encounters.

This chapter explores how the built component of neighborhoods shapes their ecological character and your quality of life. I've chosen to focus on two relationships between you and nature that are relevant at the neighborhood scale. The first is how the housing density of your neighborhood predicts the different types of birds you live amongst and whether you will see a coyote when you step out the door. I'll show you that, if you live in a suburban-density neighborhood, you live amongst the greatest number of birds of any species in your region and almost as many bird species as in undeveloped areas. Similarly, you may also be living with more coyotes than you suspect and more than in rural or urban neighborhoods. I'll provide some pointers on how to help out the chimney swift, a city bird in steep decline, and how to lessen the chance that an encounter with a coyote will be negative.

The second relationship between you and nature relevant to the neighborhood scale that I've included in this chapter is the effect of green stormwater infrastructure on water quality and urban flooding. In chapter 6, I described how green stormwater infrastructure can alleviate the Urban Stream Syndrome and I suggested ways that you could implement green stormwater infrastructure on your property. In this chapter, I'll look at how the use of green stormwater infrastructure measures designed to manage a neighborhood's stormwater, such as stormwater ponds, vegetated swales, and bioretention basins, contribute to fewer pollutants entering local streams and less urban flooding, an increasing problem in neighborhoods nationwide. Since you've already learned about best practices for stormwater management on your property, in this chapter I'll show you how to collect much-needed data about its effectiveness. At this point in the book, I'm beginning to focus on broader spaces that you call home, beyond your yard, your street, your park, or your greenway. It's by thinking at this larger scale that I hope you'll come to a deeper understanding of the direct and not so direct ways that you are connected to other species and natural processes, and how you act together to shape your urban ecosystem.

Your neighborhood's housing density determines which species will be your neighbors

Housing density is an easy way to differentiate among neighborhoods. There are very low-density residential neighborhoods at the edges of cities or farther away, with single-family homes peeking out from dense foliage and streets without sidewalks, or perhaps a subdivision with more open, manicured one-acre lots surrounded by farmland. Medium-density or suburban neighborhoods are the two-car garage, three bedrooms with fenced yard variety where neighbors are just a few feet away on the other side of a dining room window. And then there are higher density neighborhoods of several stripes, such as blocks of streets with low-rise apartment buildings and once single-family homes converted to multiple units, or rows of residential towers interspersed with parking lots and office and other commercial buildings. Of course, neighborhoods vary in all kinds of ways that don't have anything to do with housing density, but the measure is useful to broadly distinguish among the different kinds of areas that make up a city or metropolitan region.

The measure is also useful as an indicator of the degree of urbanization. In 1990, Mark McDonnell and Stewart Pickett, two of the world's foremost urban ecologists and now honorary principal fellow at the University of Melbourne in Australia and distinguished senior scientist at the Cary Institute of Ecosystem Studies in Millbrook, New York, respectively, published an influential article calling on ecologists to take advantage of spatial variation in housing density, among other measures, that is characteristic of cities.[1] McDonnell and Pickett proposed that the common arrangement of cities as high-density cores surrounded by rings of diminishing development was amenable to classical ecological study based on the gradient paradigm. The gradient paradigm states that environmental variation is ordered in space and governs variation in the occurrence and abundance of organisms and their interactions. Picture a mountain slope and adjacent valley. At the valley bottom, you find lush vegetation dominated by broad-leaved trees, shrubs, and vines. As you hike up the mountain, you notice evergreens appear among the broad-leaved trees until they dominate the forest. If you go high enough, the evergreens thin out and soon there aren't any trees at all. The gradient paradigm understands this variation in the type and amount of vegetation as the product, in part, of a spatial gradient of air temperature. McDonnell and Pickett suggested the same approach could be used in cities and their surroundings to better understand how urbanization affects the structure and functioning of ecological systems.

Since the 1990 paper, hundreds of studies have been published using McDonnell and Pickett's urban gradient approach.[2] Ecologists have used a wide variety of study designs to approximate the gradient, but the approach usually boils down to selecting sites that vary in housing, population, or building density and impervious surface cover, or selecting sites with land uses that represent variation in intensity of urbanization. For example, for a classic study on birds that I'll return to later, Robert Blair, now at the University of Minnesota, selected a treed nature preserve, a grassy recreation area, a golf course, a residential area of single-family detached houses, an office park, and downtown Palo Alto to represent a gradient of increasing urbanization in California.[3] In my case, fifteen years later, I counted birds at sites in Ottawa and Gatineau in Canada that varied in housing density, from none (sites were forested) to rural (single-family homes with three-acre lots surrounded by forest), suburban (neighborhoods with homes on third of an acre lots), and urban (dense neighborhoods with single-family homes on less than a tenth of an acre and low-rise apartment buildings).[4] In general, urban gradient sites studied by ecologists can be grouped into natural, rural, suburban, and urban categories that, in the case of the developed categories, roughly match the low-, medium-, and high-density neighborhoods I described earlier. Also, some studies may use industrial or commercial development without housing as urban sites.

Because the majority of urban gradient studies on organisms are on non-aquatic birds, we have a pretty good idea how terrestrial bird communities, the collection of avian species that inhabit an area, change in response to urbanization. The take-home message from my and others' urban gradient research is surprising. As I've said before in this book, we usually think of built areas, suburban and especially urban, as mostly devoid of wildlife and certainly not containing the numbers of individuals and species that natural areas do. Well, for terrestrial birds, this is only partly true. Total bird abundance, the number of bird individuals of any species in an area, increases with increasing urbanization, hitting a peak in suburban neighborhoods.[5] In other words, if you live in a suburban, or even urban, neighborhood, you live amongst the most non-aquatic birds anywhere in your region, including in nature preserves outside your city or town. Both urban neighborhoods and natural areas contain about 90 percent of the birds that suburban neighborhoods do, whereas rural neighborhoods are home to only about 44 percent. When it comes to the number of terrestrial bird species, urbanization does indeed reduce species richness, but more so in the densest neighborhoods than in suburban or rural neighborhoods. Suburban neighborhoods have 72 percent and rural neighborhoods have 70 percent of the species that natural areas do, whereas urban neighborhoods have 33 percent. Again, if you live in a suburban neighborhood, you live amongst not only more birds than other neighborhoods, but nearly three-quarters of the species that inhabit forests, woodlands, and fields in your region. As I described in chapter 3, your yard is just as or more important to birds in your city or suburb as nearby public greenspace and natural areas. These results show that suburban neighborhoods play a similar role at a larger spatial scale—they are home to a sizeable proportion of all the terrestrial bird species in your region and host more birds of any species than anywhere else.

Suburban neighborhoods have a relatively large number of bird species compared to other locations on the urban gradient probably because they include many different habitats. Just like butterflies in parks that contain ornamental gardens and wild nature, birds in suburban neighborhoods find a variety of habitats with differing amounts and types of resources. Compared to natural areas and rural and urban neighborhoods, suburban neighborhoods can include tracts of forest in nature preserves or along greenways, open woodlands in public parks or in school grounds, unmanaged grassy areas in undeveloped lots and along roads, street trees, lawns, a wealth of shrubs and smaller ornamental plants, and buildings, fences, and other structures. Each of these elements, and each type of edge or ecotone between them, represents a different mix of food, nest sites, and threats that different bird species are adapted to, leading to many species inhabiting suburban neighborhoods.

Of these many species, there are some that are particularly well-matched with the habitats we create in our suburbs and that, as a result, reach large population sizes that contribute to the overall larger number of birds in these places. The same is true in urban neighborhoods, where a limited number of species that are well-suited to high-density living are very abundant. Robert Blair, who led the urban gradient study in California that I mentioned above, gave the names "suburban adaptable" and "urban exploiter" to these suburb- and urban-loving species, respectively. Suburban adaptable species were those that were most abundant in the recreation area, golf course, residential area, or office park along the gradient—these sites represented intermediate intensity urbanization. Urban exploiter species were most common in downtown Palo Alto and often did not occur in any other site. Blair named species that were most common in the nature preserve and rarely occurred elsewhere as "urban avoiders."

So, who are these avian neighbors and why did they move to your neighborhood? And why do some birds choose not to move to the city at all? To describe each kind of bird, I've chosen species that epitomize the characteristics, or traits, that predispose it to live, and sometimes thrive, in certain neighborhoods—or not in the case of urban avoiders.[6] Bird species behave the way they do because it has enabled them to survive and thrive in particular environments. Our suburban and urban neighborhoods replicate the conditions of some of those environments and are therefore attractive places to live to the species used to living in those conditions. This is not to say that bird species can't change their behavior in response to new stimuli—they certainly do, as evidenced by urban birds singing at a higher pitch and at different times of day than their rural counterparts. Rather, the broad pattern represented by the urban avoider/suburban adaptable/urban exploiter classification is like an initial filtering of the birds in a region based on the environmental conditions we create in our suburbs and cities. I've also made a point of choosing species that are found across the country so that no matter where you live, you'll recognize at least a few of the avian neighbors that I'm introducing.

Urban avoiders will be the group least familiar to most readers because they have chosen to stay well away from human habitation of any kind. These are the bird species of forests, grasslands, scrublands, and deserts that behave in certain ways that are not amenable to suburban or city living and that are intolerant of disturbance of any kind, such as the noise, artificial light, and pollution that follow humans wherever we go. Urban avoiders are also adapted to native habitat conditions, like forests with large mature trees, that are rare in suburbs and cities. For instance, the cerulean warbler, a small sky-blue bird, prefers to hunt for insects on the upper leaves and twigs of 50-foot white oaks, bitternut hickories, and sugar maples. Its method of foraging, called foliage gleaning, means that it won't find much food in suburbs and cities because of the loss of insect biomass in urban areas, particularly of the kind found on trees. The veery,

The yellow-bellied sapsucker, an urban avoider species, prefers young forests that produce abundant sap.

a cinnamon-colored forest bird that sings a downward-spiraling, slightly metallic song at dusk, like the sound of altar bells rung in a silent church, is also an insectivore. The veery constructs its nest on or near the forest floor, on soft moss or against a fallen log, a habit uniquely unsuitable to urban living where soft moss and fallen logs are hard to find and where domestic cats and tramping humans are never too far away.

In contrast, suburban adaptable birds are like the neighbors who religiously tend their lawn, grill out on the back deck every Saturday evening, and bob around in the pool with their kids on Sundays. They love the suburbs. In the suburbs—and rural neighborhoods where these birds are also common—suburban adaptable birds find just about everything that their heart desires, and in spades. The northern flicker, a polka-dotted woodpecker common at lower housing densities, loves the open woodland quality of rural and suburban neighborhoods where it finds tree cavities to nest in and lots of open grassy areas to dine at. The flicker's cavity-nesting behavior is characteristic of suburban-adaptable birds, many of which, like eastern and western bluebirds, nest in nest boxes as well, or in fences, outbuildings, and even mailboxes and abandoned cars. The northern mockingbird is also attracted to open grassy areas where it forages on any insects it finds, from earthworms to bees to grasshoppers. In the fall and winter, mockingbirds eat berries from ornamental plants instead of insects. The suburbs tend to appeal to birds with the ability to eat different types of food, called omnivory, since they can take advantage of multiple resources that may be plentiful at different times of year. Seedeaters and nectarivores, like the finch, jay, and chickadee denizens of birdfeeders and many hummingbirds, also love the suburbs because their preferred food is so plentiful. The suburban adaptable category also includes species that spend some or all of their time in native habitat in nearby parks and nature preserves and that, unlike urban avoiders, don't mind the altered habitat conditions they find there.

We now come to the urban exploiters, those birds that love to live in dense neighborhoods and city centers. Each year in my Urban Ecology class, I ask students to think of the original habitat of the rock pigeon, the official name of the bird that dominates avian communities in city centers worldwide and the poster child for urban exploiters. As a hint, I ask them to think of a natural habitat that resembles the side of a skyscraper and its window ledges. It never takes long for someone to shout "a cliff face!" in response. In urban neighborhoods and city centers, the rock pigeon finds replicas of the ledges and caves where it nests in the wild, as well as abundant food on the ground where it is used to foraging. The house sparrow, a stocky gray and brown bird with a distinctive black eye mask, is another urban exploiter that nests in cavities and forages on the ground for whatever is available. I've seen house sparrows nest in a horizontal metal pipe supporting traffic lights at a busy intersection and they are a common sight in outdoor eating areas in urban neighborhoods across the country. Other urban exploiters of note are the peregrine falcon that nests on clifflike skyscrapers and regularly enjoys a meal of pigeon in the neighborhood, and the chimney swift, that, unlike the other urban exploiters I've described, is declining dramatically despite its close association with built structures (see the sidebar *Uncapped: why and how to safely welcome chimney swifts into your home*).

The northern mockingbird, a suburban adaptable species.

In addition to being home to many birds of many different species, suburban neighborhoods are where coyotes tend to roam. As recently as 1900, coyotes only occurred in the western two-thirds of the United States where they hunted opportunistically in the plains, open woodlands, scrub, and deserts of that part of the country.[7] Since then, they have moved into cities and suburbs as residential development spread within their original range, and most strikingly, into the eastern third of the conterminous United States and all the way up into Alaska, a range expansion of 40 percent. Reports of coyotes in large cities like Chicago and New York surfaced in the 1990s, with more and more throughout the country ever since.

In my city, Charlotte, North Carolina, the Mecklenburg County Division of Nature Preserves and Natural Resources began to receive reports of coyote sightings from troubled residents in the early 2010s. In response, in 2012, the Division launched a coyote sighting website to gather information from residents about when and where they encountered coyotes. In the calendar year following the launch, residents logged

Uncapped: why and how to safely welcome chimney swifts into your home

I'll start by addressing the elephant in the room. Swifts nesting in your chimney are not a source of disease to you, your family, or your pets. On the contrary, your pets and children will be enthralled by the sweet sounds of baby birds coming from right inside the house! Your kids will even be able to get a look at the nestlings by carefully using a mirror and flashlight, or a smartphone, from the open damper. Once the baby swifts fledge, you'll be treated to their twittering, soaring flight high above you on a warm summer evening and their ingestion of twelve thousand flying termites, mosquitoes, flies, and other pests *each* day.[8] As a bonus, you'll be helping out a species listed as Vulnerable—the next category is Endangered—on the global IUCN Red List of Threatened Species in part because of a 67 percent decline in population size since the 1960s according to the North American Breeding Bird Survey. Chimney swifts moved to the city when Europeans arrived in North America and their built settlements, including chimneys, spread across the land. Before that time, the species nested in large hollow trees. The reduction in chimney swift population sizes in the last seventy years is most likely due to a combination of a loss in flying insect biomass in urban areas, the capping or removal of suitable chimneys for nesting and roosting, and natural habitat loss here and in their wintering grounds in South America.[9]

If you have a chimney with a brick or stone masonry flue in your home, uncap it and close the damper from March to October. A single pair of chimney swifts will build a small, basket-like nest on the wall of the flue as early as April and raise up to ten young over the next four months. In November, put the cap back on and use your fireplace as usual for the winter. Then, in early March, have the chimney inspected and cleaned, the cap removed, and close the damper to welcome a new brood. Consider adding your nesting swift observations to iNaturalist or eBird (see the sidebars *How to use iNaturalist* and *eBird: birding in the twenty-first century* in chapters 2 and 3, respectively) and limiting the use of pesticides in your yard (see the sidebar *Death by a thousand cuts: strategies to minimize the stress you place on biodiversity* in chapter 4) to provide an abundant food source for the birds. Happy swifts will gladly take care of your mosquito problem in exchange for a cozy place to raise a family.

The rock pigeon, the quintessential urban exploiter species.

over 1,200 sightings. Stuart Wine, a master of arts in geography student under my supervision at the time used these encounter data to figure out why coyotes were being seen in some locations and not others.[10] Among the variables Stuart tested in his models, the area of intensively managed clearings, such as lawns, golf courses, parks, and powerline right-of-ways, within a mile and a quarter of sightings had a large positive effect on the likelihood of a resident seeing a coyote. This corroborated what other researchers had found, namely that urban coyotes are most strongly associated with the greenspaces typical of suburban neighborhoods, where medium-density housing sits within a network of interconnected parks, golf courses, cemeteries, and greenways that coyotes call home.

In these greenspaces, coyotes find high-quality habitat where they can avoid humans. Stanley Gehrt at the Ohio State University, whose Urban Coyote Research Project has been studying coyotes in the Chicago Metropolitan Area for twenty years, has extensive evidence of this fact. Motivated by reports of coyotes responding to urbanization positively in some ways—by eating anthropogenic foods like trash and pets—but negatively in others—by avoiding areas with housing and commercial development, Gehrt and Hance Ellington, now at the University of Florida, compared the space use and movements of thirty-five GPS-collared coyotes in natural, suburban, and urban landscapes to find out if context influenced coyote behavior.[11] Natural landscapes were mostly grassland and forest preserves in the outskirts of the Chicago Metropolitan Area; suburban landscapes were areas of low- and medium-density housing interspersed with parks, golf courses, and cemeteries; and urban landscapes, encompassing central Chicago, were dominated by high-density housing and commercial and industrial development, with greenspace found only along railroad tracks, in junkyards and landfills, or in small parks along the lakeshore.

Gehrt and Ellington's findings help to tease apart how coyotes behave in different kinds of neighborhoods. Coyotes in the suburban neighborhoods in their study had smaller home ranges than their peers in natural landscapes, indicating that the suburbs provide coyotes with more food, shelter, and other resources per unit area than forest and grassland preserves. In fact, Gehrt and his colleagues' prior research has reported pup survival to be five times higher in the Chicago Metropolitan Area than in rural landscapes, an outcome likely associated with more and higher-quality resources in suburban neighborhoods.[12] Coyote home ranges in suburban neighborhoods were also more fragmented than those in natural landscapes because coyotes were mostly restricting their activity to the golf courses, parks, and cemeteries in neighborhoods rather than the residential areas. In the urban neighborhoods of central Chicago, coyote home ranges became much larger, larger even than those in natural landscapes, and more fragmented. Although coyotes needed a larger area in urban neighborhoods to find enough resources, they still mostly limited themselves to the available greenspaces. They also spent more time encamped, or staying put in one location, in urban neighborhoods than suburban ones, presumably trying to hide from humans in these more populated areas.

In sum, it appears that coyotes do all they can to avoid encounters with humans in suburban and urban neighborhoods. However, this isn't to say that they never wander into yards. Stuart's analysis of Mecklenburg

County coyote sighting data identified a second important factor underlying the likelihood that residents would encounter a coyote: neighborhood median household income. Residents living in wealthier neighborhoods were more likely to report seeing a coyote where they lived. We hypothesized that this was because wealthier residents tended to have yards with more trees, shrubs, and other plantings that provide coyotes with places to hide or rest and are excellent habitat for rodents and rabbits, major components of a coyote's diet. This positive relationship between vegetative cover and income is referred to as the luxury effect, a term coined by Diane Hope, then at Arizona State University, and her colleagues to describe a positive association between median household income and woody plant diversity in the neighborhoods of Phoenix and surrounding areas.[13] I'll describe the luxury effect in more detail in the next chapter. For now, suffice it to say that wealthier residents have the means to invest in plantings and landscaping that create attractive conditions for coyotes in their yards.

Vegetative cover is just one of several characteristics that might make your yard a more inviting space for coyotes. In Edmonton, a city of a million people in northern Canada, Maureen Murray, now at the Lincoln Park Zoo in Chicago, and Colleen St. Clair at the University of Alberta tracked nineteen coyotes, eight of which had mange, to determine the features that attracted coyotes to yards and whether coyotes were more likely to visit yards during the day or at night.[14] Only two of the coyotes they monitored preferred residential areas more than other land covers in their home ranges; the rest generally avoided yards and housing, especially during the day. When coyotes did venture into backyards, they chose yards that were not fenced, contained accessible trash, birdseed, or compost, or crabapples and other fruit on the ground, and had three times more low vegetative cover. Ripped bags of trash tended to attract repeat visits by coyotes, much more so than open compost piles or accessible bird seed. Of concern, diseased coyotes were four times less likely to avoid residential areas in their home ranges, visited residential areas more during the day, and were nine times more likely to be drawn to backyards with trash, compost, or bird seed than healthy coyotes. Of thirty-eight yards surveyed by Murray and St. Clair that showed evidence

Low vegetative cover in your yard is attractive to coyotes.

of coyotes bedding down under houses or decks, 82 percent were used by diseased coyotes.

If you are a dog or free-roaming cat owner and you know there are coyotes in your neighborhood, you'll have noticed that Murray and St. Clair's study did not include pets as possible coyote food. For many pet owners, the threat of losing their pet to a coyote is a major cause of concern. So, what does the research on suburban and urban coyote diets tell us about their preferences? Based on studies in Seattle, San Diego, Los Angeles, Tucson, Chicago, and Albany, coyotes primarily eat wild mammals and fruit.[15] For example, in the outer suburbs of the Los Angeles metropolitan area, 75 to 94 percent of food items in coyote scats were natural in origin, mostly rodents (39 to 47 percent) and rabbits and

The eastern cottontail is a common food item of urban coyotes.

hares (12 to 13 percent), with some wild fruit (3 to 16 percent), and in the medium- and low-density housing surrounding Seattle, coyotes ate mostly fruit (43 to 57 percent) and wild mammals (25 to 29 percent). In all the studies to date, cats represented no more than 2 percent of food items found in scats, except for areas of medium-density housing in Seattle where they were 13 percent. As for dogs, I didn't find any reports of their remains in scats, only dog food. Therefore, in general, coyotes do not prey on pets. However, findings from Stanley Gehrt's Urban Coyote Research Project in the Chicago Metropolitan Area, led by Seth Newsome, now at the University of New Mexico, show that although suburban coyotes much prefer natural prey such as squirrels, voles, and rabbits, which typically represent more than 70 percent of their diet, they can eat mostly anthropogenic foods (a combination of trash and feral cats, not distinguished in the study) if natural prey are not readily available.[16]

What, then, are the takeaways of urban coyote research pertinent to readers with concerns for their or their pets' safety? First, I encourage you to recognize that coyotes are a natural and important part of urban ecosystems. They occur in every type of neighborhood, where they often occupy the role of apex predator. Consider them as mascots of a complex, diverse, and healthy ecosystem where you live that has much to offer you and your neighbors. Second, remember that coyotes try as hard as they can to avoid humans. They keep to greenspaces in residential areas and avoid housing; they are active at night rather than at dawn and dusk like their non-urban counterparts; if they do occur in high-density neighborhoods with many people, they spend a lot of time hiding to avoid them; and finally, they prefer to eat natural foods like wild mammals and fruit. Third, although coyotes do their best to stay out of our way, we do encounter them from time to time and they do, when they need to in order to survive, venture into yards and occasionally prey on cats. Maureen Murray and Colleen St. Clair's research from Edmonton demonstrates that these behaviors may be particularly acute in diseased coyotes, posing an additional risk to the health of pets and possibly humans. Because coyote encounters do occur, it's important to be prepared (see the sidebar *Be W.I.L.E.E.: Well Informed to Lessen Everyday Encounters*). As long as you take the necessary steps to lessen your chance of a negative encounter with a coyote—and hopefully, have the opportunity for a positive one, like my thrilling experience of spotting a coyote in a powerline right-of-way near my house—you should feel confident of sharing your neighborhood with this emblem of wild America.

Green stormwater infrastructure in your neighborhood improves water quality and lowers the risk of urban flooding

I was on my way home from dropping off my son at daycare and had just exited the interstate into my neighborhood. The remnants of Tropical Storm Eta were in the process of dumping nearly five inches of rain that morning alone. I glanced over to the sports field on my left as I stopped at the first stop sign, a habit of mine to watch the lacrosse players that often

Be W.I.L.E.E.: Well Informed to Lessen Everyday Encounters

An encounter with a coyote in your neighborhood, although possibly frightening, will in all likelihood end well for both parties. Attacks by urban coyotes are exceedingly rare—as the Humane Society points out, being killed by a popped champagne cork is more likely to happen to you than being bitten by a coyote, even where coyotes are very common. Attacks typically happen when coyotes are intentionally fed by people or when a person tries to rescue a pet from attack. In most cases, coming across a coyote will pose no threat, especially if you follow the guidelines below to minimize the risk of a negative encounter. For more information, consult the Humane Society of North America (https://www.humanesociety.org/resources/coyotes-people-encounters) and the Urban Coyote Research Project (https://urbancoyoteresearch.com/coyote-info/how-avoid-conflicts-coyotes).

How to Be W.I.L.E.E.

- **Do not feed coyotes.** Coyotes who become habituated to humans because they have been intentionally fed pose a threat to people. Under no circumstances should you offer food to a coyote.

- **Remove sources of food from your property.** Keep trash secure in sturdy bins with tight-fitting lids and use a contained composter with a lid and never compost meat, poultry, or fish scraps. Avoid feeding pets outdoors—if you must feed outdoors, bring any left-over food and water indoors when your pet is done eating and drinking. Clean up fallen fruit and bird seed from the ground. The latter may attract squirrels and other rodents, which attract coyotes.

- **Keep your cat indoors and your dog on a leash,** including on walks in greenspaces. Unsupervised pets in fenced yards are also at risk. Although fences may deter coyotes in some places, they are not a guarantee. Consider installing a roll bar along the top of your fence to prevent coyotes from getting the purchase they need to hop over.

- **If you do encounter a coyote, stand your ground and haze it.** Never run from a coyote. Stand tall and wave your arms and yell at the coyote to go away. Use noisemakers and throw things towards the coyote. If the coyote runs away and then stops to look back at you, continue your hazing as you walk or run toward it. Your goal is to have the coyote leave the area entirely.

practiced there. It took me a few seconds to register what I was seeing. The sports field seemed to have disappeared, as had the park in which it sat. I had trouble recognizing the area—all the landmarks were gone, and I couldn't get a sense of distances. The area was brown all over. When I realized that the brown color was water, I clued in to the fact that the creek at the back of the park, 600 feet away—that is, one and a half times the length of a football field—had flooded. When I got home, I learned that flash flooding was occurring across the state—so much so that the governor declared a state of emergency. The next day, it was announced that at least eleven people had died as a result, including children.[17]

The flooding of the sports field that I witnessed was an instance of urban flooding, an increasing problem that has only recently garnered national attention. In 2019, the National Academies of Science, Engineering, and Medicine defined urban flooding as "the accumulation of floodwaters that result when the inflow of storm water exceeds the capacity of a drainage system to infiltrate water into the soil or to carry it away."[18] Where I live, and in many parts of the country, stormwater flows directly into the local network of creeks, either overland or by way of gutters and drains embedded in the streets. The streets in my neighborhood, and their drains and gutters, were designed almost eighty years ago. Since that time, two major factors have disrupted the delicate balance between the amount of stormwater produced in the neighborhood and the capacity of the local creek to absorb it. First, my neighborhood has become more developed. A block of apartment buildings with surface parking was added, as was a school with its own parking lots. More recently, buyers have been replacing the original 1,600-square-foot bungalows with homes of 4,000 square feet or more. The increase in impervious surface cover from the increased development means that more runoff is heading to the streets and creeks instead of infiltrating into the soil—that is, more runoff than the streets were engineered to manage and more runoff than the creeks evolved to accommodate. Second, over roughly the same time period, the frequency and severity of rainstorms in my region have increased. In 2016 compared to 1958, the Southeast experienced 49 percent more two-day storms producing enough rainfall to be expected once every five years and the most intense storms dumped 27 percent more precipitation.[19] These increases were middle of the road compared to other regions in the continental United States, which saw anywhere between a 2 percent drop and 92 percent increase in the frequency of two-day, five-year storms, and a 9 to 55 percent increase in rainfall during the heaviest storms. So, while my streets and creeks were getting overwhelmed by more runoff than expected due to more impervious surfaces, they were also being inundated by more rainfall than planned. With nowhere else to go, runoff floods low-lying intersections where I live and inundates the buildings and facilities in creek floodplains.

Urban flooding, including of streams, at intersections and in parking lots, where storm drains have been blocked by debris, in buildings from sewer backups and seepage, and as a result of coastal storm surge and increasingly high tides, occurs across the United States. A majority of seven hundred stormwater and floodplain managers from 350 municipalities in forty-eight states surveyed about urban flooding reported that urban flooding had occurred in their communities (83 percent), that their communities had been affected by moderate or larger floods (51 percent), that some or all of the flooding was located outside of the one-hundred-year floodplain (85 percent), and that less than 10 percent of damages from moderate floods were covered by the National Flood Insurance Program (65 percent).[20] In addition, 46 percent of respondents described urban flooding as occurring in numerous locations or in most locations in their communities. The reason that I'm relying on survey results to describe the spatial extent of urban flooding is that, unlike large riverine or coastal floods that are readily monitored, there is very little data on where and when localized urban flooding occurs (to help rectify this, see the sidebar *Reporting urban flooding to mitigate future risk*). There is also no nationwide estimate of the economic and social impacts of urban flooding, which include loss of life if people are trapped in buildings or attempt to drive through floodwaters in their cars, asthma and other respiratory illnesses from mold and mildew in damaged buildings, loss of residential or commercial property and small businesses, and productivity losses from traffic rerouting, school closures, and utility outages. And, although there is no estimate for urban

Reporting urban flooding to mitigate future risk

As of yet, there is no nationwide effort to collect data on incidences of urban flooding. Instead, cities are taking the initiative to collect data in their jurisdictions so they can alert residents to flood risks, possibly in advance of flooding occurring, and get an idea of the amount and movement of stormwater to better manage it in the future. The navigation app, Waze, known for its community-driven sharing of traffic, accident, and construction locations, now includes a flood reporting option that generates data that cities like Norfolk, Virginia, use to map flood risk.[21] And the City of Miami, where low elevations, sprawling development, and increasingly frequent and severe storms have combined to make flooding a major issue, has partnered with ISeeChange, an app that collects user observations and stories of weather and climate change where they live, to better understand and manage localized flooding. Check online to see if your city is collecting data on urban flooding or use the Waze or ISeeChange apps to report your observations. Once we get a much better idea of where and when urban flooding is occurring, hydrologists, engineers, urban planners, and community advocates will be able to help design cities and suburbs to manage the stormwater of the future.

flooding itself, we do know that flooding in general is concentrated in the poorest communities in the nation—in other words, those who can least afford its consequences.[22]

The increased runoff in my neighborhood, from impervious surfaces and rainfall, also poses a major threat to local and regional water quality. Stormwater from agricultural and urban areas is responsible for 85 percent of water quality impairments nationwide, up from 15 percent in 1970 when pollution from factories and wastewater treatment plants was more of a problem.[23] Runoff pollution is a type of non-point-source pollution because it originates from multiple locations and activities in cities and suburbs. There is no single discharge pipe releasing pollutants into a waterway. Rather, the sources of runoff pollution are so various as to be almost overwhelming. The major sources are atmospheric deposition, vehicular transportation, and metallic building envelopes.[24] Urban atmospheric pollutants, such as benzene and other volatile organic compounds, nitrogen oxides, polycyclic aromatic hydrocarbons (PAHs), and heavy metals such as nickel, copper, lead, and zinc, are deposited on surfaces and washed into drains and gutters when it rains or dissolved in rainwater itself. Vehicle exhaust contributes many of these pollutants to the atmosphere, whereas vehicle wear, vehicle washing, road abrasion by tires, and road maintenance add microplastics, phthalates, nonylphenols (NPs), nonylphenol ethoxylates (NPEOs), road salts, and sand and grit to surfaces washed by stormwater. The corrosion of metallic building envelopes adds more heavy metals to this mix, and roof membranes and building paints add pesticides and polychlorinated biphenyls (PCBs), as well as more phthalates, NPs and NPEOs. Rubber mulch and artificial turf, fertilizer application, construction and industrial activities, littering, pet and wildlife waste—think pigeon feces, sewer misconnections whereby household appliances are incorrectly connected to stormwater systems, and stormwater pipe coatings themselves round out the list of quantifiable sources of the pollutants in runoff, many of which are harmful to human health.

Green stormwater infrastructure can alleviate the problems of urban flooding and the pollution of surface waters in cities and suburbs. In the previous chapter, I described green stormwater infrastructure as a variety of measures, such as rain barrels, rain gardens, permeable pavement, and disconnected downspouts, that manage rainfall where it lands rather than directing it into the gutters and storm drains of conventional or gray infrastructure. More broadly, green infrastructure includes any approach that relies on soil and/or plants or stormwater harvest and reuse to remove pollutants and slow the flow of runoff to surface waters. This encompasses all of the green spaces in your neighborhood where rainfall infiltrates into the ground or is taken up by plants, the measures like disconnected downspouts and rain barrels that you can implement in your yard, and larger designed structures intended to manage the runoff from a neighborhood.

Green stormwater infrastructure includes any approach that relies on soil and/or plants or stormwater harvest and reuse to remove pollutants and slow the flow of runoff to surface waters.

Common examples of the latter include stormwater or retention ponds, infiltration basins, bioretention basins, and vegetated swales, all of which store runoff and filter pollutants to varying degrees. The stormwater pond is the type you are probably most familiar with. Your neighborhood may have one, or you may have seen one next to a shopping mall or office park. Stormwater piped from surrounding development is stored in the pond, and the sediments and pollutants it carries sink to the bottom, are consumed by bacteria, algae, and animals in the water, or are taken up by shoreline vegetation. The pond may have a pre-treatment bay that collects larger-sized sediments as the water initially slows down, and one or more fountains that oxygenate the water to prevent anaerobic conditions and the release of pollutants from accumulated sediment. Unlike stormwater ponds, which store large amounts of standing water, infiltration basins, bioretention basins, and vegetated swales are designed to treat smaller volumes of runoff that drain away in a day or two. Infiltration basins are shallow, grassy depressions that allow stormwater, and the pollutants it carries, to sink into the underlying soil. Bioretention basins are commonly located in medians and other rights-of-way and in parking lot islands. The plant-filled basins filter the pollutants from stormwater as it infiltrates into the soil and an underlying layer of sand or gravel. In some cases, an underdrain carries filtered stormwater downstream. Rain gardens are a type of bioretention basin lacking the sand or gravel layer. Vegetated swales are wide, shallow ditches that direct runoff from the surrounding landscape downstream and can be grass-covered (grassy swales) or plant-filled (bioswales). Vegetated swales slow the flow of stormwater so it has a chance to infiltrate the soil or be taken up by plants. If you've seen a grassy ditch in your neighborhood, it's likely to have been a designed vegetated swale.

Each of these types of structures has been tested using models and at field sites to determine the degree to which it reduces the flow of stormwater to downstream systems and the amount and type of pollutants that it removes from stormwater. It's much less common for the cumulative impacts of multiple green stormwater infrastructure measures implemented across neighborhoods and their watersheds to be investigated, especially using field observations of water quantity and quality in streams. Michael Pennino, now at the United States Environmental Protection Agency, and his colleagues took up this challenge using data from Montgomery County, Maryland, adjacent to Washington, D.C., and Baltimore County surrounding Baltimore City.[25] Approximately 8 percent of Baltimore County and 12 percent of Montgomery County are drained by green stormwater infrastructure, some of it in place for at least a decade. Pennino focused his analyses on small urban watersheds averaging 3.5 square miles in area and with more than 10 percent impervious surface cover where stream flow and/or water quality data was available and stormwater ponds, bioretention basins, infiltration basins, swales, and similar measures were in place. Watersheds of this size probably encompass at most a handful of neighborhoods depending on the extent of development and represent a large swath of the urban gradient in the region.

Pennino and his colleagues found that green stormwater infrastructure significantly reduced the impacts of runoff on the region's streams.

Three types of green stormwater infrastructure you might find in your neighborhood: a stormwater pond, an infiltration basin that overflows into a bioretention basin in the background, and a grassy swale.

Streams draining watersheds with more than 5 percent of their area managed by green stormwater infrastructure experienced a 44 percent reduction in peak flow from runoff, 26 percent less-frequent peaks, 27 percent longer-lasting flows from runoff, and 26 percent less-variable amounts of runoff than streams draining watersheds with no green stormwater infrastructure. These large reductions in how much and how often runoff reaches streams and the severity of runoff events—less severe events are when runoff flows in a stream over a longer period of time and runoff amounts are less variable, read less extreme—have the potential to lead to less urban flooding. Watersheds with more green stormwater infrastructure also exported 44 percent less nitrate and 48 percent less total nitrogen to streams, thereby helping to alleviate the polluting impacts of runoff on local and regional aquatic systems.

As I described earlier, green stormwater infrastructure includes a variety of approaches to managing rainfall where it lands, including green spaces where rainfall infiltrates into the soil or is intercepted or absorbed by trees and other plants. A recent nationwide study focused on this type of green stormwater infrastructure and its effects on stream hydrology. Gary Conley of 2ndNature, a stormwater modeling and management firm, and his colleagues used satellite imagery and stream gage data from 1985 to 2019 for 372 urban watersheds spread across the climate regions of the country to determine if the amount of vegetated space in watersheds influenced downstream hydrology.[26] In line with Pennino's results and controlling for watershed size and the differing climates and urban extents in the dataset, Conley found that a 10 percent increase in watershed greenness was associated with an 8 percent reduction in high flow, a 2 percent reduction in high flow frequency, and an 8 percent reduction in flow variability in streams. Thus, green spaces help to manage stormwater in cities and suburbs and lessen the risk of urban flooding.

Green stormwater infrastructure isn't without its drawbacks, however. Just like for gray infrastructure, the performance of green stormwater infrastructure depends on proper design and construction, placement, and maintenance, without which it may produce unintended consequences.[27] For example, stormwater ponds may become attractive breeding habitat for mosquitoes and Canada geese and hotspots of unsightly algal growth and unpleasant odors. Measures that rely on infiltration of the soil, such as infiltration or bioretention basins, may also become mosquito breeding habitat if they do not drain quickly enough and could be sources of groundwater contamination if not sited properly. Green stormwater infrastructure itself could also be a source of pollutants to stormwater. Underlying sediment may wash out from permeable pavement, green roofs can be sources of phosphorus to runoff, soils and other materials used in construction may leach heavy metals, phthalates, and bisphenol-A (BPA), and the pollutants accumulated in sediments in stormwater ponds, bioretention basins, and other measures may be released into the water under certain conditions.

To better understand if, when, and where these malfunctions and unintended consequences occur, we need to collect much more data on the real-world performance of green stormwater infrastructure measures, large and small. Green stormwater infrastructure measures that rely on soil and/or plants to function are living systems that change and evolve over time and function differently in differing contexts, be those neighborhoods of varying housing densities or locations near or far from sources of runoff, such as roofs or roads. As the climate continues to change, in possibly unexpected ways, and as development in the United States continues apace, we need much more data on how green stormwater infrastructure responds to these stressors in different cities and suburbs over the medium and long term. And although we know that green stormwater infrastructure is effective at the watershed scale, we do not know how many measures, of what types, and where to place them to see positive downstream effects. Infiltration measures appear to be more effective at reducing peak flow in streams than approaches like stormwater ponds and wetlands that store runoff, so should every road be lined with a filtration strip and every roundabout or cul-de-sac encircle a rain garden?[28] And again, in what contexts will different watershed-level designs be most appropriate? Infiltration measures typically treat stormwater from smaller areas, so their increasing use will exacerbate the need for monitoring data by multiplying the number of sites needed to manage a neighborhood's runoff. Green stormwater infrastructure has enormous potential to transform how cities and suburbs manage stormwater,

EnviroDIY: every bit of data makes a difference

EnviroDIY (www.envirodiy.org) is one of several initiatives and tools developed by the Stroud Water Research Center (www.stroudcenter. org), an independent, nonprofit organization with a mission to advance knowledge and stewardship of freshwater ecosystems through research, education, and restoration. The purpose of EnviroDIY is to foster the development and widespread use of low-cost, easy-to-use, do-it-yourself, open-source hardware and software for real-time monitoring of the environment. If you're technologically or mechanically handy and avid to expand the monitoring of freshwater systems to better understand and mitigate our impacts on them, then the EnviroDIY community of scientists, educators, and citizens is for you.

EnviroDIY members join forums where they share their ideas and experience developing, testing, and using homegrown data loggers, sensors, communications technology, software, and training for environmental monitoring. For less experienced do-it-yourselfers, the EnviroDIY team has created a manual for building, installing, and maintaining a water quality monitoring station. The station relies on the EnviroDIY-developed Mayfly data logger that relays measurements from water conductivity, temperature, depth, and turbidity sensors via the internet to a laptop. You can deploy an EnviroDIY monitoring station in your local stream to record the impacts of runoff from storms on water quantity and quality, and then share your real-time observations with other members, including universities, municipal agencies, and freshwater conservation organizations on the Monitor My Watershed portal (www.monitormywatershed.org). These local stream data are extremely valuable supplements to the United States Geological Survey's (USGS) nationwide network of monitoring stations and can help scientists understand where, when and why local flooding occurs. Initial comparisons of EnviroDIY and USGS station measurements indicate that they collect comparable data.[29] You can also use the EnviroDIY monitoring station, or a custom set-up using the Mayfly data logger and various sensors, such as soil moisture and water velocity sensors, to collect and share data on the performance of your local green stormwater infrastructure measures. Other tools developed by the Stroud Water Research Center and part of the WikiWatershed toolkit (www.wikiwatershed.org) are the Leaf Pack Network and a water quality mobile app that instruct members on how to assess the quality of their local stream using observations of aquatic insects and tree leaves. The Leaf Pack Network is a great tool for educators and their students to explore the ecology of freshwater ecosystems.

but to really harness this potential, we need to implement a lot more of it and check on how it's working.

I've already suggested ways that you can implement green stormwater management practices in your yard in chapter 6. You may also have a stormwater pond, bioretention basins, and/or grassy swales in your neighborhood or where you work. In either case, you can share valuable data about the functioning of your local green stormwater infrastructure measures with other enthusiasts, scientists, and engineers (see the sidebar *EnviroDIY: every bit of data makes a difference*). If your neighborhood is drained by an accessible stream, you can also collect and share data on streamflow and water quality to help assess the effectiveness of your neighborhood's stormwater management approach, be it green, gray, or some combination of the two. These monitoring efforts will be critical to designing green stormwater infrastructure networks that help our neighborhoods adapt to future development and climate patterns so that urban flooding and freshwater pollution from runoff begin to seem like a thing of the past.

＊

In this chapter, I've introduced you to aspects of your neighborhood that help define its character. At a basic level, I've described neighborhoods in relation to their housing density: rural, suburban, or urban. These neighborhood types differ in the number of dwellings they contain and in their number and type of vegetation, which influence the wild animals and natural processes that occur in each. A suburban neighborhood where manicured yards with low-lying shrubs and birdfeeders wrap around a golf course is attractive habitat for coyotes and for many birds of many species, and pollutes local watercourses when runoff picks up pesticides and fertilizers applied to lawns. A denser urban neighborhood is also home to many birds, although of fewer species, that nest in or on buildings and rely on our discarded food and other trash. Rain and runoff that wash over urban neighborhoods pick up pollutants from vehicle exhaust, buildings, and road surfaces that add to freshwater pollution.

Just as the houses and vegetation in neighborhoods shape their character, so do the wild animals and natural processes influenced by them.

We are happier in neighborhoods with more species, but also apprehensive of coyotes lurking in parks and powerline rights-of-way. The streets and buildings in our neighborhoods may flood regularly and the water quality of the local creek, and even the drinking water reservoir where we live, may be poor. We can learn to adapt to the less desirable aspects of our neighborhood's character by discouraging coyotes from visiting our yards and using nature to slow and filter stormwater. As the climate continues to change, we will need to continue to adapt to the changing character of our neighborhoods. We should pay attention to the changes in natural processes where we live and in the species we live amongst, just as we would to the prospect of a new grocery store or an increasingly potholed road. By recognizing that nature is an essential part of neighborhood character and taking steps to enhance its benefits and minimize its drawbacks, we can transform our neighborhoods into the flourishing ecosystems they have the potential to be.

CHAPTER 8

YOUR CITY

In the 1930s, the Home Owners' Loan Corporation (HOLC) color-coded the neighborhoods of 239 cities in America.[1] The corporation was established as an emergency agency by the federal government in the wake of the Great Depression to prevent foreclosures by refinancing mortgages in default. Local real estate appraisers, developers, and lenders assigned grades to neighborhoods to represent the likelihood of residents repaying mortgage loans: A or "Best," B or "Still Desirable," C or "Definitely Declining," and D, or "Hazardous." The bases of the grading system are found in the notes on each neighborhood that accompany the maps, in which agents described the terrain, types of buildings, sales and rental histories, and types of inhabitants. It was this last piece of information that made its way into the descriptions of the favorable and detrimental influences on each neighborhood and ultimately determined its grade. "Hazardous" neighborhoods were those with large Black or immigrant populations and were colored red on maps. "Best" neighborhoods were wealthy and non-Latinx White. The differential access to low-interest mortgages between Whites and Blacks created by so-called redlining, or the designation of Black neighborhoods as "Hazardous" in HOLC maps, is one of the reasons why the typical Black household has just 13 percent of the wealth of the typical non-Latinx White household in America.[2] Today, 74 percent of neighborhoods that received a D grade nearly a century ago are home to households with low-to-moderate incomes and 63 percent are dominated by communities of color, whereas

91 percent of neighborhoods graded A in the 1930s have middle-to-upper median family incomes and 85 percent are predominantly White.[3]

Jeremy Hoffman at the Science Museum of Virginia and his colleagues were curious whether redlining could in part explain these disparities.[4] Using the *Mapping Inequality* database of digitized HOLC maps created by the Digital Scholarship Lab at the University of Richmond and present-day satellite measurements of summer land surface temperature, canopy cover, and impervious surface cover, Hoffman measured the greenness and imperviousness of neighborhoods by grade and calculated the difference in temperature between each neighborhood and the average of all HOLC-mapped neighborhoods in a city. In 94 percent of cities, "Hazardous" neighborhoods were warmer than average and "Best" neighborhoods were cooler, with the difference between "Hazardous" and "Best" at least 5°F in nearly half of these (49 percent). Residents of "Hazardous" neighborhoods experience these higher summer temperatures in large part because they are surrounded by just under half the canopy cover typical of "Best" neighborhoods and one and three-quarter times the impervious surface cover.

The HOLC grading of neighborhoods in America initiated a period of disinvestment in low-income communities and communities of color that transformed their physical living spaces. The unavailability of low-interest mortgages in neighborhoods graded D forced homeowners in default to lose their properties and created areas where much of the housing was rented. Landlords of rental properties in low-income neighborhoods do not typically invest in costly landscaping and may even pave over yards, and tenants do not have the means to beautify their living spaces with vegetation even if they were permitted to do so. Neighborhoods receiving low HOLC grades with low land values may also have been foci of development where once single-family properties with canopied yards became apartment complexes, shopping malls, or gas stations. At the municipal level, planners may have prioritized neighborhoods with low-income communities and communities of color for large public housing projects and elevated highways that ate up greenspace, and wealthier and White neighborhoods for street trees and public parks. As the cities mapped by the HOLC grew in population, I imagine neighborhoods receiving low grades as places that changed a lot over time and where land was planned, developed, and traded largely independent of the people who lived there, became less treed with each passing year. Conversely, A- and B-graded neighborhoods remained owned by their residents, who were deeply invested in maintaining the value of their landscaped properties on walkable streets and near public parks.

Adding to these forces acting on the greenness of HOLC neighborhoods, and more generally on neighborhoods with residents of differing incomes, races, and ethnicities, is the differential capacity of White, wealthy homeowners to influence public decision-making. White, wealthy homeowners have the time, money, education, power, and social capital to attract public investment in new trees and greenspace and to prevent their loss.[5] Case in point, my 76 percent White and relatively wealthy neighborhood of mostly single-family homeowners successfully blocked the development of 3.7 acres of forest owned by the school district and adjoining the wild bit of nature in Butterfly Park that I described in chapter 5. My neighbors had the time, energy, and know-how to organize an effective campaign against the sale of the land that included a petition with almost 1,500 signatures—that's about 40 percent of the neighborhood's adult population, a website, a community event with hot dogs and a free workout, an op-ed explaining the intricacies of the sale of surplus school district land and the benefits of preserving greenspace in an urban neighborhood, attendance at county commission meetings with professionally printed signs, and coverage by print and TV news outlets in the city. In the end, my neighbors convinced all but one county commissioner to ask the school district to take the land off the market and to buy the $3.85 million parcel itself if the school district refused.

An important point that I'd like you to take away from this example is the staggering fact that a community of residents convinced their local elected officials to spend nearly $4 million dollars to preserve a small piece of forest in one of the largest and most rapidly growing cities in the country. Yes, this group of neighbors had advantages that other residents don't have, but the fact remains that they convinced decision-makers to conserve urban nature. In this chapter, I'll show you the enormous power that you hold to influence how land is used in your city, town, or county and explain that seemingly small land use decisions add up to significant gains in habitat for local animals and plants. Since most people are not active participants in their local government, I'll provide you with a list of doable ways you can get involved that make a difference to urban nature conservation. Picking up where I left off in previous chapters on the extinction of experience, street trees, and the luxury effect, I'll continue to explore how nature is inequitably distributed among a city's residents based on their income, race, and ethnicity and the reasons why this is the case. I'll explain how unequal access to public nature in our cities, towns, and counties affects the health, well-being, and prosperity of all residents regardless of where they live, and describe the importance of acting on behalf of those who may not have as influential a voice to rectify past and present environmental injustices. In this last chapter of the book focused on a space in your urban ecosystem, I hope to show you that your connections to nature extend beyond the places you normally frequent in your city or town, and that city-wide nature is as important as nature in your yard.

Your vote and your voice are key to conserving nature in your city

The International Union for Conservation of Nature, a global consortium of governments, non-governmental organizations, academics, indigenous groups, and business associations, maintains the world's most comprehensive running tab on the extinction risks of plants, animals, and fungi on Earth, called the IUCN Red List of Threatened Species. The Red List is often referred to as the Barometer of Life because it contains risk assessments for so many species—more than 147,500, including nearly all mammals, birds, and amphibians. Red List assessments detail the habitat and ecology of a species, its geographic range and estimated global population size, its use and trade by humans, conservation actions taken on its behalf, and the threats it faces. This information is synthesized into a category describing the species' risk of extinction—from the least to the most risk, they are Least Concern, Near Threatened, Vulnerable, Endangered, Critically Endangered, Extinct in the Wild, and Extinct. For example, in the United States, approximately 9 percent of mammal species, 7 percent of bird species, and 18 percent of amphibian species are classified as threatened"—that is, Vulnerable, Endangered, or Critically Endangered—in the Red List.[6] For the majority of these American species and other threatened species around the world, the most common threat to their survival is human land use: globally, the top three reasons species are listed as threatened in the Red List are the expansion of agriculture or aquaculture (affects 64 percent of threatened species), logging (47 percent of threatened species), and residential and commercial development (32 percent of threatened species).[7] Human land use is also the primary reason that even species listed as Least Concern are declining. The conservation organization Partners in Flight identified habitat loss due to urbanization as the dominant threat to ninety-eight declining bird species in Canada and the United States, including the prothonotary warbler, wrentit, and whiskered screech-owl that the Red List considers Least Concern.[8] Our conversion of wildlife habitat into row crops, subdivisions, or wood products is clearly the primary cause of the phenomenal loss of biodiversity we are presently witnessing, more so than invasive alien species, pollution, and hunting and trapping, the next three most common reasons threatened species have been classified as such in the Red List.

Habitat loss due to human land use as the dominant cause of species decline is not surprising. After all, if you destroy a species' living space, then its numbers will necessarily diminish. What is surprising is that one of the major drivers of habitat loss, urbanization, is administered parcel by parcel at the municipal or county level. In America, local governments create and implement the policies and regulations that dictate the use of private land. Federal and state governments indirectly influence local land use through legislation such as the Clean Water Act that regulates stormwater management or the California Environmental Quality Act that requires that city and county development plans limit their impacts on the environment by providing fiscal and tax incentives; by funding and building roads; and, in the case of states, by specifying local financing laws, building codes, and the judicial review of land use permits. However, what really determines where and how subdivisions, retail businesses, schools, and office parks are built are comprehensive plans, subdivision regulations, and local ordinances, incredibly detailed regulations that specify everything from street tree spacing and sidewalk width to the type and density of buildings that are permitted on a site. It is these policies and regulatory tools that determine how much original wildlife habitat is lost when development occurs and how much new habitat is added in the form of street trees, parks, and landscaping. In other words, the implementation of local policies and regulations directly affects the amount of habitat in cities, towns, and counties and hence, the impact of urbanization on species of animals and plants, a major threat to their survival.

An excellent example of the impact of local government policies and regulations on the amount of wildlife habitat in urban areas comes from Greater Metropolitan Atlanta, the twenty-eight-county area surrounding the City of Atlanta, with a current population of just over six million.[9] Metro Atlanta's counties all lie within the Piedmont Uplands, a region of rolling hills, rivers, and oak-hickory-pine forests. Juxtaposed with this uniformity of terrain and trees, counties have developed differing planning practices and development regulations and have experienced varying levels of canopy loss as the area's population grew rapidly over the last several decades. This backdrop of similar biogeographical characteristics but differing approaches to development prompted Jeffrey Dorfman at the University of Georgia and his colleagues to test whether county policies and regulations were responsible for tree canopy coverage on public and private lands during the decade between 1991 and 2001. Controlling for impervious surface area change, population change, and land use types in counties, Dorfman's model identified three factors that each positively influenced tree canopy: the inclusion of tree-preserving clauses in a county's tree ordinance, planning and zoning regulations that protected and enhanced tree canopies and promoted quality growth projects such as conservation subdivisions and infill development, and the actual number of quality growth projects in the county.

A tree ordinance is a set of regulations that stipulate the preservation, removal, and planting of trees on public and private lands. Possible clauses in tree ordinances that directly impact canopy cover on a property include the requirement to save a certain proportion, say 10 percent, of a site that is slated for single-family homes as original tree canopy, the requirement to obtain a permit to remove trees on developed private property, the requirement to preserve exceptional trees like large, old oaks on public and private lands, and requirements for street and parking lot trees in new and existing development. Dorfman estimated that the presence of one of this type of tree-preserving clause in a county's tree ordinance was associated with a 1 percent increase in county canopy cover over the study decade. Given that Dorfman identified nine such clauses in metro Atlanta County tree ordinances, the maximum increase in county tree canopy coverage between 1991 and 2001 due to tree-preserving clauses was a little more than 9 percent. This is remarkable considering that the maximum observed loss of canopy in Atlanta's counties over this period was a little more than 12 percent. Therefore, the presence of tree-preserving clauses in a county's tree ordinance has the potential to offset three-fourths of possible tree canopy loss due to development. This is on top of the increase in canopy coverage if quality growth projects are built and planning and zoning emphasizes the preservation and planting of trees.

The metro Atlanta example illustrates the great potential of local planning policies and regulations to minimize the loss of wildlife habitat due to development and therefore significantly improve the lot of plant and animal species in urban areas. This potential has not gone unnoticed by ecologists. As a rule, ecologists are passionate about conserving nature. Many, like myself, gravitate toward the field because of their curiosity about, but also love of, nature. Whether they focus on one species or many, they translate this curiosity and love into figuring out where individuals and species live and why, and how they go about their lives. In the face of the rapid and large decline in biodiversity since the 1970s, ecologists have been keen to use the knowledge they produce to conserve the species they have dedicated their careers to studying. Because they know that planners can make a big difference to the amount of habitat and its quality in urban areas, ecologists, yours truly among them, have published lists of recommendations for land use planning to promote nature conservation. Articles with titles like "The Application of Ecological Principles to Urban and Urbanizing Landscapes" and "Designing Metropolitan Landscapes for Biodiversity" are commonplace in the ecological literature.[10]

The problem with these lists, as with other attempts to translate science, such as climate science, into practice, is that planners don't read them. Planners tend to rely on their own or close colleagues' direct experience to inform how they incorporate nature conservation into their work rather than the peer-reviewed scientific literature. This disconnect between scientific research and practice has been called the research-implementation gap, or more aptly, the knowing-doing gap.[11] During my doctoral studies at Carleton University in Canada, I, along with my advisor, Lenore Fahrig, and fellow students in her lab, hypothesized that aspects of the lists and recommendations produced by ecologists might partly explain why they weren't being consulted by planners.[12] We read twenty-one sets of recommendation for land use planning published by ecologists and identified five characteristics that, to our thinking, limited their practicality for planners. With few exceptions, the lists we reviewed exemplified all five characteristics.

First, recommendations were species-specific in the sense that a planner would need information on exactly where a certain species or type of species was located in their jurisdiction to be able to implement the recommendation. Species-specific ecological recommendations are very difficult for planners to use because by and large we have very little reliable information about where most species occur—although as iNaturalist and eBird take off, no pun intended, this may soon change. Second, recommendations were not prescriptive. For example, one recommendation called for the "establishment of landscape-level goals for retention, maintenance, or restoration of particular habitats or structures as well as limits to specific problematic conditions."[13] Even I, as an ecologist, wouldn't know how to implement this recommendation. Third, lists included a large number of recommendations, as many as 121 in one case. We thought that such a list would be passed over by a planner with limited time and money to spend on conservation. Exacerbating the multiplicity of recommendations was the fact that none of the lists ordered their recommendations according to their importance to nature conservation. It's very unlikely that a planner would be able to implement every single recommendation in a list, so without the ecological expertise needed to know which recommendation has a bigger impact on nature conservation than others, the list becomes nearly unusable, or at the very least ineffective. Fourth, non-sequential recommendations are also problematic when one recommendation in a list contradicts its neighbor—something that occurred in a third of the lists we reviewed. This leaves a planner unsure which of two conflicting recommendations to implement if their relative importance is unstated. The fifth and perhaps most significant characteristic that we thought limited the use of ecological recommendations by planners was the glaring oversight of not considering the other goals that planners aim to achieve in their jurisdictions, such as providing transportation and housing for residents. Recommendations from several lists called for removing buildings and roads near waterways or preserving large habitat patches regardless of land ownership and development pressures. For a planner tasked with accommodating a growing human population, recommendations that ignore all planning goals but nature conservation are inapplicable in the local context. It's hard to imagine how a planner would implement them if the job of locating housing and roads necessarily comes first.

As a result of our review of existing ecological recommendations, my colleagues and I decided to try our hand at a more practical list that we hoped could readily be used by planners. We came up with five sequential steps that could be used by any planner anywhere and were based on the latest ecological science. A planner following our steps would first need to select a land cover map for their jurisdiction and distinguish between land covers that they considered "natural," like forest, and those that were "non-natural" or dominated by human use, like residential development or row crop agriculture. This distinction is intended to identify the land covers that are dominated by nature and that the planner therefore wants to conserve. The second step in our framework is when the planner lists the constraints on nature conservation in their jurisdiction, such as population growth and the maintenance or promotion of economic activities of importance, like agriculture or mining or logging, depending on the context in question. This second step essentially frontloads the objectives other than nature conservation that planners typically need to address right off the bat before they can consider other priorities.

The next three steps in our list are based on ecological science and numbered in order of their importance to nature conservation. Step 3 in the framework recommends that the planner maximize the amount and diversity of natural land cover in their jurisdiction, especially near water. Step 4 states that the planner should promote activities and practices in non-natural land covers that minimize disturbance to nature. And the final step, Step 5, advises the planner to aggregate non-natural land covers associated with high intensity uses, especially away from water.

What this all means in practice is that, once the planner has accounted for the housing, transportation, and economic needs of residents of their jurisdictions, they should first locate parcels of natural land that could be conserved, perhaps by public purchase (Step 3). These parcels of land should preferentially be rare natural land cover types that are located near water. Rare natural land cover types are preferred because their conservation preserves the diversity of wildlife habitats in the jurisdiction and thus, the diversity of species: It's better to lose a bit of oak-hickory-pine forest that can be found just about anywhere than to lose the rare wetland or bit of prairie that is home to species that are found nowhere else in the area. The planner should also work to increase the cover of trees and other vegetation in built areas, minimize fertilizer and pesticide use, and promote modes of transportation other than gas-powered vehicles—in a nutshell, the actions that you can take to conserve nature described in this book (Step 4). Finally, the planner should prioritize land in or near existing developed areas for new housing and plan for existing roads to carry more traffic rather than build new roads (Step 5). Infill development and conservation subdivisions are ways to cluster housing. Infill development adds housing to vacant land in existing neighborhoods or increases the density of housing in previously low-density areas by replacing single-family dwellings with townhomes, for example. Conservation subdivisions are designed to limit housing to a portion of a parcel of land by building at a higher density than if housing was spread across the parcel. This leaves the remainder of the parcel for conservation, recreation, or low intensity uses like grazing. My and others' research has shown that clustering residential development by building at higher densities over smaller areas has less of a negative effect

Clustering development by building higher-density housing, like the duplexes shown here, allows for habitat conservation—the forest in the background—and minimizes effects on wildlife compared to sprawl.

on wildlife than building sprawling low-density housing.[14] The same is true for roads.[15] The negative effects of roadkill are lessened if traffic is concentrated on fewer roads and fewer roads are built as a result. If a planner clusters housing and bundles traffic preferably away from water as we suggest in our framework, then large areas of natural land cover, aka wildlife habitat, near water should be left over.

The most interesting thing about the framework I've just described is its intended sequence of implementation. Protecting natural land cover, preferably of a rare type and preferably near water, is the first ecological step in our framework because it's the most important thing a planner can do to conserve nature in their jurisdiction. If the only parcel of natural land cover that a planner can conserve because of the demands of growth, land values, or other constraints is a small one next to an interstate or industrial area, then the planner should protect this parcel. Protecting large contiguous areas of wildlife habitat, the outcome of the last and least important step in our framework, matters less than just simply conserving wildlife habitat wherever it is and whatever size it is. This reflects recent ecological understanding that the total amount of wildlife habitat in a landscape, regardless of whether it is in one large patch or many small ones, has a larger positive effect on wildlife than the fragmentation, or the spatial arrangement, of that habitat.[16]

The second interesting outcome of the sequential application of our steps is that a planner should prioritize greening existing developed areas to minimize disturbance to wildlife (Step 4) over housing densification (Step 5). Although building compact communities of higher housing densities is of benefit to wildlife, minimizing the many negative impacts of existing development is more important. This prioritization also ties in with the health and well-being of residents. As I've described in this book, a very dense neighborhood with little greenspace is not conducive to the presence of wildlife and it's not great for people either. Healthy and safe living spaces for people include street trees, parks, and greenways. That's why planners should prioritize adding vegetation to developed areas that lack it—even high-density neighborhoods can accommodate pocket or linear parks—over densification at all costs.

My colleagues and I did our best to design ecological recommendations for land use planning that a planner might find more useful, but we still ignored many aspects of a planner's job that might impede the implementation of our steps. There are complex regulatory, judicial, political, social, economic, and spatial contingencies that come into play when trying to figure out how to prioritize a parcel of land for one use and not another. It would have been much better if we had had planners on our team who could have told us whether our steps would work and how we could improve them. Like many well-intentioned ecologists before us, we devised guidelines for best practice without talking to the practitioners. This is like telling a nurse how to do their job without ever having stepped foot in a hospital.

To begin to rectify this, I decided to ask planners what they needed from ecologists. Rather than ecologists telling planners what to do to conserve nature, it was high time that planners had the opportunity to tell ecologists about how nature conservation occurred in their jurisdictions, the ecological knowledge they needed to effectively conserve

Planners should prioritize greening existing developed areas over housing densification. Pocket parks (left) and linear parks (right) add greenery to very dense city centers.

nature, and how that knowledge should be conveyed. To start this conversation, my colleagues and I surveyed 233 planners in cities, towns, and counties in ten southeastern US states, from West Virginia to Mississippi to Florida to North Carolina.[17] We received responses from planners of big cities and small towns and of urban and rural counties in proportion to the numbers of such places in states. Our responses also came from just as many politically conservative planners as liberal ones.

In line with my and my colleagues' reasoning underpinning our ecological land use planning framework, the planners we surveyed wanted recommendations from ecologists that were not species-specific, more feasible, in order of importance, and that included other planning concerns. Planners also wanted recommendations tailored to their region and shared hundreds of questions they had for ecologists about how best to conserve nature in their local contexts. This feedback is an extremely valuable roadmap for a future of collaboration between planners and ecologists. I'm hoping that as this and other research like it moves forward, we'll begin to see the research-implementation gap shrink, with the doing side moving closer to the knowing side by a substantial margin.

The planners my colleagues and I surveyed also clued us in to the importance of two groups of stakeholders when it comes to conserving nature at the municipal or county level: local elected officials and the public. Planners identified local elected officials as the most important entity in conserving nature and support from local elected officials and the community as the top two most helpful ways to promote nature conservation in their jurisdictions. They also listed greater awareness and education among the public and elected officials as one of the top two most feasible ways of addressing important nature conservation concerns, the other being new plans and policies. Separate research from the Research Triangle in North Carolina and Seattle, Washington, reported that public support and support from elected officials were the top two factors that surveyed planners identified as likely to lead to increased nature conservation, with the exception of conservation funding.[18] In Des Moines, Iowa, the same research showed public support tied for top spot with conservation training and information, again except for conservation funding.

I hope that these results, as well my discussion of the importance of local plans, policies, and regulations to nature conservation in urban areas earlier in this chapter, convince you of the truly awesome power that you and your local elected officials hold when it comes to enhancing nature in your city, town, or county. You can wield this power in two ways. First, you can participate in your local government's conservation planning activities. Planners across the country are telling us that this makes a big difference to nature conservation and in the Research Triangle in North Carolina, Toddi Steelman, now at Duke University, and George Hess at North Carolina State University have even found that the more stakeholders, like you, who participate in creating and implementing open space, or natural area, plans, the more likely it is that plans are effectively carried out and that open space is effectively protected.[19] You can also wield your power by choosing and influencing local elected officials. They are the ones who ultimately approve plans, policies, and regulations, which I've shown have a large effect on the amount of wildlife habitat in your city, town, or county. What's more, the southeastern planners my colleagues and I surveyed ranked local legislation as the number one driver of nature conservation where they work.

How to make the most of your vote and your voice to enhance nature in your city, town, or county

Being involved in local government is a rewarding experience. You will meet new people, develop new relationships, and build community all the while advancing the cause of nature conservation where you live. Over time, you are likely to find that local representatives, planners, and community organizers share some of your values and priorities and that working together, you can create real change in your city, town, or county. Here is a list of five ways you can participate in local government so that your vote and your voice for nature are heard.

1. **Get informed.** Read or listen to the local news and follow your local planning, parks, natural resources, and/or forestry departments on social media to find out about planning initiatives and nature-related issues in your municipality or county. Join your neighborhood association and/or local non-profit groups dedicated to nature conservation. Active members of these organizations will know a lot about how your local government works and may already have campaigns in place that you can participate in.

2. **Vote in local elections!** Average voter turnout for local elections in American cities is only 26 percent.[20] With numbers so low, your vote for a candidate can make a large difference in the outcome. To make your vote count even more, follow up with the candidates you support on social media, by phone, by letter, or by email. Let them know about the nature-related issues that are important to you and what you think they should do about them.

3. **Attend public meetings** of your city, town, or county's elected representatives. There is usually an opportunity for residents to voice their viewpoints at the start or end of each meeting and you may have the ability to add items to the agenda that you'd like addressed.

4. **Provide your feedback to planners.** Respond to surveys, submit your comments on draft plans and ordinances, attend open houses, and participate in focus groups, visioning workshops, and other events intended to solicit community input.

5. **Serve on a board, commission, or committee**. Depending on the size of your local government, you may have the opportunity to play a major role in creating plans and regulations that incorporate meaningful protection for nature. At the very least, you will be able to directly advise local government staff on planning, transportation, trees, recreation, and other topics that intersect with nature conservation.

To help you get started exercising your power to change the balance of nature where you live, I've listed five ways that you can get involved in municipal or county planning and decision-making in the sidebar *How to make the most of your vote and your voice to enhance nature in your city, town, or county*. Recall from my description of an urban ecosystem in chapter 2 that the localized interactions among ecosystem elements imply that each one of us, and each one of our actions, is critically involved in ecosystem functioning where we live. This applies to lowering your thermostat in the winter to minimize the citywide Heat Island Effect, as I described in that chapter, but also to any single action that you take to get involved in the workings of your local government. Even a very small effort is unbelievably worthwhile.

The uneven spatial distribution of public nature in cities disadvantages low-income residents and residents of color

In 2018, two meta-analyses of the effects of resident income and race or ethnicity on the distribution of trees in urban areas were published.[21] Like the study of how people's connection to nature might influence their pro-environmental behavior that I described in chapter 3, investigations of urban tree cover inequity in relation to income and race or ethnicity vary a great deal. They measure tree cover, income, race, and ethnicity in a multiplicity of ways; use different units of analysis—the parcel or neighborhood, this last defined in various ways; analyze tree cover on public or private land, or both; and focus on different cities. All these factors may influence a study's outcome, making it difficult to state unequivocally whether tree cover differs based on resident income and race or ethnicity, and in which contexts this effect, if it exists, applies. So, the fact that Shannon Watkins at the University of California San Francisco and Ed Gerrish at the University of South Dakota recently undertook two comprehensive meta-analyses, or studies of studies intended to synthesize a field's findings, is a real boon to our understanding of how nature is inequitably distributed among the residents of a city, a critical issue that impacts the health and well-being of all urban and suburban dwellers.

Gerrish and Watkins first published their meta-analysis of the effect of income on the distribution of urban tree cover, so I'll start there.

They compiled the results of sixty-one studies, mostly from the United States, of the effects of absolute income, measured as median household income, for example, or relative income, measured as poverty rate, on tree cover, measured using satellite imagery or field counts, in parcels and neighborhoods of varying sizes in multiple cities. To be included in the meta-analysis, studies had to have measured trees in some way, although they could have measured shrubs and grass too. Gerrish and Watkins combed through each of the sixty-one studies and noted how the variables of interest, income and tree cover, were measured; whether they were measured on public and/or private land and over what areal extent; whether the authors included other variables that could also explain tree cover, like housing density, housing age, and race or ethnicity; and the characteristics of the cities in which studies took place, like their population size and climate.

Taking all these factors into account, Gerrish and Watkins found an overall, statistically significant, positive effect of resident income on urban tree cover. Properties or neighborhoods with residents of higher incomes have more trees or tree cover. This positive effect persists even if resident race or ethnicity, housing density, and housing age are taken into account. It applies equally well to private and public land and small or large cities with arid or humid climates. It also doesn't matter whether absolute or relative income is measured or whether tree cover is estimated from satellite imagery or calculated from ground-level counts. The only variation in the effect is that it is stronger at the neighborhood, rather than the parcel, level. Therefore, we can confidently say that a person's income, yours or mine, and the income of their neighbors is positively associated with greater tree cover where they live—along streets, in parks, and on their properties—regardless of the person's and their neighbor's race or ethnicity and a variety of contextual and methodological factors.

I've mentioned this effect in my descriptions of the inequities in access to nature in chapter 3 and the distribution of street trees in chapter 4, and when I explained the positive effect of income on coyote sightings in Charlotte in chapter 7. In that chapter, I called it the luxury effect, the term coined for the positive effect of median household income on woody plant diversity in the neighborhoods of Phoenix and surrounding areas, and the one I'll use here for the relationship described by Gerrish and Watkins.

Researchers don't know why the luxury effect exists—I'm not aware of any studies demonstrating its causes—but they have suggested explanations for it. First, with respect to public land, the fact that tree cover is inequitably distributed between poor and rich neighborhoods implies that local governments and their agents, including non-governmental organizations, allocate more funding and provide more tree planting and maintenance services where residents are wealthier. In chapter 4, I described how, in Tampa, Florida, and New York City, neighborhoods where household incomes are higher are those with more street tree cover. Wealthier neighborhoods also have a greater number of public parks and more public park acreage per person than poorer neighborhoods, and parks in wealthier neighborhoods have more trails, aesthetic and natural elements, and tree shade.[22] It's important to recognize that the inequitable distribution of tree cover on public land is probably more a representation of past policies and practices than present ones. Trees live for a long time and their presence reflects the decisions made by the people who planted them, although this isn't to say that present discrimination based on income is not occurring.

The inequitable distribution of tree cover on public land could also be due to wealthier residents having the means to maintain or plant street trees themselves, and/or having the time, education, and influence to attract more public investment in street trees and public parks. Of note, less wealthy people face a number of barriers to participation in local planning including lack of transportation and childcare, event scheduling during work hours, and lack of knowledge of government processes.[23]

On private land, the luxury effect could be the result of residents with more income having the means to invest in landscaping and plants on their properties—the explanation my co-authors and I put forth to explain why coyotes were more often sighted in wealthier neighborhoods. However, we don't know whether the luxury effect on private land is due to the income of residents or rather, to their education level. Gary Luck has suggested that income is a better predictor of the area available for trees and other vegetation, and education is a better predictor of the trees and vegetation that a resident actually adds to their property, assuming a positive association between education and an understanding of and appreciation for the benefits of nature.[24] We also don't know whether income explains tree cover or if it's the other way around. The luxury effect may be due to wealthier people being able to afford to live in more attractive neighborhoods that have more trees and vegetation on public and private land. For example, in Phoenix, Diane Hope and her colleagues found that wealthier neighborhoods tended to be at higher elevations where woody plant diversity was naturally greater.[25]

I'll now turn to the second meta-analysis carried out by Watkins and Gerrish that looked at the effect of race and ethnicity on the distribution of urban tree cover.[26] Watkins and Gerrish found forty-two studies, again the majority from the United States, that investigated the influence of the race or ethnicity of residents—Black, Latinx, Asian, or a combination of these—on the tree cover of parcels and neighborhoods in multiple cities. Just as for their meta-analysis on income, Watkins and Gerrish made note of how race or ethnicity and tree cover were measured by study authors; whether tree cover was measured on private and/or public land; whether authors included other variables in their analyses, such as income, that could explain the distribution of tree cover; and the population size and climate of the cities where studies occurred.

The outcome of this second meta-analysis is not as straightforward as that of the first. Overall, considering all races or ethnicities, public and private land combined, and controlling for income, housing density, and housing age, there is no effect of race or ethnicity on urban tree cover. In other words, if you take into account a person's income, as well as the housing density and age of housing where they live, the fact that they are Black, Latinx, or Asian does not predict the tree cover on public and private land in their neighborhood. Yet, Watkins and Gerrish did find notable effects of race and ethnicity when they looked at public and private land separately. Black, Latinx, and/or Asian people tend to live in neighborhoods with less tree cover on public land, irrespective of their income, the density of houses, and housing age. This inequity in the distribution of tree cover on public land is especially pronounced in cities with arid climates. At the same time, Black people tend to live in

Parks in lower-income neighborhoods and neighborhoods with more residents of color (left) have fewer trails, aesthetic and natural elements, and tree shade than parks in wealthier or White neighborhoods (right).

neighborhoods with more tree cover on private land, again controlling for their income, housing density, and housing age.

So, unlike for income, we cannot say unequivocally that urban tree cover is inequitably distributed among residents based on their race or ethnicity. However, we can say that people of color live in neighborhoods with less tree cover on public land and that Black people live in neighborhoods with more tree cover on private land. In chapters 3 and 4, I described the inequity in public parks and street tree cover for Black and Latinx people. Neighborhoods with more residents of color have fewer parks, less park acreage per person, and parks in these neighborhoods have fewer trails, aesthetic and natural elements, and tree shade. In Tampa, Black and Latinx residents live along streets with less street tree cover, with the same being true for Latinx residents in New York City.

Given the racial and ethnic disparity in urban tree cover on public land, local government officials, employees, and agents may be basing their decisions and choices about the allocation of public funds and services for trees in rights-of-way and in parks, in part, on the race or ethnicity of residents. As with the inequity in public tree cover in relation to income, this racial and ethnic disparity is likely the result of past and present policies and practices. Less public tree cover in neighborhoods with more residents of color may also be the result of residents of color being excluded from planning processes. Nationwide, about 76 percent of planners are White and non-Latinx, whereas 8 percent are Asian, 5 percent are Black, and just under 3 percent are Latinx (my survey of Southeastern planners told a similar story: About 90 percent of respondents were White and non-Latinx).[27] This dire lack of diversity may deter residents of color from participating in community outreach by planners due to distrust and/or the assumption that they are not the intended audience. White planners may also lack the cultural competency to effectively engage with communities of color, not knowing the best means with which to reach out, who to reach out to, and where to hold events, for instance.[28] And they may not be communicating about public trees in a relevant way that connects with what residents of color care about. Street trees and trees in public parks are valued, or not, by different people for a variety of reasons. Finding out how and why trees are important to communities is essential to meeting their needs.

As Watkins and Gerrish expected, the inequitable distribution of tree cover on public land is heightened in cities with arid climates. Arid climates support grassland and desert biomes where few trees grow naturally. Cities located in these areas rely on planting for their tree cover to a greater extent than cities with humid climates where trees are more commonly found. If public funding and services for tree planting are biased against residents of color, then tree cover should be more inequitably distributed on public land in cities with arid climates, as Watkins and Gerrish found. This pattern is worrying because of the importance of tree cover along streets, in parks, and in public school grounds in this era of increasing urban temperatures. Residents of color in cities with arid climates are especially disadvantaged when it comes to coping with extreme heat.

Watkins and Gerrish explained the fact that neighborhoods with more Black residents have more tree cover on private land in three, non-mutually exclusive ways. First, White flight to the suburbs resulted in some older, inner-city neighborhoods with mature trees in yards being occupied predominantly by Black people, thereby creating a positive association between private tree cover and the proportion of Black residents in neighborhoods. Second, Black residents may prefer more tree cover in their yards and therefore, plant more trees or move to more treed properties. If this is the case, the inequity in tree cover on public land in neighborhoods with more Black residents is even more unjust than at first blush if one considers the deprivation of a valued amenity as itself a form of injustice. Third, Black residents may be planting more trees in their yards to compensate for the low street tree cover and the lack of public parks in the neighborhoods where they live.

It is now time to ask two important questions about the disparity in urban tree cover on public land between rich and poor neighborhoods and between neighborhoods with more or less White people. First, does it matter that White and/or wealthy residents have more tree cover on public land where they live and, if it does, why? Second, what can we, as urban residents, do about it? Before I tackle these questions, let me state that my answers are my personal reflections as a White and wealthy city dweller and that others may have different, but just as or more valid, responses. Also, my aim is not to provide all-encompassing answers to these very complex issues, but to initiate a discussion about them that hopefully helps to redress what I see as grave injustices.

Regarding the first question, my answer is "Yes!" As I've intimated above, I think the disparity in tree cover on public land between people based on their income, race, and ethnicity is unjust. I believe all urban residents deserve equal access to public nature. To my understanding, our societal contract stipulates that the benefits of the public purse are intended to be distributed equally among residents in a way that is blind to a person's identity, with the exception that accommodations may be needed so that benefits, like urban nature, are truly accessible to all. Part of the reasoning underlying this social contract is the alleviation of the lack of nature for those who do not have the means to provide it for themselves on private land—as it stands, the system is doing the exact opposite. I also think that the current distribution of urban nature on public land disadvantages everyone, whether you live in a neighborhood with lots of public nature or not. I see our society as economically, politically, and culturally poorer if a substantial proportion of its people are

Becoming aware of and combatting the inequitable distribution of public nature in your city, town, or county

Here are four ways that I think each of us can help to distribute nature and its benefits more equitably to all the residents of a city, regardless of their race, ethnicity, or income:

1. **Learn about the environmental inequities in your city and the reasons for them.** Check online for local data, news, and articles that describe inequities in tree cover, pollution, air temperature, and water and soil quality where you live. We all need to become much more aware of how the environmental quality of our neighborhood compares to others in our cities and the reasons for any differences. You may even come across some local solutions that you can participate in or otherwise support.

2. **Speak up!** Say something about the environmental inequities where you live and what you think should be done about them to your neighborhood association, local nature conservation group, and your local elected officials and planners at public meetings, during workshops, and if you sit on a board, commission, or committee (see the other sidebar in this chapter, *How to make the most of your vote and your voice to enhance nature in your city, town, or county*). I know this may be difficult, but we all need to start talking about environmental inequities based on income, race, and ethnicity much more than we do.

3. **If you are a person of color, run for local office.** Only 5 percent of people who have ever run for elected office in the United States are Black and 6 percent are Latinx, despite Black and Latinx people making up 12 percent and 15 percent of the adult population, respectively.[29] Even serving on your local school board or commission can make a difference by emphasizing equal access to nature among schoolyards. And your representation will encourage others to speak up for their communities or to get involved themselves.

4. **Hold your planners to account.** Best practice in planning involves engaging with diverse communities, which means planners must address barriers to public participation encountered by low-income people and people of color, including transportation, meeting schedules, language, trust, and relevance. Consult the American Planning Association's *Planning with Diverse Communities* for more information, including a checklist for planners to effectively include diverse communities in participatory planning. Share this resource with the planners in your community and use it as justification when you insist that the time, location, and format of an event prevent a diversity of stakeholders from participating.

less healthy in mind and body than they could be if they had access to urban nature and therefore, do not have the opportunity to contribute their talents to the greater good to as great an extent as they otherwise could. There's also the problem of the extinction of experience and the positive feedback between knowing nature, caring for it, and conserving it. Because of this, I see the inequitable distribution of public urban nature as boding very ill for the health of our planet.

Now that you know my perspective on the first question, here's my answer to the second. Although I don't know what will work best to eliminate the inequity in urban nature on public land and I know that changing this pattern will be very difficult and will take time, I also know that I must and can do something. In line with my thinking throughout this book, I strongly believe that each of us has a part to play in the urban ecosystem where we live, including in eliminating the inequitable distribution of nature in our cities. Also, in line with the intent of this book to offer feasible recommendations for action, I've thought about what a person who is not an elected official, a planner, or a community activist, and who is busy with their job, kids, and other aspects of their life, might reasonably do to help move the needle. What I've come up with are a few recommendations that I think most people can do, and that I believe will make a difference in the long run (see the sidebar *Becoming aware of and combatting the inequitable distribution of public nature in your city, town, or county*). Following these recommendations will not magically reverse the disparity in public urban nature among neighborhoods in our cities but doing so is a step in the right direction and, in my opinion, a step that is long overdue.

The connections between you and nature in your urban ecosystem reach beyond those that you experience when you are in your yard or at your park or greenway, or when you are walking or driving along your street or through your neighborhood. Your relationship with nature extends across your city, town, or county through your interactions with other people. It's by learning from others about where and why nature is distributed in your city; creating relationships with neighbors, other residents passionate about nature conservation, planners, and your local elected officials; having honest dialogues about the conservation and inequitable distribution of nature in your city; and adding your unique perspective to the public discourse by voting in local elections or standing for election yourself that will make a difference to the nature you find along your street, in your park, in your greenway, and in your neighborhood, and in all the other streets, parks, greenways, and neighborhoods of your city. Talking about the importance of everyday nature to all the lives in a city—rich or poor, White, Black, or Latinx—and how to equalize access to it should be commonplace. It's up to each of us to bring up the topic the next time we meet.

CHAPTER 9

CONCLUSION

ONE OF THE REASONS THAT I LOVE STUDYING URBAN NATURE IS THAT it gives me the sense of uncovering a secret every time I learn something new. I've got nothing against studying the ecology of places untouched by human influence—although these are becoming few and far between these days—but for me, discovering and describing ecological patterns in a place obviously dominated by them is not that exciting. Instead, I opt for the thrill of finding a southern two-lined salamander in the stream that drains a major business district near my house or spotting a pair of peregrine falcons checking what's on the menu in my neighborhood. To me, and to most people, these observations are unexpected. We've all been taught that nature in the urban and suburban places is an oxymoron. Where humans occur in great numbers, other species do not. But the more I look around me and the more urban ecology research I do, the more I'm beginning to suspect that nature is alive and well where we live. My education and training tell me that I live in an urban ecosystem, but my local experience has shown me how vibrant and dynamic that ecosystem is. Humans can be just as connected to nature in cities as elsewhere. We just need to become more aware of these connections and nurture them so that they thrive.

I hope the preceding chapters have made you more aware of your place in your urban ecosystem and have provided you with the tools to nurture the connections that matter to you. The tour of the urban or suburban place you call home that I've organized in this book has taken you from your yard, along your street, into your park and along your greenway,

Nature is alive and well where we live (from top to bottom): mallard nest, mourning dove, great blue heron, brown-headed cowbird, northern water-snake, and Carolina wren.

and throughout your neighborhood and your city. Along the way, I've highlighted some key ways that you affect nature and that it affects you.

First, with respect to how you influence nature, the main messages in this book are these:

- **How you manage nature in your yard matters just as much or more to birds than how much greenspace there is nearby.** Research from Ottawa, Phoenix, Chicago, and Hobart shows that the number of bird species in urban and suburban places depends more on the habitat in your yard than on the habitat in public greenspaces and undeveloped land. Small changes to how you manage nature in your yard can help to welcome a variety of birds to where you live, including birds that also rely on native habitats like forest and threatened species.

- **Driving along your street risks wildlife becoming roadkill, which reduces population sizes and increases local extinction.** The species most at risk of being road-killed are locally abundant species, large mammal and bird species, long-lived species that must move among different habitat types to complete their life cycle like turtles, and species that are attracted to roads and roadsides but do not avoid traffic when there. Driving less and driving the speed limit are simple ways that you can reduce roadkill risk where you live, and adding your roadkill observations to iNaturalist will help inform the use of wildlife crossing signs where and when they are needed.

- **Maintaining wild nature in your park enhances the number and types of butterflies you find there.** Little bits of wild nature like forest or grassland in your public park increase its habitat diversity and therefore the number of different butterfly species you find there. Wild nature in parks is also a refuge for butterflies when conditions in more managed areas change. You can help promote butterfly populations of a variety of different species by helping your community maintain wild nature in your park and by adding a pollinator pitstop to your yard.

- **The success of urban stream restoration in your greenway depends on how you manage stormwater in your yard.** Research to date indicates that urban restoration projects focused on short lengths of stream channels and their floodplains do not improve aquatic biodiversity or water quality. This is because restored reaches still receive large amounts of polluted stormwater from developed watersheds. A cure for the Urban Stream Syndrome includes reducing the amount of stormwater coming from your property and implementing out-of-channel restoration practices, which have been shown to increase the number of aquatic species in urban streams.

- **Your neighborhood's housing density determines which species will be your neighbors.** If you live in a suburban-density neighborhood, you live amongst the largest total number of birds anywhere in your region and amongst more species than in other neighborhoods. You also very likely share your neighborhood with coyotes, which tend to keep to greenspace, but may frequent yards if your neighborhood has a high median family income. As urbanization expands into undeveloped landscapes in the coming years, learning to safely share our living spaces with the other species in our neighborhoods, from chimney swifts to coyotes, will be a necessary part of living in an urban ecosystem.

- **Your vote and your voice are key to conserving nature in your city.** Habitat loss due to land use change is the primary threat to the persistence of wildlife. In the United States, a major cause of land use change, urbanization, is administered locally by municipal and county elected officials and planning agencies. According to planners in the Southeast, garnering support from local elected officials is the most useful and feasible way to increase the amount of habitat in urban and suburban landscapes. Voting and communicating with your local elected officials are essential to conserving nature across your city.

Second, with respect to how nature influences you, the main messages are these:

- **Experiencing nature in your yard leads to love and care for the environment.** Frequent and regular contact with nature in your yard helps you and your kids get to know nature better, value its beauty and benefits, and ultimately develop an emotional connection with it. A deeper connection with nature leads to pro-environmental behavior—in other words, the actions that we will each need to take to lessen the global loss of species. Regularly spending a few minutes on a nature activity with your kids in your yard will help them develop a connection to nature that will last into adulthood.

- **The trees along your street make you healthier, safer, and richer.** Street trees sequester enough carbon dioxide, absorb enough air pollution, take up or intercept enough stormwater, save building occupants enough energy, and add enough to home sales prices each year to rightfully be considered critical urban infrastructure. Street trees also reduce violent crime and encourage us to walk or bike more often, lowering our body mass indices in the process. Unfortunately, street tree populations in many cities in the United States are declining. You can help reverse this trend by planting a street tree and/or caring for the ones on your property or at your workplace.

- **Wild nature in your park relieves stress and mental fatigue and improves your mood.** Attention Restoration Theory and Stress Reduction Theory explain how exposure to nature restores our mental capacities, relieves stress, and makes us happier. Wild nature is especially good at fostering mental well-being. To enjoy these benefits of the little bit of wild nature in your park, visit it for about an hour and a half each week. The practice of forest bathing can help you soak up relaxation and happiness among the trees.

- **Nature along your greenway boosts the mental and physical health benefits of exercise.** Compared to exercising indoors or outdoors in a built environment, "green" or "blue" exercise along your greenway will leave you feeling more revitalized, restored, and energetic, and with a greater sense of enjoyment and satisfaction from the experience. You will also likely be less tense, angry, anxious, and stressed, all of which acts to encourage you to exercise again.

229

If there are phytoncide-producing trees along your greenway, you will also experience enhanced immune activity and increased levels of cardioprotective, anti-diabetic, and anti-obesity compounds in your blood. Just five minutes of light intensity exercise along your greenway is enough to boost your mood and lower stress.

- **Green stormwater infrastructure in your neighborhood improves water quality and lowers the risk of urban flooding.** Green storm-water infrastructure, like the disconnected downspouts and rain barrels in your yard and the stormwater ponds, bioretention basins, and vegetated swales in your neighborhood, uses plants and soil to filter pollutants and reduce and slow the flow of stormwater to local aquatic systems. This last helps to reduce the frequency and severity of urban flooding, a problem that impacts neighborhoods nationwide and is set to worsen due to climate change. You can help scientists, engineers, and planners more effectively deploy green stormwater infrastructure by collecting data on its performance in your neighborhood.

- **The uneven spatial distribution of public nature in cities disad-vantages low-income residents and residents of color.** Neigh-borhoods where median family incomes are lower or where more people of color live have less public tree cover along city streets and in parks. These patterns may be due to local governments and their agents basing their decisions about the allocation of public funds and services for trees, in part, on the wealth, race, or ethnicity of residents. They may also result from wealthy and/or White residents having greater access to planning processes related to trees and their maintenance. Citywide inequities in tree cover matter because they are unjust and, by depriving a significant portion of a city's popula-tion of the physical and mental health benefits of nature, weaken a city's economy, politics, and culture. Educating yourself and others about the inequities in access to nature in your city is part and parcel of conserving nature and creating healthier cities for all.

These main messages are a very small sample of the multitude of ways that humans relate to nature where they live. In closing this book,

I hope this book has inspired you to get reacquainted with nature where you live.

I'd like to draw your attention to one more important resource that will expose you to very different, but complementary, interactions between yourself and nature. In 2021, I attended the virtual Nature of Cities Festival that brought together more than two thousand participants from seventy-two countries to share their stories and experience of urban nature from their diverse perspectives. For a glorious five days, I explored the Ecological Urban Arts Exhibition of fine art; watched films and read poetry on urban nature; began to understand the role that urban nature plays in human culture, learning, community-making, and spirituality; delved deeper into urban nature as a critical element of environmental justice, equitable food systems, and democracy; and discussed urban nature-based solutions to seemingly intractable environmental problems like climate change. Each of these ways of conceptualizing and understanding urban nature allows us to explore and deepen our connection with it. My wish is that this book has inspired you to re-acquaint yourself with nature where you live and to get to know all the wondrous ways it intersects with your life.

NOTES

CHAPTER 1

1. Jennifer Y. Lamb, and Matthew P. Davis. "Salamanders and Other Amphibians Are Aglow with Biofluorescence." *Scientific Reports* 10 (2020): 2821; Alberto Joven, Ahmed Elewa, and András Simon. "Model Systems for Regeneration: Salamanders." *Development* 146 (2019): dev167700.

2. Judith A. Leech, William C. Nelson, Richard T. Burnett, Shawn Aaron, and Mark E. Raizenne. "It's About Time: A Comparison of Canadian and American Time–Activity Patterns." *Journal of Exposure Analysis and Environmental Epidemiology* 12 (2002): 427–32.

3. R.E.A. Almond, M. Grooten, and T. Petersen, eds. *Living Planet Report 2020: Bending the Curve of Biodiversity Loss*. Gland, Switzerland: WWF, 2020.

4. Kenneth V. Rosenberg, Adriaan M. Dokter, Peter J. Blancher, John R. Sauer, Adam C. Smith, Paul A. Smith, Jessica C. Stanton *et al.* "Decline of the North American Avifauna." *Science* 366 (2019): 120–24.

5. Bradford C. Lister, and Andres Garcia. "Climate-Driven Declines in Arthropod Abundance Restructure a Rainforest Food Web." *Proceedings of the National Academy of Sciences* 115 (2018): E10398; Caspar A. Hallmann, Martin Sorg, Eelke Jongejans, Henk Siepel, Nick Hofland, Heinz Schwan, Werner Stenmans *et al.* "More Than 75 Percent Decline Over 27 Years in Total Flying Insect Biomass in Protected Areas." *PLoS ONE* 12 (2017): 10.

6. Sandra Díaz, Josef Settele, Eduardo S. Brondízio E.S., Hien T. Ngo, Maximilien Guèze, John Agard, Almut Arneth *et al.*, eds. *Summary for Policymakers of the Global Assessment Report on Biodiversity and Ecosystem Services of the Intergovernmental Science–Policy Platform on Biodiversity and Ecosystem Services*. Bonn, Germany: IPBES secretariat, 2019.

7. Protected Planet Report 2020. "Chapter 3 Coverage." Updated May 2021. https://livereport.protectedplanet.net/chapter-3; James R. Allan, Hugh P. Possingham, Scott C. Atkinson, Anthony Waldron, Moreno Di Marco, Stuart H. M. Butchart, Vanessa M. Adams *et al.* "The Minimum Land Area Requiring Conservation Attention to Safeguard Biodiversity." *Science* 376 (2022): 1094–101.

8. Kim Parker, Juliana Menasce Horowitz, Anna Brown, Richard Fry, D'Vera Cohn, and Ruth Igielnik. *What Unites and Divides Urban, Suburban and Rural Communities*. Washington, DC: Pew Research Center, 2018.

CHAPTER 2

1. Camilo Mora, Derek P. Tittensor, Sina Adl, Alastair G. B. Simpson, and Boris Worm. "How Many Species Are There on Earth and in the Ocean?" *PLoS Biology* 9 (2011): e1001127.

2. Manu Saunders. "How Many Species Live in Your Home?" *Ecology is not a dirty word,* May 6, 2020. https://ecologyisnotadirtyword.com/2020/05/06/how-many-species -live-in-your-home/.

3. Benjamin Cull. "Potential for Online Crowdsourced Biological Recording Data to Complement Surveillance for Arthropod Vectors." *PLoS ONE* 16 (2021): e0250382; Reut Vardi, Oded Berger-Tal, and Uri Roll. "iNaturalist Insights Illuminate COVID-19 Effects on Large Mammals in Urban Centers." *Biological Conservation* 254 (2021): 108953.

4. Albert Barberán, Robert R. Dunn, Brian J. Reich, Krishna Pacifici, Eric B. Laber, Holly L. Menninger, James M. Morton *et al.* "The Ecology of Microscopic Life in Household Dust." *Proceedings of the Royal Society B: Biological Sciences* 282 (2015): 20151139.

5. Lenny Lampel, email to author, July 17, 2020.

6. Gary W. Luck. "A Review of the Relationships Between Human Population Density and Biodiversity." *Biological Reviews* 82 (2007): 607–45.

7. Marco Pautasso. "Scale Dependence of the Correlation Between Human Population Presence and Vertebrate and Plant Species Richness." *Ecology Letters* 10 (2007): 16–24.

8. A.G. Tansley. "The Use and Abuse of Vegetational Terms and Concepts." *Ecology* 16 (1935): 284–307.

9. Suzanne W. Simard, W. Jean Roach, Camille E. Defrenne, Brian J. Pickles, Eva N. Snyder, Alyssa Robinson, and Les M. Lavkulich. "Harvest Intensity Effects on Carbon Stocks and Biodiversity Are Dependent on Regional Climate in Douglas-Fir Forests of British Columbia." *Frontiers in Forests and Global Change* 3 (2020): 88.

10. Elyn R. Humphreys, T. Andrew Black, Kai Morgenstern, Tiebo Cai, Gordon B. Drewitt, Zoran Nesic, and J. A. Trofymow. "Carbon Dioxide Fluxes in Coastal Douglas-Fir Stands at Different Stages of Development After Clearcut Harvesting." *Agricultural and Forest Meteorology* 140 (2006): 6–22.

11. Ronald Kellett, Andreas Christen, Nicholas C. Coops, Michael van der Laan, Ben Crawford, Thoreau Rory Tooke, and Inna Olchovski. "A Systems Approach to Carbon Cycling and Emissions Modeling at an Urban Neighborhood Scale." *Landscape and Urban Planning* 110 (2013): 48–58.

12. Kim Parker, Juliana Menasce Horowitz, Anna Brown, Richard Fry, D'Vera Cohn, and Ruth Igielnik. *What Unites and Divides Urban, Suburban and Rural Communities.* Washington, DC: Pew Research Center, 2018.

13. Climate Central. *Hot Zones: Urban Heat Islands.* Princeton: Climate Central, 2021.

14. David M. Hondula, Matei Georgescu, and Robert C. Balling Jr. "Challenges Associated with Projecting Urbanization-Induced Heat-Related Mortality." *Science of the Total EnvironmenT* 490 (2014): 538–44.

15. Lewis H. Ziska, Dennis E. Gebhard, David A. Frenz, Shaun Faulkner, Benjamin D. Singer, and James G. Straka. "Cities as Harbingers of Climate Change: Common Ragweed, Urbanization, and Public Health." *Journal of Allergy and Clinical Immunology* 111 (2003): 290–95.

16. Lewis H. Ziska, "Climate, Carbon Dioxide, and Plant-Based Aero-Allergens: A Deeper Botanical Perspective." *Frontiers in Allergy* 2 (2021): 714724; Samuel C. Zipper, Jason Schatz, Aditya Singh, Christopher J. Kucharik, Philip. A. Townsend, and Steven P. Loheide II. "Urban Heat Island Impacts on Plant Phenology: Intra-Urban Variability and Response to Land Cover." *Environmental Research Letters* 11 (2016): 054023.

17. Ricardo Vieira Araujo, Marcos Roberto Albertini, André Luis Costa-da-Silva, Lincoln Suesdek, Nathália Cristina Soares Franceschi, Nancy Marçal Bastos, Gizelda Katz *et al*. "São Paulo Urban Heat Islands Have a Higher Incidence of Dengue Than Other Urban Areas." *Brazilian Journal of Infectious Diseases* 19 (2015): 146–55.

18. Adam G. Dale, and Steven D. Frank. "The Effects of Urban Warming on Herbivore Abundance and Street Tree Condition." *PLoS ONE* 9: e102996.

19. Omid Kardan, Peter Gozdyra, Bratislav Misic, Faisal Moola, Lyle J. Palmer, Tomáš Paus, and Marc G. Berman. "Neighborhood Greenspace and Health in a Large Urban Center." *Scientific Reports* 5: 11610; Wei-Lun Tsai, Amy J. S. Davis, and Laura E. Jackson. "Associations Between Types of Greenery Along Neighborhood Roads and Weight Status in Different Climates." *Urban Forestry & Urban Greening* 41 (2019): 104–17; Blair Alexandra Burley. "Green Infrastructure and Violence: Do New Street Trees Mitigate Violent Crime?" *Health & Place* 54 (2018): 43–49; Angel Hsu, Glenn Sheriff, Tirthankar Chakraborty, and Diego Manya. "Disproportionate Exposure to Urban Heat Island Intensity Across Major US Cities." *Nature Communications* 12 (2021): 2721; Shannon Lea Watkins, and Ed Gerrish. "The Relationship Between Urban Forests and Race: A Meta-Analysis." *Journal of Environmental Management* 209 (2018): 152–68.

20. S.T.A. Pickett, M.L. Cadenasso, J.M. Grove, C.H. Nilon, R.V. Pouyat, W.C. Zipperer, and R. Costanza. "Urban Ecological Systems: Linking Terrestrial Ecological, Physical, and Socioeconomic Components of Metropolitan Areas." *Annual Review of Ecology and Systematics* 32 (2001): 127–57.

21. Lauren Frayer. "Air Pollution in Northern India is Causing Partial Lockdowns in New Delhi." *NPR*, November 16, 2021. https://www.npr.org/2021/11/16/1056263662/air-pollution-in-northern-india-is-causing-partial-lockdowns.

22. Nancy B. Grimm, J. Morgan Grove, Steward T A. Pickett, and Charles L. Redman. "Integrated Approaches to Long-Term Studies of Urban Ecological Systems." *BioScience* 50 (2000): 571–84.

23. Lillian Collins, Grant D. Paton, and Sara A. Gagné. "Testing the Likeable, Therefore Abundant Hypothesis: Bird Species Likeability by Urban Residents Varies Significantly with Species Traits." *Land* 10 (2021): 487.

24. Marina Alberti, John M. Marzluff, Eric Shulenberger, Gordon Bradley, Clare Ryan, and Craig Zumbrunnen. "Integrating Humans into Ecology: Opportunities and Challenges for Studying Urban Ecosystems." *BioScience* 53 (2003): 1169–79.

CHAPTER 3

1. Gustave Axelson. "EBirders Surpass 1 Billion Observations And Break Global Big Day Records." *All About Birds*, June 25, 2021. https://www.allaboutbirds.org/news/ebirders-surpass-1-billion-observations-and-break-global-big-day-records/.

2. Audrey L. Mayer, Brian Buma, Amélie Davis, Sara A. Gagné, E. Louise Loudermilk, Robert M. Scheller, Fiona K. A. Schmiegelow, Yolanda F. Wiersma, and Janet Franklin. "How Landscape Ecology Informs Global Land-Change Science and Policy." *BioScience* 66 (2016): 458–69.

3. Alessandro Ossola, Dexter Locke, Brenda Lin, and Emily Minor. "Yards Increase Forest Connectivity in Urban Landscapes." *Landscape Ecology* 34 (2019): 2935–48; Hashem Akbari, L. Shea Rose, and Haider Taha. "Analyzing the Land Cover of an Urban Environment Using High-Resolution Orthophotos." *Landscape and Urban Planning* 63 (2003): 1–14; Alison Loram, Philip H. Warren, and Kevin J. Gaston. "Urban Domestic Gardens (XIV): The Characteristics of Gardens in Five Cities." *Environmental Management* 42 (2008): 361–76.

4. Karl L. Evans, Stuart E. Newson, and Kevin J. Gaston. "Habitat Influences on Urban Avian Assemblages." *Ibis* 151 (2009): 19–39.

5. Dagmar Haase, Clemens Jänicke, and Thilo Wellmann. "Front and Back Yard Green Analysis with Subpixel Vegetation Fractions from Earth Observation Data in a City." *Landscape and Urban Planning* 182 (2019): 44–54.

6. Adam C. Smith, Charles M. Francis, and Lenore Fahrig. "Similar Effects of Residential and Non-Residential Vegetation on Bird Diversity in Suburban Neighbourhoods." *Urban Ecosystems* 17 (2014): 27–44.

7. Susannah B. Lerman, and Paige S. Warren. "The Conservation Value of Residential Yards: Linking Birds and People." *Ecological Applications* 21 (2011): 1327–39.

8. J. Amy Belaire, Christopher J. Whelan, and Emily S. Minor. "Having our Yards and Sharing Them Too: The Collective Effects of Yards on Native Bird Species in an Urban Landscape." *Ecological Applications* 24 (2014): 2132–43; G.D. Daniels, and J. B. Kirkpatrick. "Does Variation in Garden Characteristics Influence the Conservation of Birds in Suburbia?" *Biological Conservation* 133 (2006): 326–35.

9. S.K. Willson, I. A. Okunlola, and J. A. Novak. "Birds Be Safe: Can a Novel Cat Collar Reduce Avian Mortality by Domestic Cats (Felis Catus)?" *Global Ecology and Conservation* 3 (January 1, 2015): 359–66.

10. Karin T. Burghardt, Douglas W. Tallamy, and W. Gregory Shriver. "Impact of Native Plants on Bird and Butterfly Biodiversity in Suburban Landscapes." *Conservation Biology* 23, no. 1 (2009): 219–24; Desirée L. Narango, Douglas W. Tallamy, and Peter P. Marra. "Nonnative Plants Reduce Population Growth of an Insectivorous Bird." *Proceedings of the National Academy of Sciences* 115 (2018): 11549–54.

11. Mark A. Davis, Matthew K. Chew, Richard J. Hobbs, Ariel E. Lugo, John J. Ewel, Geerat J. Vermeij, James H. Brown *et al.* "Don't Judge Species on Their Origins." *Nature* 474 (2011): 153–54.

12. Travis E. Wilcoxen, David J. Horn, Brianna M. Hogan, Cody N. Hubble, Sarah J. Huber, Joseph Flamm, Madeline Knott *et al.* "Effects of Bird-Feeding Activities on the

Health of Wild Birds." *Conservation Physiology* 3, no. 1 (December 21, 2015): cov058; Kate E. Plummer, Kate Risely, Mike P. Toms, and Gavin M. Siriwardena. "The Composition of British Bird Communities Is Associated with Long-Term Garden Bird Feeding." *Nature Communications* 10 (2019): 2088; Gillian N. Robb, Robbie A. McDonald, Dan E. Chamberlain, S. James Reynolds, Timothy J. E. Harrison, and Stuart Bearhop. "Winter Feeding of Birds Increases Productivity in the Subsequent Breeding Season." *Biology Letters* 4 (2008): 220–23.

13. Rachel L. White, Katie Eberstein, and Dawn M. Scott. "Birds in the Playground: Evaluating the Effectiveness of an Urban Environmental Education Project in Enhancing School Children's Awareness, Knowledge and Attitudes Towards Local Wildlife." *PLoS ONE* 13 (2018): e0193993.

14. Robert M. Pyle. "The Extinction of Experience: A Loss of Neighborhood Species Endangers Our Experience of Nature." *Horticulture* 56 (1978): 64–67.

15. Thomas F. Juster, Hiromi Ono, and Frank P. Stafford. *Changing Times of American Youth: 1981–2003*. Ann Arbor, Michigan: Institute for Social Research, University of Michigan, 2004. http://ns.umich.edu/Releases/2004/Nov04/teen_time_report.pdf.

16. Sandra L. Hofferth, "Changes in American Children's Time–1997 to 2003." *electronic International Journal of Time Use Research* 6 (2009): 26–47.

17. Rhonda Clements. "An Investigation of the Status of Outdoor Play." *Contemporary Issues in Early Childhood* 5 (2004): 68–80.

18. Judith A. Leech, William C. Nelson, Richard T. Burnett, Shawn Aaron, and Mark E. Raizenne. "It's About Time: A Comparison of Canadian and American Time–Activity Patterns." *Journal of Exposure Analysis and Environmental Epidemiology* 12 (2002): 427–32.

19. Lincoln R. Larson, Gary T. Green, and H. K. Cordell. "Children's Time Outdoors: Results and Implications of the National Kids Survey." *Journal of Park and Recreation Administration* 29 (2011): 1–20.

20. Natural England. *Childhood and Nature: A Survey on Changing Relationships with Nature Across Generations*. Worcester, UK: Natural England, 2009. http://publications.naturalengland.org.uk/publication/5853658314964992.

21. See note 7 above; Diane Hope, Corinna Gries, Weixing Zhu, William F. Fagan, Charles L. Redman, Nancy B. Grimm, Amy L. Nelson, Chris Martin, and Ann Kinzig. "Socioeconomics Drive Urban Plant Diversity." *Proceedings of the National Academy of Sciences* 100 (2003): 8788–92.

22. Shannon Lea Watkins, and Ed Gerrish. "The Relationship Between Urban Forests and Race: A Meta-Analysis." *Journal of Environmental Management* 209 (2018): 152–68.

23. Alessandro Rigolon. "A Complex Landscape of Inequity in Access to Urban Parks: A Literature Review." *Landscape and Urban Planning* 153 (2016): 160–69.

24. Masachi Soga, Kevin J. Gaston, Tomoyo F. Koyanagi, Kiyo Kurisu, and Keisuke Hanaki. "Urban Residents' Perceptions of Neighbourhood Nature: Does the Extinction of Experience Matter?" *Biological Conservation* 203 (2016): 143–50.

25. Margaret Renkl. "This 'Shazam' for Birds Could Help Save Them." *New York Times*, July 26, 2021. https://www.nytimes.com/2021/07/26/opinion/cornell-birdsong-id-app.html.

26. Julie Whitburn, Wayne Linklater, and Wokje Abrahamse. "Meta-Analysis of Human Connection to Nature and Proenvironmental Behavior." *Conservation Biology* 34 (2019): 180–93.

27. Robert R. Dunn, Michael C. Gavin, Monica C. Sanchez, and Jennifer N. Solomon. "The Pigeon Paradox: Dependence of Global Conservation on Urban Nature." *Conservation Biology* 20 (2006): 1814–16.

28. See note 14 above.

29. Kenneth V. Rosenberg, Adriaan M. Dokter, Peter J. Blancher, John R. Sauer, Adam C. Smith, Paul A. Smith, Jessica C. Stanton *et al.* "Decline of the North American Avifauna." *Science* 366 (2019): 120–24.

CHAPTER 4

1. Sara A. Gagné, Jennifer L. Bates, and Richard O. Bierregaard. "The Effects of Road and Landscape Characteristics on the Likelihood of a Barred Owl (*Strix varia*)–Vehicle Collision." *Urban Ecosystems* 18 (2015): 1007–20.

2. Richard O. Bierregaard. "Barred Owls: A Nocturnal Generalist Thrives in Wooded, Suburban Habitats." In *Urban Raptors: Ecology and Conservation of Birds of Prey in Cities,* edited by Clint W. Boal, and Cheryl R. Dykstra, 138–51. Washington, DC: Island Press, 2018.

3. See note 1 above.

4. Martin A. Schlaepfer, Michael C. Runge, and Paul W. Sherman. "Ecological and Evolutionary Traps." *Trends in Ecology & Evolution* 17 (2002): 474–80.

5. Lenore Fahrig, John H. Pedlar, Shealagh E. Pope, Philip D. Taylor, and John F. Wegner. "Effect of Road Traffic on Amphibian Density." *Biological Conservation* 73 (1995): 177–82.

6. Kurt H. Riitters, and James D. Wickham. "How Far to the Nearest Road?" *Frontiers in Ecology and the Environment* 1 (2003): 125–29.

7. Lenore Fahrig, and Trina Rytwinski. "Effects of Roads on Animal Abundance: An Empirical Review and Synthesis." *Ecology and Society* 14 (2009): 21; Raphaela Pagany. "Wildlife–Vehicle Collisions—Influencing Factors, Data Collection and Research Method." *Biological Conservation* 251 (2020): 108758.

8. James H. Baxter–Gilbert, Julia L. Riley, Christopher J. H. Neufeld, Jacqueline D. Litzgus, and David Lesbarrères. "Road Mortality Potentially Responsible for Billions of Pollinating Insect Deaths Annually." *Journal of Insect Conservation* 19 (2015): 1029–35.

9. S. Loss, Tom Will, and Peter P. Marra. "Estimation of Bird–Vehicle Collision Mortality on U.S. Roads." *Journal of Wildlife Management* 78 (2014): 763–71.

10. See note 7 above.

11. H. Howell, and Richard A. Seigel. "The Effects of Road Mortality on Small, Isolated Turtle Populations." *Journal of Herpetology* 53 (2019): 39–46; Brian A. Crawford, Clinton T. Moore, Terry M. Norton, and John C. Maerz. "Integrated Analysis for Population Estimation, Management Impact Evaluation, and Decision–Making for a Declining Species." *Biological Conservation* 222 (2018): 33–43.

12. Clara Grilo, Luis Borda–de–Água, Pedro Beja, Eric Goolsby, Kylie Soanes, Aliza le Roux, Elena Koroleva *et al.* "Conservation Threats from Roadkill in the Global Road Network. *Global Ecology and Biogeography* 30 (2021): 2200–10.

13. Kristina Chyn, Te–En Lin, Yu–Kai Chen, Chih–Yun Chen, and Lee A. Fitzgerald. "The Magnitude of Roadkill in Taiwan: Patterns and Consequences Revealed by Citizen Science." *Biological Conservation* 237 (2019): 317–26.

14. David L. Wagner, Eliza M. Grames, Matthew L. Forister, May R. Berenbaum, and David Stopak. "Insect Decline in the Anthropocene: Death by a Thousand Cuts." *Proceedings of the National Academy of Sciences* 118 (2021): e2023989118.

15. Trina Rytwinski, and Lenore Fahrig. "The Impacts of Roads and Traffic on Terrestrial Animal Populations." In *Handbook of Road Ecology*, edited by Rodney van der Ree, Daniel J. Smith, and Clara Grilo, 237–46. Chichester, UK: John Wiley & Sons, Ltd, 2015.

16. Fraser Shilling, Tricia Nguyen, Malak Saleh, Min Khant Kyaw, Karla Tapia, Gabrielle Trujillo, and Mireya Bejarano *et al.* "A Reprieve from US Wildlife Mortality on Roads During the COVID–19 Pandemic." *Biological Conservation* 256 (2021): 109013.

17. United States Environmental Protection Agency. "Fast Facts on Transportation Greenhouse Gas Emissions." Accessed August 29, 2022. https://www.epa.gov/green vehicles/fast–facts–transportation–greenhouse–gas–emissions.

18. James M.W. Ryalls, Ben Langford, Neil J. Mullinger, Lisa M. Bromfield, Eiko Nemitz, Christian Pfrang, and Robbie D. Girling. "Anthropogenic Air Pollutants Reduce Insect–Mediated Pollination Services." *Environmental Pollution* 297 (2022): 118847.

19. Nguyen Tien Hoang, and Keiichiro Kanemoto. "Mapping the Deforestation Footprint of Nations Reveals Growing Threat to Tropical Forests." *Nature Ecology & Evolution* 5 (2021): 845–53.

20. United States Environmental Protection Agency. "Global Emissions by Economic Sector." Accessed August 29, 2022. https://www.epa.gov/ghgemissions/global–green house–gas–emissions–data#Sector.

21. Chris Wilcox, Erik Van Sebille, and Britta Denise Hardesty. "Threat of Plastic Pollution to Seabirds Is Global, Pervasive, and Increasing." *Proceedings of the National Academy of Sciences* 112, no. 38 (2015): 11899–904.

22. Jean C. Buzby, Hodan Farah Wells, and Jeanine Bentley. "ERS's Food Loss Data Help Inform the Food Waste Discussion." *Amber Waves*, June 3, 2013. https://www.ers .usda.gov/amber–waves/2013/june/ers–food–loss–data–help–inform–the–food–waste –discussion/.

23. Daniel L. Hernández, Dena M. Vallano, Erika S. Zavaleta, Zdravka Tzankova, Jae R. Pasari, Stuart Weiss, Paul C. Selmants, and Corinne Morozumi. "Nitrogen Pollution Is Linked to US Listed Species Declines." *Bioscience* 66, no. 3 (2016): 213–22.

24. Tyson Wepprich, Jeffrey R. Adrion, Leslie Ries, Jerome Wiedmann, and Nick M. Haddad. "Butterfly Abundance Declines over 20 Years of Systematic Monitoring in Ohio, USA." *PLOS ONE* 14, no. 7 (2019): e0216270.

25. Ralf Schulz, Sascha Bub, Lara L. Petschick, Sebastian Stehle, and Jakob Wolfram. "Applied Pesticide Toxicity Shifts Toward Plants and Invertebrates, Even in GM Crops." *Science* 372, no. 6537 (2021): 81–84.

26. Sarah E. Hobbie, Jacques C. Finlay, Benjamin D. Janke, Daniel A. Nidzgorski, Dylan B. Millet, and Lawrence A. Baker. "Contrasting Nitrogen and Phosphorus Budgets in Urban Watersheds and Implications for Managing Urban Water Pollution." *Proceedings of the National Academy of Sciences* 114, no. 16 (2017): 4177–82.

27. Scott R. Loss, Tom Will, Sara S. Loss, and Peter P. Marra. "Bird–Building Collisions in the United States: Estimates of Annual Mortality and Species Vulnerability." *Condor* 116, no. 1 (January 2014): 8–23; Scott R. Loss, Tom Will, and Peter P. Marra. "Direct Mortality of Birds from Anthropogenic Causes." *Annual Review of Ecology, Evolution, and Systematics* 46, no. 1 (2015): 99–120.

28. Benjamin M. Winger, Brian C. Weeks, Andrew Farnsworth, Andrew W. Jones, Mary Hennen, and David E. Willard. "Nocturnal Flight–Calling Behaviour Predicts Vulnerability to Artificial Light in Migratory Birds." *Proceedings of the Royal Society B: Biological Sciences* 286 (2019): 20190364.

29. Emma Coulthard, John Norrey, Chris Shortall, and W. Edwin Harris. "Ecological Traits Predict Population Changes in Moths." *Biological Conservation* 233 (May 1, 2019): 213–19.

30. See note 15 above; Daniel A. Soluk, Deanna S. Zercher, and Amy M. Worthington. "Influence of Roadways on Patterns of Mortality and Flight Behavior of Adult Dragonflies near Wetland Areas." *Biological Conservation* 144, no. 5 (May 1, 2011): 1638–43; Anders Paper Møller, Helga Erritzoe, Johannes Erritzoe. "A Behavioral Ecology Approach to Traffic Accidents: Interspecific Variation in Causes of Traffic Casualties Among Birds." *Zoological Research* 32 (2011): 115–27.

31. Matthew J. Aresco, "The Effect of Sex–Specific Terrestrial Movements and Roads on the Sex Ratio of Freshwater Turtles." *Biological Conservation* 123, no. 1 (May 1, 2005): 37–44.

32. Roy V. Rea, and Roy V. Rea Sr. "Of Moose and Mud." *Public Roads* 69 (2005). https://highways.dot.gov/public–roads/septemberoctober–2005/moose–and–mud; Sergio A. Lambertucci, Karina L. Speziale, Thomas E. Rogers, and Juan M. Morales. "How Do Roads Affect the Habitat Use of an Assemblage of Scavenging Raptors?" *Biodiversity and Conservation* 18, no. 8 (July 1, 2009): 2063–74; Francis D. Meunier, Christophe Verheyden, and Pierre Jouventin. "Use of Roadsides by Diurnal Raptors in Agricultural Landscapes." *Biological Conservation* 92, no. 3 (March 1, 2000): 291–98; Ronald L. Mumme, Stephan J. Schoech, Glen E. Woolfenden, and John W. Fitzpatrick. "Life and Death in the Fast Lane: Demographic Consequences of Road Mortality in the Florida Scrub–Jay." *Conservation Biology* 14, no. 2 (2000): 501–12; Cheryl S. Brehme, Jeff A. Tracey, Leroy R. McClenaghan, and Robert N. Fisher. "Permeability of Roads to Movement of Scrubland Lizards and Small Mammals." *Conservation Biology* 27 (2013): 710–20; Charles R. Brown, and Mary Bomberger Brown. "Where Has All the Road Kill Gone?" *Current Biology* 23, no. 6 (March 18, 2013): R233–34.

33. K.A. Zeller, D.W. Wattles, L. Conlee, and S. Destefano. "Response of Female Black Bears to a High–Density Road Network and Identification of Long–Term Road Mitigation Sites." *Animal Conservation* 24, no. 2 (2021): 167–80.

34. Arild Husby, and Magne Husby. "Interspecific Analysis of Vehicle Avoidance Behavior in Birds." *Behavioral Ecology* 25, no. 3 (May 1, 2014): 504–8.

35. See note 32 above.

36. Julie Bouchard, Adam Ford, Felix Eigenbrod, and Lenore Fahrig. "Behavioral Responses of Northern Leopard Frogs (*Rana Pipiens*) to Roads and Traffic: Implications for Population Persistence." *Ecology and Society* 14, no. 2 (October 14, 2009): 23.

37. Marc J. Mazerolle, Matthieu Huot, and Mireille Gravel. "Behavior of Amphibians on the Road in Response to Car Traffic." *Herpetologica* 61 (2005): 380–88.

38. Conservation Evidence. "Install Culverts or Tunnels as Road Crossings." Accessed August 29, 2022. https://www.conservationevidence.com/actions/884#.

39. Conservation Evidence. "Install Barrier Fencing and Underpasses Along Roads." Accessed August 29, 2022. https://www.conservationevidence.com/actions/2571; Conservation Evidence. "Install Overpasses Over Roads/Railways." Accessed August 29, 2022. https://www.conservationevidence.com/actions/2526.

40. Marcel P. Huijser, Christa Mosler–Berger, Mattias Olsson, and Martin Strein. "Wildlife Warning Signs and Animal Detection Systems Aimed at Reducing Wildlife–Vehicle Collisions." In *Handbook of Road Ecology*, edited by Rodney van der Ree, Daniel J. Smith, and Clara Grilo, 198–212. Chichester, UK: John Wiley & Sons, Ltd, 2015.

41. M.P. Huijser, P. McGowen, J. Fuller, A. Hardy, A. Kociolek, A.P. Clevenger, D. Smith, and R. Ament. *Wildlife–Vehicle Collision Reduction Study: Report to Congress.* McLean, VA: United States Department of Transportation, Federal Highway Administration, 2008.

42. Joseph Stromberg. "Why scientists have mapped 29,777 instances of roadkill across California." *Vox*, April 4, 2015. https://www.vox.com/2015/4/4/8341263/road-kill–maps; R.J. Safford, J.S. Ash, J.W. Duckworth, M.G. Telfer, and C. Zewdie. "A New Species of Nightjar from Ethiopia." *Ibis* 137 (1995): 301–07.

43. Stéphanie Périquet, Lizanne Roxburgh, Aliza le Roux, and Wendy J. Collinson. "Testing the Value of Citizen Science for Roadkill Studies: A Case Study from South Africa." *Frontiers in Ecology and Evolution* 6 (2018): 15.

44. Diemer Vercayie, and Marc Herremans. "Citizen Science and Smartphones Take Roadkill Monitoring to the Next Level." *Nature Conservation* 11 (July 28, 2015): 29–40.

45. David P. Waetjen, and Fraser M. Shilling. "Large Extent Volunteer Roadkill and Wildlife Observation Systems as Sources of Reliable Data." *Frontiers in Ecology and Evolution* 5 (2017): 89.

46. Adam Millard–Ball. "The Width and Value of Residential Streets." *Journal of the American Planning Association* 88, no. 1 (January 2, 2022): 30–43.

47. E. Gregory McPherson, Natalie van Doorn, and John de Goede. "Structure, Function and Value of Street Trees in California, USA." *Urban Forestry & Urban Greening* 17 (June 1, 2016): 104–15.

48. F.D. Cowett, and N.L. Bassuk. "Statewide Assessment of Street Trees in New York State, USA." *Urban Forestry & Urban Greening* 13, no. 2 (January 1, 2014): 213–20; Anne B. Cumming, Daniel B. Twardus, and William D. Smith. *National Forest Health Monitoring Program: Maryland and Massachusetts Street Tree Monitoring Pilot Projects.* Newtown Square, Pennsylvania: United States Department of Agriculture, Forest Service, 2006; Tom Treiman, Nick Kuhn, Justine Gartner, and Ann Koenig. *Missouri's 2010 Street Tree Inventory.* Colombia, Missouri: Missouri Department of Conservation, 2011.

49. See note 48 above; Davey Resource Group. "Indiana's Street Tree Species Distribution." Accessed August 29, 2022. http://www.in.gov/dnr/forestry/files/Fo-INSpecies-DistributionUrbanTrees709.pdf; Anne B. Cumming, Daniel B. Twardus, Robert Hoehn, David J. Nowak, Manfred Mielke, Richard Rideout, Helen Butalla, and Patricia Lebow. *National Forest Health Monitoring Program: Wisconsin Street Tree Assessment 2002–2003.* Newtown Square, Pennsylvania: United States Department of Agriculture, Forest Service, 2008.

50. Shawn M. Landry, and Jayajit Chakraborty. "Street Trees and Equity: Evaluating the Spatial Distribution of an Urban Amenity." *Environment and Planning A: Economy and Space* 41, no. 11 (November 1, 2009): 2651–70.

51. Jian Lin, Qiang Wang, and Xiaojiang Li. "Socioeconomic and Spatial Inequalities of Street Tree Abundance, Species Diversity, and Size Structure in New York City." *Landscape and Urban Planning* 206 (February 1, 2021): 103992.

52. See note 47 above.

53. Tom Treiman, Nick Kuhn, Justine Gartner, and Ann Koenig. *Missouri's 2010 Street Tree Economics.* Colombia, Missouri: Missouri Department of Conservation, 2011.

54. American Society of Civil Engineers, Region 9. *California's Surface Transportation Report Card: An Analysis of Roads, Bridges, and Transit.* American Society of Civil Engineers, 2018.

55. Missouri House of Representatives. "Report of the 21st Century Missouri Transportation Systems Task Force: Recommendations to Support Economic Competitiveness, Transportation Reliability, and Highway Safety." Accessed August 29, 2022. https://house.mo.gov/billtracking/bills181/commit/rpt1723/Transportation.pdf.

56. Wei–Lun Tsai, Leah Yngve, Yuhong Zhou, Kirsten M. M. Beyer, Andrew Bersch, Kristen M. Malecki, and Laura E. Jackson. "Street–Level Neighborhood Greenery Linked to Active Transportation: A Case Study in Milwaukee and Green Bay, WI, USA." *Landscape and Urban Planning* 191 (November 1, 2019): 103619.

57. Wei–Lun Tsai, Amy J. S. Davis, and Laura E. Jackson. "Associations between Types of Greenery along Neighborhood Roads and Weight Status in Different Climates." *Urban Forestry & Urban Greening* 41 (May 1, 2019): 104–17.

58. Blair Alexandra Burley. "Green Infrastructure and Violence: Do New Street Trees Mitigate Violent Crime?" *Health & Place* 54 (November 1, 2018): 43–49.

59. Frances E. Kuo, and William C. Sullivan. "Aggression and Violence in the Inner City: Effects of Environment via Mental Fatigue." *Environment and Behavior* 33, no. 4 (July 1, 2001): 543–71.

60. Green Cities: Good Health. "Crime & Public Safety." Accessed August 29, 2022. https://depts.washington.edu/hhwb/Thm_Crime.html.

61. Richard J. Hauer, and Ward Peterson. *Municipal Tree Care and Management in the United States: A 2014 Urban & Community Forestry Census of Tree Activities.* Stevens Point, Wisconsin: College of Natural Resources, University of Wisconsin–Stevens Point, 2016. https://www.uwsp.edu/cnr/Documents/MTCUS%20%20Forestry/Municipal%202014%20Final%20Report.pdf.

62. See note 47 above.

63. See note 48 above.

64. Jacqueline W.T. Lu, Erika S. Svendsen, Lindsay K. Campbell, Jennifer Greenfeld, Jessie Braden, Kristen L. King, and Nancy Falxa-Raymond. "Biological, Social, and Urban Design Factors Affecting Young Street Tree Mortality in New York City." *Cities and the Environment* 3 (2010): 1–15.

CHAPTER 5

1. Galen Cranz. *The Politics of Park Design: A History of Urban Parks in America*. Cambridge, MA: The MIT Press, 1989.

2. Jeffrey Smith. *The Rural Cemetery Movement: Places of Paradox in Nineteenth-Century America*. Lanham, MD: Lexington Books, 2017.

3. Galen Cranz, and Michael Boland. "Defining the Sustainable Park: A Fifth Model for Urban Parks." *Landscape Journal* 23, no. 2 (January 1, 2004): 102–20.

4. Kong-Wah Sing, Wan F.A. Jusoh, Nor Rasidah Hashim, and John-James Wilson. "Urban Parks: Refuges for Tropical Butterflies in Southeast Asia?" *Urban Ecosystems* 19, no. 3 (September 1, 2016): 1131–47.

5. Robert H. MacArthur. "Population Ecology of Some Warblers of Northeastern Coniferous Forests." *Ecology* 39, no. 4 (1958): 599–619.

6. Michael L. Rosenzweig. *Species Diversity in Space and Time*. Cambridge: Cambridge University Press, 1995.

7. Christoffer Lange-Kabitz, Michael Reich, and Asmus Zoch. "Extensively Managed or Abandoned Urban Green Spaces and Their Habitat Potential for Butterflies." *Basic and Applied Ecology* 54 (August 1, 2021): 85–97.

8. Claudia Bräuniger, Sonja Knapp, Ingolf Kühn, and Stefan Klotz. "Testing Taxonomic and Landscape Surrogates for Biodiversity in an Urban Setting." *Landscape and Urban Planning* 97, no. 4 (September 30, 2010): 283–95.

9. Erik Öckinger, Åse Dannestam, and Henrik G. Smith. "The Importance of Fragmentation and Habitat Quality of Urban Grasslands for Butterfly Diversity." *Landscape and Urban Planning* 93, no. 1 (October 30, 2009): 31–37.

10. Lian Pin Koh, and Navjot S. Sodhi. "Importance of Reserves, Fragments, and Parks for Butterfly Conservation in a Tropical Urban Landscape." *Ecological Applications* 14, no. 6 (2004): 1695–708.

11. Masahiko Kitahara, and Koichi Fujii. "An Island Biogeographical Approach to the Analysis of Butterfly Community Patterns in Newly Designed Parks." *Researches on Population Ecology* 39, no. 1 (June 1, 1997): 23–35.

12. James Barron. "A Secret Section of Central Park Reopens." *New York Times*, May 10, 2016. https://www.nytimes.com/2016/05/11/nyregion/a-secret-section-of-central-park-reopens.html; Central Park Conservancy. "Restoration of the Hallett Nature Sanctuary." Accessed August 29, 2022. https://www.centralparknyc.org/restoration/hallett.

13. Virginie M. Stevens, Camille Turlure, and Michel Baguette. "A Meta-Analysis of Dispersal in Butterflies." *Biological Reviews* 85, no. 3 (2010): 625–42.

14. The Trust for Public Land. *City Park Facts 2021: Acreage and Park System Data*. Distributed by The Trust for Public Land. https://www.tpl.org/2021-city-park-facts.

15. Marie-Hélène Lizée, Thierry Tatoni, and Magali Deschamps-Cottin. "Nested Patterns in Urban Butterfly Species Assemblages: Respective Roles of Plot Management,

Park Layout and Landscape Features." *Urban Ecosystems* 19, no. 1 (March 1, 2016): 205–24.

16. Clàudia Pla-Narbona, Constantí Stefanescu, Joan Pino, Francisco J. Cabrero-Sañudo, Enrique García-Barros, Miguel L. Munguira, and Yolanda Melero. "Butterfly Biodiversity in the City Is Driven by the Interaction of the Urban Landscape and Species Traits: A Call for Contextualised Management." *Landscape Ecology* 37, no. 1 (January 1, 2022): 81–92.

17. Richard A. Fuller, Katherine N. Irvine, Patrick Devine-Wright, Philip H. Warren, and Kevin J. Gaston. "Psychological Benefits of Greenspace Increase with Biodiversity." *Biology Letters* 3, no. 4 (August 22, 2007): 390–94.

18. Rachel Kaplan, and Stephen Kaplan. *The Experience of Nature: A Psychological Perspective*. New York: Cambridge University Press, 1989.

19. Stephen Kaplan, and Rachel Kaplan. *Cognition and Environment: Functioning in an Uncertain World*. New York: Praeger, 1983.

20. Roger S. Ulrich. "Aesthetic and Affective Response to Natural Environment." In *Behavior and the Natural Environment*, edited by Irwin Altman, and Joachim F. Wohlwill, 85–125. Boston: Springer, 1983.

21. Roger S. Ulrich,. "Visual Landscapes and Psychological Well-being." *Landscape Research* 4, no. 1 (March 1, 1979): 17–23.

22. Roger S. Ulrich, Robert F. Simons, Barbara D. Losito, Evelyn Fiorito, Mark A. Miles, and Michael Zelson. "Stress Recovery during Exposure to Natural and Urban Environments." *Journal of Environmental Psychology* 11, no. 3 (September 1, 1991): 201–30.

23. Patrik Grahn, and Ulrika A. Stigsdotter. "Landscape Planning and Stress." *Urban Forestry & Urban Greening* 2, no. 1 (January 1, 2003): 1–18.

24. Mathew P. White, Ian Alcock, Benedict W. Wheeler, and Michael H. Depledge. "Would You Be Happier Living in a Greener Urban Area? A Fixed-Effects Analysis of Panel Data." *Psychological Science* 24, no. 6 (June 1, 2013): 920–28.

25. Helen Hoyle, James Hitchmough, and Anna Jorgensen. "All about the 'Wow Factor'? The Relationships between Aesthetics, Restorative Effect and Perceived Biodiversity in Designed Urban Planting." *Landscape and Urban Planning* 164 (August 1, 2017): 109–23; Giuseppe Carrus, Massimiliano Scopelliti, Raffaele Lafortezza, Giuseppe Colangelo, Francesco Ferrini, Fabio Salbitano, Mariagrazia Agrimi, Luigi Portoghesi, Paolo Semenzato, and Giovanni Sanesi. "Go Greener, Feel Better? The Positive Effects of Biodiversity on the Well-Being of Individuals Visiting Urban and Peri-Urban Green Areas." *Landscape and Urban Planning* 134 (February 1, 2015): 221–28; Karin Kragsig Peschardt, and Ulrika Karlsson Stigsdotter. "Associations between Park Characteristics and Perceived Restorativeness of Small Public Urban Green Spaces." *Landscape and Urban Planning* 112 (April 1, 2013): 26–39.

26. Dörte Martens, Heinz Gutscher, and Nicole Bauer. "Walking in 'Wild' and 'Tended' Urban Forests: The Impact on Psychological Well-Being." *Journal of Environmental Psychology* 31, no. 1 (March 1, 2011): 36–44.

27. Elizabeth K. Nisbet, and John M. Zelenski. "Underestimating Nearby Nature: Affective Forecasting Errors Obscure the Happy Path to Sustainability." *Psychological Science* 22, no. 9 (September 1, 2011): 1101–6.

28. Mathew P. White, Ian Alcock, James Grellier, Benedict W. Wheeler, Terry Hartig, Sara L. Warber, Angie Bone, Michael H. Depledge, and Lora E. Fleming. "Spending at Least 120 Minutes a Week in Nature Is Associated with Good Health and Wellbeing." *Scientific Reports* 9 (2019): 7730.

29. MaryCarol R. Hunter, Brenda W. Gillespie, and Sophie Yu-Pu Chen. "Urban Nature Experiences Reduce Stress in the Context of Daily Life Based on Salivary Biomarkers." *Frontiers in Psychology* 10 (2019): 722.

30. Qing Li, Toshiaki Otsuka, Maiko Kobayashi, Yoko Wakayama, Hirofumi Inagaki, Masao Katsumata, Yukiyo Hirata *et al.* "Acute Effects of Walking in Forest Environments on Cardiovascular and Metabolic Parameters." *European Journal of Applied Physiology* 111, no. 11 (November 1, 2011): 2845–53; Qing Li. "Effect of Forest Bathing Trips on Human Immune Function." *Environmental Health and Preventive Medicine* 15, no. 1 (January 1, 2010): 9–17.

CHAPTER 6

1. LandDesign, Inc. *Little Sugar Creek Greenway Master Plan*. Charlotte, North Carolina: Mecklenburg County Park and Recreation Department, 2003. https://www.mecknc .gov/ParkandRec/Parks/Greenways/LittleSugarCreekGreenway/Pages/Masterplan.aspx.

2. E.S. Bernhardt, M.A. Palmer, J.D. Allan, G. Alexander, K. Barnas, S. Brooks, J. Carr *et al.* "Synthesizing U.S. River Restoration Efforts." *Science* 308, no. 5722 (April 29, 2005): 636–37.

3. The Mountains Recreation and Conservation Authority. *The Tujunga Wash Greenway and Restoration Project*. Los Angeles: The Mountains Recreation and Conservation Authority, 2018. https://mrca.ca.gov/wp-content/uploads/2018/06/MRCA.TWash -brochure-.pdf.

4. Cedric Rose. "Lick Run finally comes back to life." *Cincinnati Magazine*, February 25, 2021. https://www.cincinnatimagazine.com/article/lick-run-finally-comes-back-to -the-surface/; Project Groundwork. "Lick Run Greenway." Accessed August 29, 2022. https://www.projectgroundwork.org/lickrun/.

5. Christopher J. Walsh, Allison H. Roy, Jack W. Feminella, Peter D. Cottingham, Peter M. Groffman, and Raymond P. Morgan. "The Urban Stream Syndrome: Current Knowledge and the Search for a Cure." *Journal of the North American Benthological Society* 24, no. 3 (September 2005): 706–23.

6. Emily S. Bernhardt, and Margaret A. Palmer. "Restoring Streams in an Urbanizing World." *Freshwater Biology* 52, no. 4 (2007): 738–51.

7. Barbara A. Doll, Garry L. Grabow, Karen R. Hall, James Halley, William A. Harman, Gregory D. Jennings, and Dani E. Wise. *Stream Restoration: A Natural Channel Design Handbook*. Raleigh, NC: North Carolina Stream Restoration Institute and North Carolina Sea Grant, 2003.

8. Christy R. Violin, Peter Cada, Elizabeth B. Sudduth, Brooke A. Hassett, David L. Penrose, and Emily S. Bernhardt. "Effects of Urbanization and Urban Stream Restoration on the Physical and Biological Structure of Stream Ecosystems." *Ecological Applications* 21, no. 6 (2011): 1932–49; Elizabeth B. Sudduth, Brooke A. Hassett, Peter Cada, and Emily S. Bernhardt. "Testing the Field of Dreams Hypothesis: Functional Responses to

Urbanization and Restoration in Stream Ecosystems." *Ecological Applications* 21, no. 6 (2011): 1972–88.

9. Margaret A. Palmer, Holly L. Menninger, and Emily Bernhardt. "River Restoration, Habitat Heterogeneity and Biodiversity: A Failure of Theory or Practice?" *Freshwater Biology* 55, no. s1 (2010): 205–22; Scott W. Miller, Phaedra Budy, and John C. Schmidt. "Quantifying Macroinvertebrate Responses to In-Stream Habitat Restoration: Applications of Meta-Analysis to River Restoration." *Restoration Ecology* 18, no. 1 (2010): 8–19; Michael B. Griffith, and Michael G. McManus. "Consideration of Spatial and Temporal Scales in Stream Restorations and Biotic Monitoring to Assess Restoration Outcomes: A Literature Review, Part 1." *River Research and Applications* 36 (2020): 1385–97.

10. Daniel J. Bain, Erin M. Copeland, Marion T. Divers, Marijke Hecht, Kristina G. Hopkins, Justin Hynicka, Michael Koryak *et al.* "Characterizing a Major Urban Stream Restoration Project: Nine Mile Run (Pittsburgh, Pennsylvania, USA)." *JAWRA Journal of the American Water Resources Association* 50, no. 6 (2014): 1608–21.

11. See note 4 above.

12. Nathan J. Smucker, and Naomi E. Detenbeck. "Meta-Analysis of Lost Ecosystem Attributes in Urban Streams and the Effectiveness of Out-of-Channel Management Practices." *Restoration Ecology* 22, no. 6 (2014): 741–48.

13. Michael E. Dietz, and John C. Clausen. "Stormwater Runoff and Export Changes with Development in a Traditional and Low Impact Subdivision." *Journal of Environmental Management*, Microbial and Nutrient Contaminants of Fresh and Coastal Waters, 87, no. 4 (June 1, 2008): 560–66.

14. Front Yard Initiative. *Green Stormwater Infrastructure in New Orleans: 2020 Residential Survey Results*. New Orleans: The Urban Conservancy, 2021. https://www.urban conservancy.org/wp-content/uploads/2021/07/FYI-Survey-Report.pdf.

15. Melissa A. Kenney, Peter R. Wilcock, Benjamin F. Hobbs, Nicholas E. Flores, and Daniela C. Martínez. "Is Urban Stream Restoration Worth It?" *JAWRA Journal of the American Water Resources Association* 48, no. 3 (2012): 603–15.

16. Jules Pretty, Jo Peacock, Martin Sellens, and Murray Griffin. "The Mental and Physical Health Outcomes of Green Exercise." *International Journal of Environmental Health Research* 15, no. 5 (October 1, 2005): 319–37.

17. J. Thompson Coon, K. Boddy, K. Stein, R. Whear, J. Barton, and M. H. Depledge. "Does Participating in Physical Activity in Outdoor Natural Environments Have a Greater Effect on Physical and Mental Wellbeing than Physical Activity Indoors? A Systematic Review." *Environmental Science & Technology* 45, no. 5 (March 1, 2011): 1761–72; Diana E. Bowler, Lisette M. Buyung-Ali, Teri M. Knight, and Andrew S. Pullin. "A Systematic Review of Evidence for the Added Benefits to Health of Exposure to Natural Environments." *BMC Public Health* 10, no. 1 (August 4, 2010): 456; Nancy Qwynne Lackey, Deborah A. Tysor, G. David McNay, Leah Joyner, Kensey H. Baker, and Camilla Hodge. "Mental Health Benefits of Nature-Based Recreation: A Systematic Review." *Annals of Leisure Research* 24, no. 3 (May 27, 2021): 379–93.

18. Tytti P. Pasanen, Liisa Tyrväinen, and Kalevi M. Korpela. "The Relationship between Perceived Health and Physical Activity Indoors, Outdoors in Built

Environments, and Outdoors in Nature." *Applied Psychology: Health and Well-Being* 6, no. 3 (2014): 324–46.

19. See note 17 above; Ian Lahart, Patricia Darcy, Christopher Gidlow, and Giovanna Calogiuri. "The Effects of Green Exercise on Physical and Mental Wellbeing: A Systematic Review." *International Journal of Environmental Research and Public Health* 16, no. 8 (January 2019): 1352.

20. Qing Li, Ari Nakadai, Hiroki Matsushima, Yoshifumi Miyazaki, Alan M. Krensky, Tomoyuki Kawada, and Kanehisa Morimoto. "Phytoncides (Wood Essential Oils) Induce Human Natural Killer Cell Activity." *Immunopharmacology and Immunotoxicology* 28, no. 2 (January 1, 2006): 319–33.

21. Q. Li, K. Morimoto, A. Nakadai, H. Inagaki, M. Katsumata, T. Shimizu, Y. Hirata *et al*. "Forest Bathing Enhances Human Natural Killer Activity and Expression of Anti-Cancer Proteins." *International Journal of Immunopathology and Pharmacology* 20 (2007): 3–8.

22. Q. Li, K. Morimoto, M. Kobayashi, H. Inagaki, M. Katsumata, Y. Hirata, K. Hirata *et al*. "Visiting a Forest, but Not a City, Increases Human Natural Killer Activity and Expression of Anti-Cancer Proteins." *International Journal of Immunopathology and Pharmacology* 21 (2008): 117–21.

23. Q. Li, K. Morimoto, M. Kobayashi, H. Inagaki, M. Katsumata, Y. Hirata, K. Hirata *et al*. "A Forest Bathing Trip Increases Human Natural Killer Activity and Expression of Anti-Cancer Proteins in Female Subjects." *Journal of Biological Regulators and Homeostatic Agents* 22, no. 1 (March 2008): 45–55.

24. Qing Li. "Effect of Forest Bathing Trips on Human Immune Function." *Environmental Health and Preventive Medecine* 15 (2010): 9–17.

25. Q. Li, M. Kobayashi, Y. Wakayama, H. Inagaki, M. Katsumata, Y. Hirata, K. Hirata *et al*. "Effect of Phytoncide from Trees on Human Natural Killer Cell Function." *International Journal of Immunopathology and Pharmacology* 22 (2009): 951–59.

26. Qing Li, Toshiaki Otsuka, Maiko Kobayashi, Yoko Wakayama, Hirofumi Inagaki, Masao Katsumata, Yukiyo Hirata *et al*. "Acute Effects of Walking in Forest Environments on Cardiovascular and Metabolic Parameters." *European Journal of Applied Physiology* 111, no. 11 (November 1, 2011): 2845–53.

27. See note 19 above.

28. See note 17 above.

29. Giovanna Calogiuri, Hildegunn Nordtug, and Andi Weydahl. "The Potential of Using Exercise in Nature as an Intervention to Enhance Exercise Behavior: Results from a Pilot Study." *Perceptual and Motor Skills* 121, no. 2 (October 1, 2015): 350–70.

30. Marianne Lacharité-Lemieux, Jean-Pierre Brunelle, and Isabelle J. Dionne. "Adherence to Exercise and Affective Responses: Comparison between Outdoor and Indoor Training." *Menopause* 22, no. 7 (July 2015): 731–40.

31. Stella-Maria Hug, Ralf Hansmann, Christian Monn, Pius Krütli, and Klaus Seeland. "Restorative Effects of Physical Activity in Forests and Indoor Settings." *International Journal of Fitness* 4 (2008): 25–38.

32. Anna Kajosaari, and Tytti P. Pasanen. "Restorative Benefits of Everyday Green Exercise: A Spatial Approach." *Landscape and Urban Planning* 206 (February 1, 2021): 103978.

33. Jo Barton, and Jules Pretty. "What Is the Best Dose of Nature and Green Exercise for Improving Mental Health? A Multi-Study Analysis." *Environmental Science & Technology* 44, no. 10 (May 15, 2010): 3947–55.

CHAPTER 7

1. M.J. McDonnell, and S.T.A. Pickett. "Ecosystem Structure and Function along Urban-Rural Gradients: An Unexploited Opportunity for Ecology." *Ecology* 71 (1990): 1232–37.

2. Mark J. McDonnell, and Amy K. Hahs. "The Use of Gradient Analysis Studies in Advancing Our Understanding of the Ecology of Urbanizing Landscapes: Current Status and Future Directions." *Landscape Ecology* 23, no. 10 (December 1, 2008): 1143–55.

3. Robert B. Blair, "Land Use and Avian Species Diversity Along an Urban Gradient." *Ecological Applications* 6, no. 2 (1996): 506–19.

4. Sara A. Gagné, and Lenore Fahrig. "Do Birds and Beetles Show Similar Responses to Urbanization?" *Ecological Applications* 21 (2011): 2297–312.

5. Péter Batáry, Kornélia Kurucz, Marcela Suarez-Rubio, and Dan E. Chamberlain. "Non-Linearities in Bird Responses across Urbanization Gradients: A Meta-Analysis." *Global Change Biology* 24, no. 3 (2018): 1046–54.

6. Michael L. McKinney. "Urbanization, Biodiversity, and Conservation: The Impacts of Urbanization on Native Species Are Poorly Studied, but Educating a Highly Urbanized Human Population about These Impacts Can Greatly Improve Species Conservation in All Ecosystems." *BioScience* 52, no. 10 (October 1, 2002): 883–90.

7. James W. Hody, and Roland Kays. "Mapping the Expansion of Coyotes (Canis Latrans) across North and Central America." *ZooKeys* 759 (May 22, 2018): 81–97.

8. The Wildlife Center of Virginia. "Chimney Swifts as Neighbors." Accessed August 29, 2022. https://www.wildlifecenter.org/chimney-swifts-neighbors.

9. Birds of the World. "Chimney Swift." Accessed August 29, 2022. https://birdsoftheworld.org/bow/species/chiswi/cur/introduction.

10. Stuart Wine, Sara A. Gagné, and Ross K. Meentemeyer. "Understanding Human–Coyote Encounters in Urban Ecosystems Using Citizen Science Data: What Do Socioeconomics Tell Us?" *Environmental Management* 55, no. 1 (January 1, 2015): 159–70.

11. E. Hance Ellington, and Stanley D. Gehrt. "Behavioral Responses by an Apex Predator to Urbanization." *Behavioral Ecology* 30 (2019): 821–29.

12. Stanley D. Gehrt, Justin L. Brown, and Chris Anchor. "Is the Urban Coyote a Misanthropic Synanthrope? The Case from Chicago." *Cities and the Environment* 4 (2011): 3.

13. Diane Hope, Corinna Gries, Weixing Zhu, William F. Fagan, Charles L. Redman, Nancy B. Grimm, Amy L. Nelson, Chris Martin, and Ann Kinzig. "Socioeconomics Drive Urban Plant Diversity." *Proceedings of the National Academy of Sciences* 100 (2003): 8788–92.

14. Maureen H. Murray, and Colleen Cassady St. Clair. "Predictable Features Attract Urban Coyotes to Residential Yards." *Journal of Wildlife Management* 81, no. 4 (2017): 593–600.

15. T. Quinn. "Coyote (Canis latrans) Food Habits in Three Urban Habitat Types of Western Washington." *Northwest Science* 71 (1997): 1–5; James G. MacCracken. "Coyote Foods in a Southern California Suburb." *Wildlife Society Bulletin* 10 (1982): 280–81; Jose M. Fedriani, Todd K. Fuller, and Raymond M. Sauvajot. "Does Availability of Anthropogenic Food Enhance Densities of Omnivorous Mammals? An Example with Coyotes in Southern California." *Ecography* 24, no. 3 (2001): 325–31; Mark F. McClure, Norman S. Smith, and William W. Shaw. "Diets of Coyotes near the Boundary of Saguaro National Monument and Tucson, Arizona." *The Southwestern Naturalist* 40 (1995): 101–25; Paul S. Morey, Eric M. Gese, and Stanley Gehrt. "Spatial and Temporal Variation in the Diet of Coyotes in the Chicago Metropolitan Area." *American Midland Naturalist* 158 (2007): 147–61; Stanley D. Gehrt, "Ecology of Coyotes in Urban Landscapes." In *Proceedings of the 12th Wildlife Damage Management Conference*, edited by D.L. Nolte, W.M. Arjo, and D.H. Stalman, 303–11. Lincoln, Nebraska: Internet Center for Wildlife Damage Management, 2007.

16. Seth D. Newsome, Heidi M. Garbe, Evan C. Wilson, and Stanley D. Gehrt. "Individual Variation in Anthropogenic Resource Use in an Urban Carnivore." *Oecologia* 178, no. 1 (May 1, 2015): 115–28.

17. Neil Vigdor, Azi Paybarah, and Christine Hauser. "At Least 11 Killed as Flash Floods Ravage North Carolina." *New York Times*, November 12, 2020. https://www.nytimes.com/2020/11/12/us/north-carolina-eta-flooding.html.

18. National Academies of Sciences, Engineering, and Medicine. *Framing the Challenge of Urban Flooding in the United States*. Washington, DC: The National Academies Press, 2019.

19. D.J. Wuebbles, D.W. Fahey, K.A. Hibbard, D.J. Dokken, B.C. Stewart, and T.K. Maycock, eds. *Climate Science Special Report: Fourth National Climate Assessment, Volume I*. Washington, DC: U.S. Global Change Research Program, 2017.

20. University of Maryland, Center for Disaster Resilience, and Texas A&M University, Galveston Campus, Center for Texas Beaches and Shores. *The Growing Threat of Urban Flooding: A National Challenge*. College Park: A. James Clark School of Engineering, 2018.

21. Ryan Murphy. "Waze Helps Track Flooding, and Could Predict the Future." *AP News*, August 5, 2018. https://apnews.com/article/d5e9d30a98ca4d63ac14c855590cc12a.

22. Oliver E.J. Wing, William Lehman, Paul D. Bates, Christopher C. Sampson, Niall Quinn, Andrew M. Smith, Jeffrey C. Neal, Jeremy R. Porter, and Carolyn Kousky. "Inequitable Patterns of US Flood Risk in the Anthropocene." *Nature Climate Change* 12, no. 2 (February 2022): 156–62.

23. Water Environment Federation Stormwater Institute. *Rainfall to Results: The Future of Stormwater*. Alexandria, Virginia: Water Environment Federation, 2015.

24. Alexandra Müller, Heléne Österlund, Jiri Marsalek, and Maria Viklander. "The Pollution Conveyed by Urban Runoff: A Review of Sources." *Science of The Total Environment* 709 (March 20, 2020): 136125.

25. Michael J. Pennino, Rob I. McDonald, and Peter R. Jaffe. "Watershed-Scale Impacts of Stormwater Green Infrastructure on Hydrology, Nutrient Fluxes, and Combined Sewer Overflows in the Mid-Atlantic Region." *Science of The Total Environment* 565 (September 15, 2016): 1044–53.

26. Gary Conley, Robert I. McDonald, Tyler Nodine, Teresa Chapman, Craig Holland, Christopher Hawkins, and Nicole Beck. "Assessing the Influence of Urban Greenness and Green Stormwater Infrastructure on Hydrology from Satellite Remote Sensing." *Science of The Total Environment* 817 (April 15, 2022): 152723.

27. Vinicius J. Taguchi, Peter T. Weiss, John S. Gulliver, Mira R. Klein, Raymond M. Hozalski, Lawrence A. Baker, Jacques C. Finlay, Bonnie L. Keeler, and John L. Nieber. "It Is Not Easy Being Green: Recognizing Unintended Consequences of Green Stormwater Infrastructure." *Water* 12, no. 2 (February 2020): 522.

28. Anne J. Jefferson, Aditi S. Bhaskar, Kristina G. Hopkins, Rosemary Fanelli, Pedro M. Avellaneda, and Sara K. McMillan. "Stormwater Management Network Effectiveness and Implications for Urban Watershed Function: A Critical Review." *Hydrological Processes* 31, no. 23 (2017): 4056–80.

29. Scott Ensign. "How Do EnviroDIY Monitoring Stations Compare with USGS Stations?" *EnviroDIY*, June 3, 2022. https://www.envirodiy.org/how-do-envirodiy-monitoring-stations-compare-with-usgs-stations/.

CHAPTER 8

1. Mapping Inequality: Redlining in New Deal America. "Introduction." Accessed August 29, 2022. https://dsl.richmond.edu/panorama/redlining/#loc=5/39.1/-94.58&text=intro.

2. Emily Moss, Kriston McIntosh, Wendy Edelberg, and Kristen Broady. "The Black-White Wealth Gap Left Black Households More Vulnerable." *The Brookings Institution*, December 8, 2020. https://www.brookings.edu/blog/up-front/2020/12/08/the-black-white-wealth-gap-left-black-households-more-vulnerable/.

3. Bruce Mitchell, and Juan Franco. "HOLC "Redlining" Maps: The Persistent Structure of Segregation and Economic Inequality." *National Community Reinvestment Coalition*, March 20, 2018. https://ncrc.org/holc/.

4. Jeremy S. Hoffman, Vivek Shandas, and Nicholas Pendleton. "The Effects of Historical Housing Policies on Resident Exposure to Intra-Urban Heat: A Study of 108 US Urban Areas." *Climate* 8, no. 1 (January 2020): 12.

5. J.M. Grove, A.R. Troy, J.P.M. O'Neil-Dunne, W.R. Burch, M.L. Cadenasso, and S.T.A. Pickett. "Characterization of Households and Its Implications for the Vegetation of Urban Ecosystems." *Ecosystems* 9, no. 4 (June 1, 2006): 578–97.

6. IUCN Red List. "Summary Statistics." Accessed August 29, 2022. https://www.iucnredlist.org/resources/summary-statistics.

7. Jonathan E.M. Baillie, Janine Griffiths, Samuel T. Turvey, Jonathan Loh, and Ben Collen, eds. *Evolution Lost: Status and Trends of the World's Vertebrates*. London: Zoological Society of London, 2010.

8. K.V. Rosenberg, J.A. Kennedy, R. Dettmers, R.P. Ford, D. Reynolds, J.D. Alexander, C.J. Beardmore *et al. Partners in Flight Landbird Conservation Plan: 2016 Revision for Canada and Continental United States*. Partners in Flight Science Committee, 2016.

9. Elizabeth Hill, Jeffrey H. Dorfman, and Elizabeth Kramer. "Evaluating the Impact of Government Land Use Policies on Tree Canopy Coverage." *Land Use Policy*, Forest transitions, 27, no. 2 (April 1, 2010): 407–14.

10. Wayne C. Zipperer, Jianguo Wu, Richard V. Pouyat, and Steward T. A. Pickett. "The Application of Ecological Principles to Urban and Urbanizing Landscapes." *Ecological Applications* 10 (2000): 685–88; Paul Opdam, and Eveliene Steingröver. "Designing Metropolitan Landscapes for Biodiversity Deriving Guidelines from Metapopulation Ecology." *Landscape Journal* 27, no. 1 (January 1, 2008): 69–80.

11. Andrew T. Knight, Richard M. Cowling, Mathieu Rouget, Andrew Balmford, Amanda T. Lombard, and Bruce M. Campbell. "Knowing But Not Doing: Selecting Priority Conservation Areas and the Research-Implementation Gap." *Conservation Biology* 22 (2008): 610–17.

12. Sara A. Gagné, Felix Eigenbrod, Daniel G. Bert, Glenn M. Cunnington, Leif T. Olson, Adam C. Smith, and Lenore Fahrig. "A Simple Landscape Design Framework for Biodiversity Conservation." *Landscape and Urban Planning* 136 (April 1, 2015): 13–27.

13. D.B. Lindenmayer, J. F. Franklin, and J. Fischer. "General Management Principles and a Checklist of Strategies to Guide Forest Biodiversity Conservation." *Biological Conservation* 131, no. 3 (August 1, 2006): 433–45.

14. Sara A. Gagné, and Lenore Fahrig. "The Trade-off Between Housing Density and Sprawl Area: Minimising Impacts to Forest Breeding Birds." *Basic and Applied Ecology* 11, no. 8 (December 1, 2010): 723–33; Sara Gagné, and Lenore Fahrig. "The Trade-off Between Housing Density and Sprawl Area: Minimizing Impacts to Carabid Beetles (Coleoptera: Carabidae)." *Ecology and Society* 15, no. 4 (November 5, 2010): 12; Nélida R. Villaseñor, Ayesha I. T. Tulloch, Don A. Driscoll, Philip Gibbons, and David B. Lindenmayer. "Compact Development Minimizes the Impacts of Urban Growth on Native Mammals." *Journal of Applied Ecology* 54, no. 3 (2017): 794–804.

15. J.A. Jaeger, L. Fahrig, and K. C. Ewald. "Does the Configuration of Road Networks Influence the Degree to Which Roads Affect Wildlife Populations?" In *Proceedings of the 2005 International Conference on Ecology and Transportation*, edited by C. L. Irwin, P. Garrett, and K. P. McDermott, 151–63. Raleigh, North Carolina: Center for Transportation and the Environment, 2005.

16. Lenore Fahrig. "Ecological Responses to Habitat Fragmentation Per Se." *Annual Review of Ecology, Evolution, and Systematics* 48, no. 1 (2017): 1–23.

17. Sara A. Gagné, Kaitlynn Bryan–Scaggs, Robert H. W. Boyer, and Wei–Ning Xiang. "Conserving Biodiversity Takes a Plan: How Planners Implement Ecological Information for Biodiversity." *Ambio* 49 (2020): 1490–505.

18. J.R. Miller, M. Groom, G.R. Hess, T. Steelman, D.L. Stokes, J. Thompson, T. Bowman, L. Fricke, B. King, and R. Marquardt. Biodiversity Conservation in Local Planning. *Conservation Biology* 23 (2009): 53–63.

19. Toddi A. Steelman, and George Hess. "Effective Protection of Open Space: Does Planning Matter?" *Environmental Management* 44 (2009): 93–104.

20. Zoltan L. Hajnal. "Why Does No One Vote in Local Elections?" *New York Times*, October 22, 2018. https://www.nytimes.com/2018/10/22/opinion/why-does-no-one-vote-in-local-elections.html.

21. Ed Gerrish, and Shannon Lea Watkins. "The Relationship between Urban Forests and Income: A Meta-Analysis." *Landscape and Urban Planning* 170 (February 1, 2018): 293–308; Shannon Lea Watkins, and Ed Gerrish. "The Relationship Between Urban Forests and Race: A Meta–Analysis." *Journal of Environmental Management* 209 (2018): 152–68.

22. Alessandro Rigolon. "A Complex Landscape of Inequity in Access to Urban Parks: A Literature Review." *Landscape and Urban Planning* 153 (2016): 160–69.

23. Ivis García, Andrea Garfinkel-Castro, and Deirdre Pfeiffer. *Planning with Diverse Communities*. Washington, DC: American Planning Association, 2019.

24. Gary W. Luck, Lisa T. Smallbone, and Rachel O'Brien. "Socio-Economics and Vegetation Change in Urban Ecosystems: Patterns in Space and Time." *Ecosystems* 12, no. 4 (June 1, 2009): 604–20.

25. Diane Hope, Corinna Gries, Weixing Zhu, William F. Fagan, Charles L. Redman, Nancy B. Grimm, Amy L. Nelson, Chris Martin, and Ann Kinzig. "Socioeconomics Drive Urban Plant Diversity." *Proceedings of the National Academy of Sciences* 100 (2003): 8788–92.

26. See note 21 above.

27. Data USA. "Urban & Regional Planners." Accessed August 29, 2022. https://datausa.io/profile/soc/urban-regional-planners#:~:text=In%202019%2C%20Urban%20%26%20regional%20planners,installers%20%26%20repairers%20make%20somewhat%20less; See note 17 above.

28. See note 23 above.

29. Seth Motel. "Who runs for office? A profile of the 2%." *Pew Research Center*, September 3, 2014. https://www.pewresearch.org/fact-tank/2014/09/03/who-runs-for-office-a-profile-of-the-2/.

INDEX